DOUBLE-EDGED SWORD

Espada: synonym for the
sword; also used to refer to
the matador himself.

———————

From the glossary of
Death in the Afternoon by
ERNEST HEMINGWAY

Sidney Franklin (1939) by Luis Quintanilla. *Courtesy of Paul Quintanilla.*

BART PAUL

Double-Edged Sword

The Many Lives of Hemingway's Friend,
the American Matador Sidney Franklin

University of Nebraska Press | Lincoln & London

*Library of Congress
Cataloging-in-Publication Data*

Paul, Bart.
Double-edged sword : the many lives
of Hemingway's friend, the American
matador Sidney Franklin / Bart Paul.
    p. cm.   Includes
bibliographical references and index.
ISBN 978-0-8032-1129-2
        (cloth : alk. paper)
1. Franklin, Sidney, 1903–1976.
2. Bullfighters—United States—
Biography. 3. Hemingway, Ernest,
1899–1961—Friends and associates.
4. Jews—United States—Biography.
5. Gays—United States—Biography.
        I. Title.
GV1108.F7P38 2009
791.8'2092—dc22
[B]   2009022904

Set in Vendetta by Bob Reitz.
Designed by A. Shahan.

In memory of Steve and Peggy Paul

When sitting in a Madrid café, Sidney Franklin was asked by an acquaintance why he, a Jewish matador, wore a cross around his neck. Sidney shrugged at the obviousness of the question and said, "The bulls are Catholic."

CONTENTS

ACT THREE

ILLUSTRATIONS

Following page 120

Any man's life told truly, is a novel,
but the bullfighter's life has an
order in the tragedy of its progression
which tends to formalize the
story into a groove. Sidney's life
has escaped this and he has truly
lived three lives, one Mexican,
one Spanish and one American
in a way that is unbelievable. The
story of those lives belongs to him
and I will not tell it to you.

From *Death in the Afternoon* by
ERNEST HEMINGWAY

INTRODUCTION

The Alternative

Madrid — 1945

IT WAS JULY 18 OF THE LAST year of the Second World War when a tall redheaded Jewish boy from Brooklyn, New York, stepped out with slippered feet onto the sand of Madrid's Plaza Monumental to become the first American *matador de toros* in Spanish bullfighting history. But by then Sidney Franklin was no kid. He had just turned forty-two the week before, an age when most successful matadors have retired to raise fighting stock or marry movie stars — equally dangerous avocations — and he had been a bullfighter for over two decades. He was thicker around the middle and his sandy red hair was now mostly gone. After a decade and a half out of the spotlight, Sidney's career was now as much of an artifice as the toupee he wedged under his *montera*, the vaguely Napoleonic cap worn by bullfighters in the first act of the *corrida de toros*. As his friend Ernest Hemingway wrote before things ended bitterly between them, Franklin had indeed lived many lives: from the streets of New York and the wilds of revolutionary Mexico to a near-death goring in Madrid to friendships with some of the most famous names of his era during a short but triumphant moment in the sun. But today none of that mattered. Today he would finally join the ranks of the greats or be carried lifeless from the ring.

Franklin stood in the passageway between the stands and the ring and watched the first bull of the afternoon — his bull — charge into the arena. He studied the animal's movement as his assistant, a *banderillero*, waved a cape gracelessly with one hand in front of the bull, doubling the charging animal to see whether it favored hooking with the right or the left horn, much as a boxer sizes up the strength of his opponent's jabs and hooks in the first round of a prizefight. Then he scanned the stands for some friendly faces, for a glimpse of those transatlantic celebrities who once long ago could not get enough of him. Whether he would have admitted it or not, he was looking for Hemingway, too.

After a few moments the *banderillero* ran to the arena fence and squeezed through a narrow opening to safety. Franklin took a deep breath, took his heavy *capote de brega* — the work cape — in his teeth and slid his big freckled hands down the cape to just the proper spot. Then he strode out into the arena to make history.

But on that hot afternoon in Madrid, the stands of the bullring, both in sun and in shade — *sol y sombra* — were poorly populated. There was a scattering of aficionados, mostly Spanish, few American. There was perhaps a diplomat here, a die-hard expatriate there, but even a second-rate Hollywood star would have been rare as few Americans were in Spain just then. So, in those first months after the end of the war in Europe, no one was terribly interested in a middle-aged Norteamericano taking his *alternativa*, the ceremony whereby the lower-ranked professional — the *novillero* — becomes elevated into the top echelon as a *matador de toros*. Not that Spain let a small thing like World War II distract it from the national passion. That summer, while the rest of Europe dug out from the rubble, Spain was going crazy with the greatest bullfight rivalry in a generation, as Córdoba's "Manolete" — Manuel Rodríguez y Sánchez — and Mexico's Carlos

Arruza went *mano a mano* in plazas throughout the country. The aficionados had seen nothing like this since the *first* world war and the rivalry of Juan Belmonte and "Joselito"—José Gómez—which only ended in 1920 with twenty-five-year-old Joselito's death from a hooking horn, which tore open his stomach, killing him within minutes. Although he often bragged to the contrary, Sidney Franklin had nowhere near the same star power as those two. His taking the *alternativa* at age forty-two was comparable to the great Negro League pitcher Satchel Paige not hitting the big leagues until well into his forties, far past his prime. Tallealto, the bull circling the arena looking for something to attack, was only four years old himself and did not know or care about Sidney's unique situation. The *banderillero* and Sidney were the first dismounted humans Tallealto had ever encountered, so there was much information for him to assimilate. Having lived his entire life unchallenged and unmolested, the animal could not know that within twenty minutes either he or the redheaded man shaking the annoying cape would be dead.

Franklin presented his profile to the bull, extending the *capote* in front of him, waiting for the first charge as he spoke to the bull in low, clipped tones. His "toro-huh-toro" had the distinctly Brooklyn lilt of a Damon Runyon tout giving the odds on the third race at Aqueduct. When the half-ton animal snorted and thundered directly at him, Sidney coolly set his feet and performed a classic *verónica*, bullfighting's basic pass, as he had done a thousand times before. The magenta and yellow cape drew the bull past him while the right horn sliced the air just inches from Sidney's thigh. There were only scattered shouts of "*olé!*" from the stands as the bull wheeled to face the man once more. Then, this middle-aged son of an immigrant Brooklyn cop shook the cape again, barked "ah-ha-toro, ah-ha" and repeated the *verónica* from the other side as the bull charged a second time.

Some old aficionados say that the regular Spanish bullfighting press did not even cover Franklin's *alternativa* ceremony that afternoon, and that it was not a regularly scheduled *corrida* anyway, but rather an exhibition event for the benefit of a youth league sponsored by the dictator Francisco Franco. July 18 was after all the ninth anniversary of the outbreak of the Spanish civil war when Franco led his troops against the old Republican government, so perhaps this is true. Others insist — incorrectly according to the record — that Franklin performed so poorly that both the bulls he faced left the arena mangled but alive, a disgraceful outcome for a bullfighter.

None of that really matters today. For this has-been to achieve what no American had ever achieved — the taking of the *alternativa* in Madrid — was a personal victory too long in coming. He had quite literally transformed himself into a modern-day dragon slayer. This American who as a boy had fancied a career on the stage, and who had begun his professional life as a silk-screen artist, had now conquered the hyper-macho world of Spanish bullfighting. In doing so, he had become a close friend and traveling companion of Ernest Hemingway, the most publicly masculine American celebrity of the twentieth century. And the redheaded kid from Brooklyn's Jackson Place had done it all without letting the world in on a little secret that if exposed would have made such accomplishments difficult, perhaps impossible, in the bullfighting world of the 1920s and 1930s. Sidney Franklin was gay.

This was not a fact that Franklin ever discussed publicly. It was not part of the persona he presented to the world, either in interviews or in his own autobiography, *Bullfighter from Brooklyn*. But by the 1950s Franklin's homosexuality was an open secret in the gossipy world of toreros, bull breeders, promoters, and aficionados. This information, however, remained either unknown or unmentioned in almost all mainstream biographies of Ernest Hemingway, even those that delve at length into the author's sexual attitudes or his open disdain for "the mincing gentry."

Sidney Franklin had first become widely known to readers in the United States in Hemingway's 1932 book on bullfighting *Death in the Afternoon*, which concluded with a section entitled, "A Short Estimate of the American, *Sidney Franklin*, as a Matador."

> He is a better, more scientific, more intelligent and more finished matador than all but about six of the full matadors in Spain today, and the bullfighters know it and have the utmost respect for him.

That assessment would not find universal agreement among the matadors themselves, especially those whose blood had been spilled by Hemingway's pen.

But this afternoon as Franklin finished his first series of passes with a half *verónica* then turned his back on the bull and sauntered away, Ernest Hemingway was nowhere to be seen among the spectators. Due to his chaotic domestic life, the civil war in Spain, and then a world war, the self-proclaimed authority on all things taurine had not been to many bullfights during the previous decade. He would not do so regularly again for another few years. More importantly, he had not seen much of his friend Sidney Franklin since 1937, when under siege by Franco's troops during the Spanish civil war, Madrid was a sandbagged city full of the rubble of buildings, the stench of death, and the rank odor of ripening literary reputations. This was a siege where legends were born and friendships died along with the volunteers of the international brigades. It was here in Madrid while this new bullring, the Plaza Monumental, was shuttered and the artillery shells flew that Sidney Franklin and Ernest Hemingway had some of their finest hours — and they had them together. Then, after five dangerous and well-publicized weeks, the eight-year friendship between the author and the closeted bullfighter began to fall apart. The cause of it all, of which neither man would speak publicly for the rest of their lives, was a woman.

As Sidney finished his opening *verónicas*, the two picadors' horses were led into the arena by members of the bullring's event staff, ring servants known as *monosabios* (wise monkeys). Sidney drew his bull across the ring until it faced the new intruder as the *monosabio* turned the armored side of the horse and rider to the bull. When the bull got a clear look at the horse with the heavy mattresslike padding hanging down its side and the stout man in the flat hat squatting on its back, the bull charged, hitting the horse full in the side, slamming it into the planks of the arena fence. The picador leaned into his lance, driving the four-and-a-half-inch blade at the end of the *pica* into the great hump of muscle above the bull's withers, then grinding away. This, according to the aficionados, is oddly the one moment of satisfaction for the bull, when he finally gets to hit something more solid than a moving cape. Fifteen minutes later, however, this momentary satisfaction will have robbed the bull of the neck strength to similarly slam the man in the suit of lights when the sharpened swords are out.

As the horse staggered to retain its feet while the bull still rooted away at it with its horns, Sidney ran up behind the bull shouting "ah-ha-toro" to begin his *quite*, the taking of the bull from the horse, a bit of business that demonstrates some of the finest capework of the *corrida* as the three matadors on the program each try in turn to outdo the others. Sidney finished drawing the bull away from the horse with a series of passes, swirling the cape around his waist in a *rebolera* like a flamenco dancer swirling her skirt prettily for the customers. The bull, with bright red blood now running down his slick rust-colored shoulders, was then faced by "El Estudiante" — one of the two full matadors on the program — for his *quite*. El Estudiante was thirty-four-year-old Luis Gómez, who had been one of Spain's leading matadors in 1938. As the senior sword on the program, Gómez would be Sidney's *padrino* in the *alternativa* to come. This ceremony of induction would occur in the natural break of events just before the third act of the bullfight, which ends with the actual killing. It was during this final phase, fifteen years before in the old ring in Madrid when he and Hemingway were inseparable, that Sidney received the emblematic wound — a horrible rectal goring deep into his abdominal cavity — that almost killed him.

The woman whose presence broke up the friendship of Sidney Franklin and Ernest Hemingway was the writer Martha Gellhorn, who would go on to become Hemingway's third wife. After their short, glamorous, and ultimately bitter marriage ended, Gellhorn downplayed her role as both literary disciple and home wrecker, although her dislike for the American bullfighter with whom she shared Hemingway's time and space during the siege of Madrid remained acute until the end of her life. To Gellhorn, Sidney was the annoying source of many unflattering stories about her that found their way into Hemingway studies, most notably Professor Carlos Baker's once definitive *Ernest Hemingway: A Life Story*. To Sidney, a close friend of Hemingway's second wife Pauline Pfeiffer, Gellhorn was the cause of misfortune and betrayal as Pauline's husband discarded her for this younger, more glamorous rival. Sidney's bitterness was aggravated by the knowledge of his own role in that betrayal, a role in which he was specifically cast by Hemingway himself. Sidney simply did not have the skill or the grace to perform a *quite* dazzling enough to draw this charging female away from the tempting target that was Ernest Hemingway.

It had all started out harmlessly enough. The two men had sailed for Europe together on the liner *Paris* in early 1937. An existing photo shows them on the rail, squinting contentedly into the sun somewhere in the mid-Atlantic, just two pals on a great new adventure, covering someone else's war as they recaptured the good times they had known together years before. Despite the comradeship shown in that snapshot, their friendship would begin to sink in just eight weeks.

Of those days, there is much that has been written, but much more that can never be positively known. Biographers for Hemingway and Gellhorn stake out rival turf as they recount the events of 1937, and their interpretations vary widely. Hemingway is presented by turns as heroic, noble, caddish, or showboating. Gellhorn is seen as both feminist icon — cutting her own literary swath in a man's world — and fortune-hunting adventuress, riding on a great man's coattails after wangling her way into his bed (and not for the first time or the last, apparently). The truth is what one wants to make of it, or perhaps the sensibilities one brings to these events. Sidney remains caught in the middle, occupying a position as dangerous as any patch of sand in the bullring. Writers on the *corrida* describe the bull's arbitrarily claimed terrain, his *querencia*, as a piece of ground where he is the most dangerous. Sidney's failure to avoid the emotional goring and tossing as he stood his ground in Ernest Hemingway's *querencia* cost him the most important friendship of his life. The specifics of that friendship's end may be as simple as what writer Lillian Ross said fifty-six years after meeting both men. Their positions were unequal from the start. "One was a genius," she said simply, "one wasn't."

Outside of bullfighting chronicles written by and for aficionados, Sidney Franklin is written of now mostly as a footnote to literary biography in terms of that friendship. Although his time with

Ernest Hemingway—like his time in Mexico or Spain—was certainly one of the lives that Sidney lived, it was hardly the only one. He loved nothing more than telling whomever crossed his path about those other lives—except of course the private one—and about the adventures and accomplishments that to him and his contemporaries truly *were* unbelievable, just as Hemingway had said they were. The author may have introduced the name Sidney Franklin to his compatriots, but as he was the first to admit, Sidney was worth the knowing. There are still those of a certain age who once followed the bullfights and who now, upon hearing Sidney's name, brighten up and begin to talk, remembering the cocky redheaded American who handled a cape so gracefully, and who handled the batterings taken outside the ring almost as well. To them, Sidney was their window into the bullring. He would be happy to know that more than thirty years after his death he is still talked about for his achievements, but would say that some of what is said is nobody's damned business. A guy has a right to his secrets. For openers, there was the matter of the name itself: Franklin it was not.

DOUBLE-EDGED SWORD

ACT ONE

——————

The Suerte de Varas (the act of the pica, *or, as it is sometimes known, the act of the horses). Like a well-made play or film, the traditional bullfight was divided into three acts, or* suertes. *The act of the horses is often the one most difficult for the uninitiated to watch, but it is the act that determines the shape and the motifs of the drama to come. Here the matador learns if the animal hooks to the right or to the left and assesses the quality of its courage as it attacks the horses while being gouged by the* vara — *the lance — of the mounted* picador.

1

The Bull

HE WAS BORN SIDNEY FRUMPKIN on July 11, 1903, one of nine surviving children to Abram and Lubba Frumpkin of Minsk and Kazan, respectively. His parents, both Orthodox Jews, emigrated from Imperial Russia in 1888. After eight years in this country and the birth of his first few children, Abram joined the New York City Police Department, eventually working out of Brooklyn's Seventy-Eighth Precinct. The borough of Brooklyn was completing the transition from a semirural community of farms, shade trees and backyard gardens to a noisy city, becoming further transformed by the new immigrants from eastern and southern Europe. The city had been an independent municipality until just five years before Sidney's birth, when it was incorporated into New York City. The *Brooklyn Eagle*, the paper that would eventually chronicle the rise of its hometown matador, was for a time edited in the late 1840s by Walt Whitman, another homeboy whose private life was also best kept from the public eye.

By the time the Frumpkin's fifth child Sidney arrived, the family was living at 14 Jackson Place in a district known as Park Slope. They were just three blocks west of Prospect Park and five blocks north of Greenwood Cemetery, the two huge green patches left in the center of Brooklyn.

Most of what is known of Sidney's childhood a century ago comes from two sources, both over half a century old. Each, although covering many of the same events, are quite different: parallel yet only partial narratives in very dissimilar voices, although the source for the mingled (and occasionally mangled) facts and fictions in both is Sidney himself. The first was a profile of Sidney by Lillian Ross that appeared in the *New Yorker* magazine under the title "El Único Matador" in 1949. The young writer traveled with Sidney for a time in Mexico as he toured with an American protégé. She extensively interviewed Sidney's former friend Ernest Hemingway in Ketchum, Idaho, in December 1947 for the article—the first that would appear in the magazine under her own byline. The persona of Sidney that comes through in "El Único Matador" is brash, confident, slangy, eccentric, and boastful—a true American character. He also occasionally appears, if not foolish, at least lacking in self-awareness. After the article appeared, Sidney remarked of Ross: "She sits there like a little mouse, looking so cute, but there's nothing but vitriol in her typewriter."

Decades after meeting Sidney, Miss Ross's memories of him remained vivid, full of detail and anecdote that did not make it into her profile. Her article, despite Sidney's grumbling, kept him in the public eye, perpetuating his rather singular celebrity. Having been befriended by Hemingway and his fourth wife, Mary, while researching the article on Sidney, Lillian Ross would go on to write "How Do You Like It Now, Gentlemen?" a famous piece on the author that appeared in the *New Yorker* in 1950. Many of Hemingway's friends shared Sidney's complaint about Ross: her extensive use of the subject's quotes without sufficient context made Hemingway look foolish. Unlike Sidney, Hemingway remained Ross's friend and defended her and her work for the rest of his life. For her part, Miss Ross returned the favor, remaining a Hemingway stalwart, her fondness and respect for him undiminished. If there are any sides to be taken in the subsequent falling out between Sidney Franklin and Ernest Hemingway, for Ross there is no contest.

The second source of information on Sidney's early life was his autobiography, *Bullfighter from Brooklyn*, which was published by Prentice Hall in 1952. There is no co-writer mentioned, and the assumption is that this is the face that Sidney wanted the public to see. To some this face is more of a mask. The book is generally considered fanciful by many who knew him. Barnaby Conrad, foremost American bullfight authority, aficionado, writer of many bullfighting books, and himself an amateur *torero* who once performed on the same bill with the great Juan Belmonte as "El Niño de California" (loosely "the California Kid"), when asked about *Bullfighter from Brooklyn* said cheerfully, "Of course it's all bullshit." One of Sidney's acquaintances from the 1940s, film director and bullfighter Budd Boetticher, said essentially the same thing, the reference to taurine excrement being the common thread.

An autobiography implies that the reader is getting the subject and author's true voice, but what is missing from *Bullfighter from Brooklyn* is Sidney's actual *voice*, the streetwise hyperbole and movie tough-guy slang that comes through so clearly in Ross's *New Yorker* piece. In contrast, Sidney personifies himself as a man of thoughtful maturity, a midcentury American sportsman, soldier of fortune, and bon vivant who became a citizen of the world, a friend of presidents and kings. He speaks modestly of the most preposterous accomplishments. He claimed to have single-handedly saved the Spanish bullfight from extinction when in 1930 the dictator Miguel Primo de Rivera, in an attempt to bring his country into the modern era, tried to ban the *corrida* outright because tourists were horrified by the bulls' gutting of the picadors' horses, an occurrence foreigners found particularly medieval and barbaric. Sidney asserts that it was he alone who arrived at the solution of armoring the horses with thick padding as is done on the breeding ranches for the *tientas*, the testing of young stock. Sidney claims to have obtained a solo audience with Primo de Rivera to pitch this solution, and that his intervention was all that kept bullfighting alive. It is a boast scoffed at by aficionados then and now. Were it true, it was still not enough to save the dictator, who died soon after being given the boot by his compatriots when they established the Spanish Republic.

Sidney likewise casts himself as the hero in many picaresque tales, the most outlandish of which is the one where for nine days he sexually services the entire female population of a Central American Indian village with the approval of the tribe's males. The laying down of these heterosexual markers right out of the most lurid men's true-story pulps stretched credulity even in 1952. That yarn itself takes up half a chapter. His entire boyhood in Park Slope only merits a page and a half. Recollections of friends and family members who knew Sidney as an adult can only partially bridge the gap between these two narratives of Miss Ross and Sidney himself. There remains then much of his early life that will stay hidden. This is exactly as Sidney would have wished.

Sidney was a small child, often sickly, who claimed to have been pronounced dead by the family doctor at age six from "brain fever." He attended PS 10 in Brooklyn but because of his health and small stature was not allowed to play sports — the great grade-school equalizer essential to the assimilation process of the children of immigrants. Sidney's sense of apartness was felt at an early age. "I didn't fit in," he said simply. He claims this was aggravated by his older sister Bella, a high school teacher who would try out modern educational theories on Sid when he was tiny, an experience that somewhat unsettled the sensitive lad. A further oddity, according to Sid, was his relationship with his older brother Samuel, a doctor, who let his little brother help him dissect cadaver pieces in his lab before dying of TB at only twenty-seven. At every turn Sidney would feel distance from the world that spawned him, even as he relished the uniqueness of his experiences.

Sidney's real problem growing up was his father. Officer Frumpkin was a tyrant and a bully whose normal tone of voice was a bellow. Sidney recalled that his father was a terror for a small boy. Sidney's niece Eve Frumkin (the *P* was dropped somewhere across the decades) said that her grandfather went by the name of "Abe," probably since his police force days. She remembered him late in life, banging his walking stick angrily on the floor to command attention from his family. He was a large, imposing man with a florid complexion and a big moustache. Lillian Ross spoke to some of Sidney's elementary school teachers in 1947, and one recalled Officer Frumpkin haranguing the teachers whenever one of his girls got into trouble. He seems to have had less interest in defending his fifth-born. Sidney claimed that his own father simply did not like him, partly because he inherited Lubba's fair hair and skin. (Eve Frumkin said that her grandfather inflicted emotional damage on his other sons as well. She described one, a successful professional, who later in life lived almost as a recluse, sleeping in a tiny room behind his office and only socializing once a week when he would visit a sister's family for a hot meal and a bath.)

Officer Frumpkin also seemed not to like Sidney's inclination to the arts. By the time the unathletic boy was twelve years old, he had found his first calling, the stage, performing skits with two girls between the acts at a local theater. His mother was all for it, but the patriarch — correctly, in his mind — sniffed something unmanly in the whole process of singing and dancing for public display. Sidney first adopted the surname "Franklin" as a stage name, supposedly to keep the old man from getting wise to his after-school activity. It didn't work. Sidney claims the name Franklin was inspired by Benjamin Franklin, founder of his favorite magazine, the *Saturday Evening Post*. (This Anglicization of his father's old country name to something more all-American was a common enough practice by first generation children at the turn of the last century, especially those who aspired to a public life. Jacob Gershovitz, born in Brooklyn five years before Sidney, became George Gershwin by the time of his earliest tin-pan alley days.) After two years of semiprofessional greasepaint, Sidney gave up the stage, later telling Lillian Ross that the whole business was too "feministic."

The artistic itch was persistent, however, and Sidney found a new creative outlet in drawing classes, the only course he truly enjoyed in Brooklyn's Commercial High School. By age seventeen Sidney dropped out of school and with this newly nurtured talent, began his own commercial silk-screen poster business. (His obituary in the *New York Times* stated that he attended art school at Columbia University, but Sidney makes no mention of this either to Lillian Ross or in his own writings.)

Many parents would have been proud of such entrepreneurial initiative, an example of a child's successful immersion into the new culture, but Officer Frumpkin was again displeased. Sidney's late brother, Sam, had been the doctor. Two other brothers, Robert and Milton, became accountants. The eldest surviving boy, Henry, became a cop like the old man. All the Frumpkin men had acceptable, if not he-man, careers for first-generation Americans growing up with the new century—careers that a parent could brag about in the butcher shop, or on the sidewalk with the fruit man, at the front stoop with the nosy neighbor lady, or with the boys down at the station house. All except Sidney. For him excuses had to be made, at least by Abe. Lubba always supported her boy in whatever he would choose to do. She was not the first mama who had to protect a sensitive boy from a brutish pop.

Sidney Franklin was still, in the terms of the day, all boy and all Brooklyn: tough, cocky, quick to get his dander up, quick to crack wise. Brooklyn had never been a place for the timid to grow up; a kid who showed weakness was as doomed as a gazelle limping across the Serengeti. In these old world neighborhoods, an aggressive attitude, a ritual in-your-face posturing, was needed just to survive. To outsiders from more genteel circumstances this pose could seem loud, belligerent, or even obnoxious. It would, however, prove to be good training for the bullfighting world, especially for a young man who was discovering that there was something different about himself that he had best keep under wraps. Still there was nothing swishy or effeminate about Sidney, and he wouldn't dare display such behavior even if he wanted to. As he grew into an adult, his voice modulated into a rich baritone. Lillian Ross said of him in middle age that his vocabulary and manner of speaking made him sound like a fight promoter—or a cop. His words were torrents of cliché, hyperbole, homily, and the well-worn adage.

The Brooklyn street of his youth, typical of the greater New York melting pot, was the world of "disses" and "dats," "dems" and "dose," a home to an urban subculture that became an American archetype, spawning a stock character of the streetwise child of immigrants with the defiant New York accent. In popular culture it would become as identifiable a character as the Southern belle, the flinty New Englander, or the Texas cowboy. (If one listens to the recording of Lou Gehrig's famous farewell speech in Yankee Stadium, instead of Gary Cooper's flat Montana intonation in the film version of the event, it almost sounds as if the Iron Horse is saying that he is the luckiest man "on the face of the oith." Gehrig, the son of German immigrants, was born in lower Manhattan less than a month before Sidney.) To those raised in Brooklyn, the accent had its own subdivisions. For example, locals said it was easy to differentiate the more high-pitched, nasal New Yorkese of the predominantly secular Jewish neighborhood of Flatbush from the lower, more guttural tones of the Italians of Bensonhurst.

This cultural mix bred the individuals who created the archetype. Brooklyn was the birthplace of Al Capone four years before Sidney's own arrival. Another child of immigrants, Capone would also grow up with the new century just a few miles north of Park Slope in the neighborhood of Williamsburg, then move with his parents to Park Slope itself when Sid was just ten. Williamsburg was home to a rich Jewish community both secular and orthodox, which was chronicled by novelist and screenwriter Daniel Fuchs (who presumably did not run with the same crowd as the Capone boy, although he and his pals did treat the drugstore phone booth where Vincent "Mad Dog" Coll was rubbed out as a tourist attraction). Another Jewish intellectual born in Brooklyn just ten months after Sidney was editor, critic, and broadcast personality Clifton Fadiman, who also happened to be Sidney's cousin.

Horse-drawn delivery drays shared the pavement with streetcars, trolleys, and the new arrival, automobiles. The town was the home of Ebbets Field, built when Sidney was just nine for the National League team, which would soon shorten its name from Brooklyn Trolley Dodgers to simply Dodgers. The new ballpark was situated two and a half miles by street from Jackson Place, much closer if a boy cut straight east through Prospect Park. Once there, Sidney could stand in line to plop down his quarter at the ticket window for a Dodger game with, if not such kids as Al Capone, George Gershwin, or Daniel Fuchs, then perhaps with the sons of some Lithuanian Jews from Brooklyn's Bath Beach, the Horwitz boys — later known as the Howards of the Three Stooges — the youngest of whom, Jerome ("Curly"), was just Sid's age. Three years after Ebbets Field was built, the Dodgers won their first National League pennant since 1900 behind the hitting of a young Casey Stengel. Down Flatbush Avenue about three miles from Ebbets Field loomed the Manhattan Bridge and, to its left, the Brooklyn Bridge. Beyond them rose the great towering iconic shapes of Manhattan itself. Sidney Frumpkin was now a young man earning his own money, beginning to make his way in this amazing city at the beginning of one of New York's own signature eras, the 1920s.

As a financially self-sufficient seventeen-year-old, Sidney was free to explore these enticing streets. He was less free to explore his own feelings and inclinations. There was no acceptable way to be a homosexual in the Brooklyn where Sidney grew up — where conforming to sexual and ethnic expectations was essential to survival — and certainly no way under the roof of Abe Frumpkin. Even Sidney's short stage career was considered incompatible with his father's interpretation of Orthodox Jewry. There would be no coming out, no confessionals at the kitchen table followed by tears and hugs. There were no role models, no support groups, no safe paths. The insular immigrant neighborhoods were as gossipy as small town America; they could be nurturing and supportive until taboos and norms were violated, then they could be scornful, cruel, or violent. Being gay was simply out of the question.

Lillian Ross in her *New Yorker* piece teases the Freudian notion

that Officer Frumpkin would not only have been called "cop" or
"flatfoot" by the kids on the street, but in the parlance of the day,
"bull" as well, so that what Sidney was doing every time he stepped
into the ring was performing a symbolic slaying of the father. After
planting this provocative kernel, she then allows Sid to cheerfully
debunk the idea. "Once I stepped into a ring, I never even *thought* of
my father." If Dr. Freud had little juice around Jackson Place, Officer
Frumpkin still had the upper hand — or fist — in his own house.

The incident that sent Sidney at the age of nineteen into Latin
America and the violent ritual of the bulls was itself an act of violence. It was also a ritual performed over and over between many
fathers and sons when fear and sexuality are in play. Sidney, now
a solid five-feet-eleven, virtually an adult with his own business
and bank account, felt free to come and go as he pleased although
still living at home. He tested the limits of that freedom in the
late spring of 1922 when he spent a weekend at the Jersey shore
with a male friend. To Lillian Ross he said he and another young
man entertained two chorus girls for a couple of nights, although
he was careful to say that nothing sexual happened. In his own
story three years later, the chorus girls disappeared from the tale
and his companion was his "business partner."

When he came home that Sunday afternoon, his father was in
a rage. Sidney claims the old man's anger was because he, blam-
ing busy telephone lines, had not called his parents to let them
know his whereabouts. If so, the policeman's response was still
extreme. Sitting on his bed, Sidney could hear his father thump-
ing up the narrow stairs from the front parlor, a sound to which
he had steeled himself over the years. The door flew open and,
without a word, Abe came after his son. Not having a *banderillero* to double the charging animal for him, Sidney did not know
whether the bull would hook from one side or the other — whether

to watch for the right hand or the left. Bullfighters refer to the horn an animal prefers as the master horn, a concept Sidney would soon learn. Before he could come up with an explanation or excuse, his father punched him in the face. Sidney claimed he did not regain consciousness until the following day.

It is pointless to speculate whether this act was in response to simply not calling, or whether his father feared what his boy and a male friend could be doing at a hotel in Asbury Park for two nights. Sidney's niece Eve said that over the last eighty-five years family memory had dimmed on the subject of the patriarch's motives, if indeed the incident is discussed at all. Abe's response today would perhaps land him in the lockup of his own Seventy-Eighth Precinct, but in 1922 it was apparently a father's prerogative to knock a son unconscious, especially if he feared the boy was becoming a *faygeleh*. In the Brooklyn of Sidney Franklin's youth, domestic violence was as common as stickball.

The explosion had been building up for years. Sidney was ready to go. He had held himself in check since he was a boy, controlling not only his temper and passions but also his curiosity — curiosity about life, about sex not furtive but unbridled, about the world. He was tired of pretending to be what he could not be: the dutiful son who would one day have the safe career, marry a nice girl who would make the folks proud, and have a family so that no one would talk. Sexuality aside, his grand sense of himself and his destiny was too great for such a conventional life. He was ready for the world and what he imagined it could hold for him in all its darkness and all its glory. He was, after all, almost nineteen and thought in such sweeping nineteen-year-old terms. So he cleaned out his bank account, ordered a trunk from Gimbels, and booked passage under the name "Sidney Franklin" on the SS *Monterrey* bound for Havana and Veracruz.

2

Que Viva Mexico

IT WAS A GRAND GESTURE SUITED to Sidney's sense of style and taste for the dramatic. Other boys might have moved in with a friend for a few days or taken a room in the city to sulk, raise hell, perhaps to feel heroically sorry for themselves, and somehow let the homefolks know that they were no longer needed. But those boys would never become bullfighters, either. "I am the sun, moon and stars to myself," he would later say. A liner to an exotic destination would sure show the old man.

The *Monterrey* docked in Veracruz after almost a week of rough passage down the Atlantic coast into the Gulf with a stop in Havana. Redheaded Sidney was now in the tropics. Many of his fellow travelers were Latin American students his own age returning home after the American school year and continuing south to Caracas, Rio, and Buenos Aires. These modern, bicultural kids were Sidney's first taste of the ancient worlds he was about to enter. Veracruz had been founded by the conqueror Cortez over a century before the Dutch settled the cozy little hamlet of Breuckelen. There is a story that before marching his soldiers, cutthroats, and adventurers two hundred miles westward across the mountains to seize the Valley of Mexico and all its treasure, Cortez burned his ships in the harbor of Veracruz so that his men would not flee back to Cuban settlements when the challenges of raping the New World became too much to bear. It was succeed or die. Sidney Frumpkin was under no such pressure, but the new world that spread out before him was as wonderfully exotic as the land of the Olmec had been to Mr. Cortez.

Ships from all over the world crowded the harbor. Men from all over the hemisphere crowded the docks. From the oil refineries and pumping stations up the coast at Tampico, filthy tankers floated Mexican crude out to the world and the smoke from their stacks could be seen smudging the horizon. After almost two decades of family, neighborhood, community, of knowing everyone and everything in his brownstone universe, Sidney was indeed a stranger in a very strange land. Even a teenage Norteamericano with a passable suit and a few hundred dollars cash in his pocket was a man of substance in such a place. Sidney found himself enchanted that first night as he gazed at the trolleys clattering by under the arc lights on rails shiny in the evening mist, at the lemonade vendors and shoeshine boys scrambling for the attention of the foreign travelers, at the Gulf of Mexico glistening beyond the ships slipping past the Sacrificios Lighthouse at the harbor entrance. It was a land of endless possibility.

Sidney had met a young man on the *Monterrey*. This new companion on life's strange journey had helped Sidney with the unfamiliar language and the chaos of debarkation; taking charge, he helped the slim young stranger with the Brooklyn accent buy his rail ticket to the capitol, where both men would travel together. If only for the few weeks that he had planned on staying, Sidney was for the first time in his life finally free — free to invent himself and accountable to no one — at least for the length of his spree. If he had toyed with the moniker "Sidney Franklin" since the days of his junior high school theatrics, he was certainly about to become a new man now. His ships burned to the waterline whether he knew it or not, Sidney Franklin and his new friend caught the morning train for Mexico City.

Veracruz with its international trade would have seemed somewhat familiar to a kid who grew up so near the port of New York. Once the train pulled out of town, Sidney left every trace of the familiar behind. From the humid gulf, the railroad cut through dunes and swamp and clouds of strange insects, then crossed a coastal plain, part savanna, part cropland and orchards, where Sidney would see exotic birds and his first mango and cactus. The train wound into the jungle foothills of the Sierra Madre Oriental heading for the same destination as Cortez. For the first years of his life, the tallest objects Sidney had ever seen were of the manmade variety just across the East River. Now the locomotive chugged through Córdoba, then Orizaba, which was founded on the site of the old Aztec garrison Ahuaializapan, and down the western side of the range before looping up to the colonial city of Puebla. If Sidney were sitting on the right side of the ancient mahogany, brass, and velour Mexican National Railway coach, its windows pulled down as relief from the heat, only to let in the dust and smoke, he could peer just to the north to see snow on the eighteen-thousand-foot peak of the old volcano Citlaltépetl, Mexico's highest mountain. Between the towns and the hamlets and the fields, Sidney saw his first wild country, the land of the eagle, the snake, the jaguar, and from Spain, the bull.

It was night when the train pulled into Mexico City. The streets were wet, the stars overhead obscured by the electric lights. Parts of the city were as civilized and cosmopolitan as the countryside Sidney had seen that day was backward and dangerous. Rich and poor, European and mestizo, modern and feudal—all were jammed together at a noisy seventy-three hundred feet that literally took Sidney's breath away. A New Yorker—even a Brooklynite—of the 1920s could be forgiven for thinking that he lived in the center of the universe. An hour on the pavement of the City of Mexico would leave Sidney with no such illusions. He supervised the porters as they navigated his Gimbels trunk to the curbstones, where horsepower came in all forms and the cabbies touted hotels, brothels, and games of chance. Even at night the depot swarmed with the exotic, the unfamiliar. Students, tycoons, tourists, and provincials all came to the capitol by rail. The sidewalk was crowded with street vendors selling strange fruits, hard pastries, and iced lemonade ladled by the glass from tin buckets. He heard the familiar sound of the hurdy-gurdy and sniffed the strange odor of mesquite smoke from sidewalk braziers. Even Hell's Kitchen—had he ever seen it—would not have prepared Sidney for the level of poverty to be witnessed in urban Mexico. Tiny Indian women, barely out of their teens but looking fifty, wrapped in black from head to toe, held up bony infants no larger than Sidney's hand for the inspection of passersby as they sold gum from the *chicle* of the sapodilla tree or begged outright, wailing in unfamiliar tongues. Maimed victims of the recent revolution sat in filth and silence, their hands outstretched.

Sidney immediately noticed the brigades of shoeshine boys— brash cheerful, barefoot, brown-skinned, brown-eyed, and insolent—chasing the new arrivals with their homemade shine boxes and steady patter, boys sometimes not yet in their teens but savvy to the ways of the world. From a traveler's footwear these little entrepreneurs could size up his country of origin, the amount of money in his pocket, and his penchant for parting with it. English or Spanish, there was no request, demand, or proposition that they had not heard, and they had an answer for each one. For Sidney, Latin boys would become a lifelong weakness. He took a cab to the center of the city, checked into a hotel, then wandered the streets for hours before dawn, filling his nostrils with whiffs of gasoline exhaust, horse manure, and the smell of the previous day's vegetables rotting in the gutters. The fate of his young traveling companion from the *Monterrey*, Sidney did not say. What Sidney did in the middle of that first intoxicating night remains his secret. He was still two weeks shy of his nineteenth birthday.

If Sidney had decided that his Mexico trip was to be a son's dramatic thumb of the nose to the old man for a few weeks, he soon changed his mind and began behaving as a young man with a purpose — starting a new life in Mexico. He secured a storefront studio with living quarters and set up a printing and poster business as he had back in New York. His first clients were American advertisers, but he soon was printing for local businesses, bridging the language gap with hand gestures and sketches, scribbling furiously on a small pad. He staffed his shop exclusively with boys of the street, soon employing fifteen in three eight-hour shifts. Sidney was like a kid in a candy shop. In later life he relished the memory of crowds of shoeshine boys fighting for his business as he gladly overpaid. His wingtip perched on the box, he offered nickel bonuses for the filthiest double-entendres of the Mexican street, coaxing the little boys into colloquial sexual descriptions until his vocabulary was as salacious as those of his new young friends. Ernest Hemingway would later remark that Sidney had a rare ear for language and dialect. It was a gift Sidney cultivated with both ease and pleasure as he began this new life as an expatriate printer. The freedom first sensed aboard ship, then in Veracruz, had become a permanent condition. Life in Mexico City was like life in any big cosmopolitan metropolis for a gay lad from the provinces.

There were no nosy neighbor ladies to watch his comings and go-
ings, no neighborhood tough guys to taunt him on his fastidious
wardrobe or choice of companions. He gravitated to people who
did not seem to care about such things and who accepted Sidney as
he was — smart, charming, boisterous, talkative, generous, always
curious, always open to something new.

His business grew quickly, first with streetcar cards for soft
drinks and cigarettes, then theatrical ads and, inevitably, bullfight
posters, or *cartels*. Sidney's artist's eye instinctively caught the inherent drama of the *corrida*. His stylized posters emphasized the
size and danger of the animal, the cool bravery of the man. Soon
a "Sidney Franklin" *cartel* became quite popular in its own right.
Mexico City at this time already had a rich engraving and poster-
making culture from which Sidney could draw inspiration, led by
such artists as José Clemente Orozco and his mentor José Guada-
lupe Posada. Young and modestly successful in a new city, Sidney
spent his free time in such establishments as El Gallo de Oro (the
Golden Cock, or Rooster), which was at the corner of Calle Nuevo
Mexico and Avenida Bolivar near his shop, and the Fénix Café, a
bullfighters' hangout. The chatty Sidney made friends easily in
the world of his clients and their friends, getting to know a smart
crowd of artists, newspapermen, actors, singers, comedians, drag
acts, and, of course, bullfight promoters. He also found himself
among what he called European "society bloods," implying sleek
young men of good families, large allowances, and time on their
hands. These were worlds where Sidney felt he should fit right in.
Once his business could support it, he dragged his new friends on
weekend excursions to the countryside, where they drove in hired
cars to explore Spanish colonial towns, isolated Indian villages, the
great haciendas, and peasant farms. Sidney absorbed the culture
and folklore along with the language, and he fell in love with the

people. But for months he claimed he did not, *would* not, attend a bullfight.

Sidney's circle of friends shows his lifelong interest in rubbing elbows with the best of the best and proving that he belonged in their company. This child of immigrants felt he was "destined to lead" as he told interviewer Lillian Ross, "it's a matter of noblesse oblige." But the sophisticates and professionals he gravitated toward in the cafés were the minority. Like Soviet Russia, Mexico had just completed a revolution of the poor.

It had been less than a decade since the peasant armies of Pancho Villa from the north and Emiliano Zapata from the south had joined forces and, temporarily victorious, ridden through the capitol. In 1914 the pale-skinned aristocrats and bourgeoisie had peered fearfully down from windows and balconies into the streets below at the bobbing sombreros that hid the dark faces of these invading horsemen — and women — wearing crossed *bandoleros* over their rags. The streets were so full of riders that, from above, their hats hid the cobblestones. The revolution was not quite over in that summer of 1922 when Sidney first arrived. It still had the twitch and venom of a just-macheted snake. It would be another year before Pancho Villa would be ambushed in Parral, in the state of Chihuahua, while driving from a wedding in his big Dodge — murdered presumably on orders from General Obregón, the new president. Obregón himself had led a revolt that deposed the old president, General Carranza, in 1920, his troops blasting Carranza from the saddle as he tried to reach Veracruz over the Sierra Madre on horseback. Carranza had in turn seized power from General Huerta in 1914 after Huerta had murdered the reformer Francisco Madero the year before. Madero — beloved briefly by Villa and Zapata — had started the whole thing by leading the revolution against the old dictator Díaz in 1910. Not that

Sidney paid any attention to such dizzying facts. He was never much interested in history except in those moments he chose to rewrite his own. He was rather a man who lived either in the here and now, or in his tweaked version of his own exploits. But as he and his pals tooled around the countryside sightseeing in rented autos, the blood was not yet dry on the Mexican sand. Unlike Russia, the wealthy never really lost their grip on Mexico.

As Sidney rewrote his history over the years, he gave two versions of his first bullfight, which he attended after being in the country for many months. To Lillian Ross in 1947 he said that the experience did absolutely nothing for him. In his autobiography published three years later, Sidney opens the book with a breathless description of that first *corrida*. He claims one of the matadors on the program was Rodolfo Gaona, a Mexican Indian who, along with Juan Belmonte and Joselito, was already considered one of the three greatest matadors of the early twentieth century — bullfighting's golden age. The second sword on the program was the Spaniard Marcial Lalanda, then only nineteen, whom Sidney describes as "strikingly lithe and graceful" his effortless capework beautiful "yet so masculine." (There are aficionados who dispute this scenario by saying that there is no record of Gaona and Lalanda appearing together in a *corrida* in Mexico in 1922.) Sidney did state that he was sickened by the evisceration of the picadors' horses, a spectacle that happened half a dozen times every afternoon in those days before the horses wore the *peto*, the thick protective padding common since 1930 (a reaction that no doubt spurred Sidney's boast in his autobiography taking credit for the addition of the padding). By the second act of the fight, the placing of the *banderillas*, he was caught up in the excitement and claimed — as usual placing himself at the center of attention — that his fellow spectators were infected by the enthusiasm of the young American who seemed inherently to understand the events in the ring like a seasoned pro. In the third act when Lalanda brought out the sword and small cape — the *muleta* — to work the bull for the kill, Sidney was hooked. Or so he says. As an artist, Sidney had no trouble recognizing artistry in another discipline, even one so foreign. What really seduced him was the adoration of the crowd for the matadors and the realization of the huge amounts of money that these men of often humble beginnings could command. To Sidney there was nothing foreign about money and fame.

3

The Wisdom of the Aztec

BULLFIGHTING: MONEY, FAME, SEX, DEATH — fame, money, and yeah, sex. This was something Sidney had not reckoned with, had not clearly understood in Brooklyn terms. This bullfighting business meant huge national recognition. It meant love, the kind of love like folks had for a guy like President Theodore Roosevelt that made the whole country go soft when he died in 1919. It was like the respect for athletic artistry that guys had for the Giants' pitcher Christy Mathewson that made it so damned sad when he got a lungful of mustard gas in training camp during the Great War. This was way better than fame. It was drama. It was love from strangers. He hadn't figured on that. Sidney was tantalized by the love part, but he understood drama. Then there was the dough, the kind of money that old J. P. Morgan had, or even better, Tom Mix, who looked like he knew how to have more fun with his dough than old J. P. Sidney would have to think about this — there must be an angle.

In these early months in Mexico, the Latin and Indian cultures surrounding him were mostly impenetrable to Sidney's adolescent sensibilities, be they scrappy New York, old country Orthodox Jewish, or boosterish Warren Harding. He could enjoy these Mexican cultures as an observer, a tourist, but they were not his own. It would only be a matter of time until he was comfortable in the bullfighter's casual *traje corto* of tight, high-waisted pants, short jacket, high-heeled country boots, and flat-brimmed hat, but for now his worldview was still closer to the fedora or the yarmulke than the sombrero *cordobés*. That first *corrida* with Gaona and La-landa would change those sensibilities. Before he would ever hear the bullfighters' name for it, he would experience the *gusanillo*, the worm that aficionados say bores into the flesh and soul of those destined to step into the bullring. The first symptom of his infection by the *gusanillo* was Sidney's belief that he could somehow understand this new spectacle and explain it intellectually. Instead, as could have been predicted, he stuck his foot in it. Late night chatter after dinner with his artistic friends led to Sidney being teased about the nature of courage, about whether a non-Latin, specifically an American, had the stuff, the courage in the blood to face the *toro bravo*. Americans simply did not have the genetic equipment to be bullfighters, his Mexican friends said.

Naturally, Sidney rose to the bait. The one thing that comes across in Sidney's own words and others' recollections is the braggadocio, the verbal combativeness, the Brooklyn pride and feistiness that let no challenge go unanswered. Sidney claimed an American could succeed at anything he put his hand to, and that a man was always superior to any animal. "Americans have more guts in their little fingers than the rest of the world put together." He was never one for understatement.

His friends howled him down, and suggested that if it were so easy, why then did he not try it? Sidney claimed that the Mexi-co City papers soon took up his boast and that the whole issue quickly became one of defending national pride, putting himself in the midst of a self-described international incident. Whatever the circumstances, the *gusanillo* was doing its work, drawing him toward the bulls. The result of this boast was that Sidney was encouraged to contact the Great Indian himself, maestro Rodolfo Gaona, for personal instruction in the art of bullfighting. The plan was for Sidney to learn enough to enter the ring just once as wealthy amateurs often did in charity exhibitions, or in *tientas* at the great bull-breeding ranches. There was no suggestion yet of any possible career. Such a notion would have seemed ridiculous, even to Sidney. He would simply learn enough to prove his point — and his courage.

The word from Sidney's friends was that the Great Indian was superstitious, so Sidney was persuaded to write his request on garish stationary decorated with cats' heads, then pester the maestro by phone before there had even been time for a reply. The matador's representatives sent word to the pushy American that he was expected at a dinner party the following night at Gaona's home on Calle Liverpool. Because of the posters Sidney had made for Gaona's *corridas* in Mexico City, he would have been known at least to Gaona's manager if not the matador himself. In his autobiography Sidney claims that his friends instructed him on proper clothing, cologne, and demeanor as if he were going on a blind date. They teased him with lurid stories about Gaona's sex life as if he would be the object of a pass from the matador (who according to Sidney's own later account was a married man with both lovely children and a fine mistress, so this is an odd invention on his part). Sidney claims this attempt to scare him off failed. He rang the bell at the Calle Liverpool mansion at the appointed hour.

Gaona, by then near the end of his career, was kind and gracious to his guest. After dinner when Sidney was able to speak to him alone over cigars and cognac, Gaona patiently listened to his unrealistic request that he wished to learn enough of the basics of bullfighting to perform once in the ring. The matador explained the danger of such an undertaking. Unless in an arena with young calves, there are no half measures, no shallow water in dealing with a full-grown bull bred to fight. The amateur is in just as deep as the professional the moment the bull is released into the ring, so this was a very serious request. Whether out of kindness, curiosity, or simply for the novelty of seeing an American try the ancient art, Gaona agreed to coach Sidney free of charge, to become his mentor. Perhaps Sidney would learn enough to both perform and survive if he stuck with it and showed sufficient aptitude. He allowed Sidney to choose capes and *muletas* from his own supply and keep them as his own. Early every morning for the next two weeks, Sidney arrived at Gaona's home to be driven by the maestro himself to a practice ring in nearby Nativitas, where a dozen young aspirants practiced under Gaona's supervision.

To the newcomer, the training of bullfighters is a strange-looking business. The most obvious thing, of course, is that there is no bull. Bulls being such dangerous — and expensive — creatures, the would-be matadors have to learn to do without, just as aspiring astronauts have to train on earth without the benefit of outer space. To an American city boy, the bullfighting world was just as otherworldly. That first morning, Sidney would have seen a dozen or so young men performing a strange pantomime in a small practice ring while old men and young women watched from the wooden grandstands. A few of the novices would have been dressed in street clothes, the well-off in slacks and polo shirts, and the poor in tee shirts and dungarees, or, if it were hot, which it constantly was in summer, in bathing briefs with shoes or sandals. Playing the part of the bull would be old men or small but wise boys carrying before them a set of bull's horns from the slaughterhouse as they pressed moderately but steadily toward the novice, who would then plant his feet and move his cape away from his body as the disembodied horns followed it. Some of the young men practicing the placing of the *banderillas* or rehearsing passes with their *muletas* faced a set of horns mounted on a single bicycle wheel pushed by a set of handles. The contraption is called a *carretilla*, and can move as quickly as the boy pushing it, turning it on a centavo. Whether handheld or on wheels, each time the horns came close, the student moved his cape or *muleta* away with a deliberate grace. To the uninitiated this ritual had a slightly ridiculous look to it, like shadowboxing in slow motion, but it was serious business. This was what the bull, in theory, would do when such a move was tried in the ring. As every novice knew, the bull was not always a predictable beast, and most matadors had scars on thigh and groin and belly to testify to those times when the animal did not follow the cape away from the body. (Students of the bullfight reckon that a matador could expect to be gored many times in the course of a career, and once a season was not unusual.) If the cape move was ill performed, the boys charging with the slaughterhouse horns gladly jabbed the novice with the horn tips, giving him a small taste of the pain to come. The idea was to practice such simple moves with such deadly dull repetition that they become unconscious, so that when a fifteen-hundred-pound animal lunges at the hundred-thirty-pound man like a derailed locomotive hurtling close enough to snag one's zipper, the man's instinct kicks in and the cape moves where it ought. An untrained person's reflex would draw the horns right to them if they jumped away. So it was practice, practice, practice.

Sidney warmed to the camaraderie of his fellow students and gamely put up with the hard, repetitious training. One exercise consisted simply of standing with one's back flat against the barrier and holding the work cape at arm's length in both hands. The student then would pivot his torso as he moved the cape first as far as his arm would extend to his right, then back all the way to his left, keeping the cloth parallel to the fence at his back — and in theory parallel to the imaginary bull in front of him. A trained matador whirls the *capote* with such ease that it seems as if it must be as light as a dinner jacket. Sidney, as all novices, would experience the unpleasant surprise at the heaviness of the *capote* the first time he picked one up. The item is a true cape with magenta silk on one side and a shell of yellow duck on the other. The exercise at the fence was to perfect the simple pass, the *verónica*, that is the matador's basic tool in the first act of the *corrida*, when the bull has just entered the ring and the man and animal are testing each other for the first time. The pass is as elemental as a left jab to a boxer. The matador simply holds the *capote* in both fists and swings it away from his body, but of course there is nothing simple about it. The pass can be pedestrian or a thing of beauty, depending on the practitioner. Like hitting an inside curveball, it's all in the wrists. Bullfighting legend says that the pass was named for Saint Veronica, the woman who held out her linen veil to Christ so that he could wipe the blood and sweat from his face; the *corrida*, like the road to Calvary, being heavy with symbolism. Sidney performed the exercise against the barrier for hours until his shoulders ached and quivered. At twenty, he was already older than many of the young men with whom he practiced, and who, unlike Sidney, had grown up in the culture. Some of the dozen, despite their passion, would not have the skill, the bravery, or the luck to go on to a career in the arena. Of those who did, some might live to see twenty-two.

In one way his café friends were right. To an American raised on images of tobacco-chewing, wisecracking Brooklyn shortstops, or grinning, broken-nosed fullbacks, the demeanor of the would-be bullfighter was worlds apart. Sidney watched the deadly serious expression of his counterparts as they practiced their capework. He would have to learn the cool, contemptuous scowl, the sneer in the face of danger, the actor's mask too dignified to show excitement or joy, much less fear. This was definitely a Latin male pose — certainly not how a fella carried himself sauntering down Flatbush Avenue on his way to the picture show. Having toyed with acting — and posing — Sidney would take to that posture soon enough. The pose extended to the haughty chin-back, hips-forward strut of the *torero* as he entered the ring, the way he wore the archaic suit of lights as if pink silk stockings were the only clothing possible for a real man to inhabit. The passion extended long after the lessons ended. It was not considered strange for such obsessed young men to clear the tables in the center of a café, grab a tablecloth, and perform *verónicas* late into the night as friends put fingers to their temples and played the part of the bull. Such parlor games were called *toreo de salón* — literally, living room bullfighting. These games and the men who played them were profoundly serious.

After two weeks of total immersion in the art of bullfighting, Sidney found himself at sea when Gaona went back to making a living, leaving the capitol for a new tour. The maestro left Sidney in the hands of a hack matador who spent more effort sponging money from the young printer than working on Sidney's footwork. It was time to move on. One of Sidney's promoter clients provided introduction to one don Abelardo, owner of the Xochitl Ranch, where fighting stock was raised for the bullring. (Don Abelardo's Xochitl *ganadería*, as Sidney refers to it in *Bullfighter from Brooklyn*, would later be known as the Xajay ranch. In his *New Yorker* interview, he used this later name, but referred to the *ganadero* as don Julio Herrera. The well-known Xajay ranch was founded in 1923 by the brothers Edmundo and Jorge Guerrero. When Sidney referred to "don Abelardo," perhaps he was thinking of some other *ganadero*. Another explanation for this inconsistency is that after more than two decades, Sidney's memory might have become vague on this matter, and thus Edmundo became "Abelardo," Jorge became "Julio," and Guerrero devolved into "Herrera." In any case, the ranch will be referred to here as the Xajay and the rancher don Jorge Guerrero.) The promoter told Sidney that once he gained enough experience, he would book him in some small festival. This would be enough to prove Sidney's point to his café pals, which was of course the purpose of the whole crazy exercise.

Sidney took a train north to the town of El Cazadero in the state of Querétaro, then was driven by automobile due north on a dirt road through gently rolling country to the ranch. There he spent several days playing with señor Guerrero's heifer calves — his first introduction to caping a living adversary. It was also Sidney's introduction to the life of the *hacendado*, the owner of vast landholdings who lived in a gracious feudal world of sleek cattle, blooded horses, plentiful peons, bountiful food, and beautiful women — most of which held great appeal for Sid. Although a century or two removed from the trolleys, front stoops, pushcarts, and curbside crap games among which he grew up, it was a world where the kid from Brooklyn quickly felt at home. These hacienda guys knew how to *live*.

When Sidney stepped off his train upon his return to Mexico City, there was more greeting him than just the crowds and noise he had left behind for a week. Bullfight posters announced that he, Sidney Franklin, was to appear in an upcoming bullfight that Sunday. To add to his shock, the poster was presumably not one of his own. It seemed that the promoter who arranged Sidney's week in the country with don Jorge assumed that on his return he would be seasoned enough to face his first bull. An American on the card of even a modest bullring such as Plaza de Chapultepec would be enough of a novelty to draw a crowd. The promoter would not be paying Sidney except in invaluable experience and exposure. Whether or not he performed well was almost beside the point. It was September, the end of the season, so it would be Sidney's last chance until the following spring. (Sidney's explanation of this as a do-or-die moment seems to contradict the notion that the usual Mexican bullfight season was based on a winter schedule extending from fall to spring. This would be the first of many seeming contradictions in the record of his long and singular career.)

Sidney was both flattered and horrified. He obviously did not think he was ready to face a full-grown bull in an organized bullfight in front of a paying crowd. This was not just playing with some calves on a ranch. Then there was the matter of the costume. Sidney had none, and as they were expensive, custom-made items, obtaining one would take weeks. The promoter had that covered, loaning Sidney a pearl-grey and gold costume that had belonged to a retired *torero*. Sidney responded in characteristic fashion. He spent the entire afternoon admiring himself at a photographer's studio.

The *traje de luces*, or suit of lights, is an outfit with roots in the eighteenth century, when bullfighting took its modern form. Tight knee britches, a short jacket over a vest, stockings, light slippers, and the little black chenille cap, the *montera*, all weighed together as much as twenty pounds. The sequined outfit does not simply button up. There are drawstrings to pull, ribbons to tie. It is all part of the ritual of transformation. Once Sidney actually squeezed his robust frame into the suit and saw himself in the mirror, it was love at first sight. "I looked like a Christmas tree." Like Narcissus staring at his image in the pond, or perhaps more accurately, like Peter O'Toole in the film *Lawrence Of Arabia* entranced by his reflection in the blade of a dagger the first time he puts on his virginally white Arabian burnoose, Sidney saw himself in his suit of lights as a man transformed. He looked at the reflection of the grinning big-eared Brooklyn boy — still only twenty — in that ancient costume, and saw his future. (To a post-Disney viewer, the *montera* has an undeniably mouse-eared shape, which accentuated Sidney's own appendages.) He claims that as the afternoon wore on the photographer finally had to throw him out of the studio so he could go home.

There was still the matter of the bull. Sidney's excitement as a new man was tempered by the knowledge of the recklessness and danger of what he was agreeing to do the following day. Sidney was the second matador on the program at the Chapultepec ring — a late-morning preliminary exhibition on September 30, 1923, that preceded the main *corrida* by several hours. One of the young men appearing with him that day was Juan Espinosa, who would fight under the name "Armillita" during a long career as both matador and *banderillero*. Juan showed Sidney how to carry his dress cape for the opening procession, but the haughty demeanor of his comrades was lost on the grinning New Yorker. Goofing across the sand, he was as amused as the crowd was at the spectacle he was creating. Then, when the first bull of the day had been killed and it was Sidney's turn, he learned that the term "moment of truth" was, in the bullring, no glib cliché. He claims that when his bull charged into the arena, he had second thoughts and, to the delight of the spectators who had come for the novelty of watching the redheaded Yanqui, got into an argument with the promoter behind the *barrera* — the red wooden fence surrounding the arena. Meanwhile, on the other side of the fence, his bull, twice the size of anything Sidney had caped on the ranch the week before, trotted triumphantly around the ring with no adversary in sight. Sidney was finally persuaded to go out and do as he had been instructed. At first, the bull charged, then stopped, although Sidney was shaking his cape and calling to it in his Brooklyn accent. He finally got the animal to charge and completed the first successful *verónica* of his career to what he remembers as the roar of the crowd. The intense repetition under Gaona's instruction, even for only a few weeks, had paid off. Sidney performed many more passes, including a difficult behind-the-back cape move invented by Gaona himself, got harmlessly tossed by the bull, then retired behind a *burladero*, one of the wooden shields spaced around the arena about eighteen inches out from narrow openings in the fence, which allowed just enough room for a man — but not enough for a bull — to slip through. As the barbed sticks were placed in the bull's shoulders by Sidney's *banderillero*, Sidney felt he could relax. His work was done. He had proved his point. An American could perform adequately in a bullring after all.

At that point Sidney had his second argument with the promoter. The bull, his withers bleeding from the picador's lance, and with the *banderillas* hanging from smaller wounds on his shoulders, was panting in the center of the ring, looking for his adversary. The third act of the *corrida*, the *faena*, remained undone. The promoter reminded Sidney that he had been billed as a *matador*. Matador does not mean bullfighter. It does not even mean head, chief, or most respected bullfighter. The word comes from the verb *matar*: to kill. Matador means *killer*. Period. So Sidney still had some unfinished business in the ring. He reasonably explained that he had not advanced to the killing part of the festival in his schooling. He had practiced neither with the *muleta* — the small semicircular red flannel cape articulated by a short stick — nor with the sword. Without such training, a guy could get murdered out there. The promoter informed Sidney that if he did not take up the *muleta* and the sword, he was in much more danger from the crowd than he was from the bull.

Sidney had seen his fellow students, as they practiced with Gaona, perform the one-handed passes with the *muleta* intended to draw the bull low and close prior to the kill. He had seen them scrunch up their faces as they sighted down the sword at the charging horns on the bicycle wheel when they rehearsed their sword thrusts. For Sidney there would be no practice. Behind the *barrera*, Juan Espinosa and Sidney's own *banderilleros* quickly gave him a run-through of what was expected of him. Then, there was nothing for him to do but go out and kill the bull.

By this, the third act, the animal has been weakened by the *pica* and the *banderillas*, but he has probably learned a thing or two as well. The matador cannot plunge the sword into the animal unless he is close enough so that one quick hook to the side by the bull can change the outcome of the whole business. The kill was to be clean and ritualistic — no hacking at the animal sideways. The sword arm had to come in over the horns so that the blade tip enters at the base of the neck, essentially between the shoulder blades. It was not unheard of for bull and man to kill one another at the same instant, which happened to the legendary Manolete in 1947, a day about which aficionados still speak with reverence. About the only thing worse for the matador than this outcome is to botch the kill so that a second try is necessary. It is also not unheard of that a matador is not able kill his bull cleanly with multiple thrusts and must leave the killing to others, exiting the ring in disgrace to boos and objects thrown from the stands. A terrified Sidney, whether by innate instinct or dumb luck, stood his ground, sighted down the *estoque* — the killing sword — which he held in his right hand as the *muleta* held in his left hand drew the bull past him. In this complicated pose with arms crossed in front of him (the cross formed by the bullfighter's arms in the face of such a black devil was yet another bit of religious symbolism), Sidney reached over the horns and thrust downward. It worked. He killed his bull with that first try. The crowd went wild, throwing hats and handkerchiefs into the arena. According to the story he told throughout his career, they carried him in triumph from the ring. Sidney had never known such adulation, such love in his life. His decision was almost made for him. After all, no other guy from the states — certainly no other kid from Brooklyn — had thought to stake out this turf. He would have the whole field to himself. He would become an American bullfighter.

ACT TWO

The Suerte de Banderillas.
This second act consists of the matador's
assistants, the banderilleros, *jabbing the*
barbed sticks, the banderillas, *into the*
shoulders of the bull to correct any defect
in the direction of the animal's charge.
By this time in the drama, for both the bull
and the matador, the course of the action
has taken a certain direction and is falling
into well-ordered grooves, although
the outcome is always in question.

4

———

El Niño de la Synagoga

SIDNEY HAD CHANGED THE DIRECTION of his charge twice in as many years, which is not too surprising for a young man of only twenty. He quickly learned that deciding to make one's living as an adored member of a risk-taking elite is not quite the same as actually becoming part of such a group. The next few years would be quite hard for Sidney, and it is remarkable that he stuck to a discipline so foreign to his upbringing, so dangerous, and something before now nearly impossible for an American to achieve. If his accomplishments were not quite what he would brag they were in later years, he still did become a bullfighter, an amazing achievement in itself. To a young man in the grip of a dream, success is a foregone conclusion. Whether he would have stuck to the task if he could have known that it would be another twenty-three years before he would take his *alternativa* is anyone's guess.

First, Sidney had to walk away from his successful poster business. This was an occupation that came easily, and that suited both his artistic and his garrulous natures. The gelt in the pockets of the gabardine slacks, money earned by his own wit and talent, was an essential part of who Sidney was since he had been in his mid-teens. His ability to support himself was what gave him his buffer against the disapproving world. It was what gave him the courage to leave his father's house, and what allowed him to travel to Mexico as a young man with a future, not as a bum. Money was also protection for a young fellow with a secret life. It would be a hard thing now to be poor — to not just starve for this new art, but to become vulnerable to the world for it. And to allow the old man to say I told you so. When his business was chugging along, Sidney could have returned to his family at any time, his head held high. Without his business, a return to Brooklyn would have been humiliating, an admission of failure, and perhaps logistically impossible. Still, Sidney shut the poster shop down, gave up his studio, and sold his equipment and supplies. He let his boys go, which would have been hard for so many reasons. He moved into a small rented room in a modest family home, paying months in advance. He had truly burned his ships this time. There was no turning back. Then, he tried to get back into the ring.

The promoter of his Chapultepec debut was willing to pay Sidney a small fee to appear in a series of exhibition fights in the southern and eastern states, but Mexican politics intervened. President Obregón's minister of defense, a General Adolfo de La Huerta (not to be confused with the dictator Victoriano Huerta the decade before), led a revolt against the government in the fall of 1923 and captured the very areas to be covered by Sidney's tour. Sidney was aboard a train that was attacked by troops of the rebel general as it wound through the Sierra Madre Oriental somewhere near Puebla. It seems the general had wanted to be named the president's hand-picked successor, but Obregón had his eye on another contender. The Mexican political situation had become slightly less violent than in recent years. The revolt was put down with La Huerta being only exiled, not hunted down and shot, which Sidney, considering the effect on his tour, might have preferred.

He spent the rest of the offseason training, returning to the world of the *ganaderías* to practice more with heifers—both by himself or in *tientas*. Early in the 1924 season Sidney claims he was invited by well-known matador Luis Freg to appear with him—presumably again as a novelty—in two exhibition fights. These were to be at Ciudad Juárez, fifteen hundred miles north of the capitol just across the border from El Paso, Texas. Spectators came to see the American tossed by the bull, and they were rarely disappointed. This day in March, however, Sidney Franklin made his first money as a matador. The pay was only a couple hundred pesos, but he was now a *novillero*, a professional bullfighter. *Novilleros* are not of the first rank, as those who have taken their *alternativa*, but they are respected members of the taurine community and no longer amateurs. Sidney then secured another exhibition in Chihuahua, and a fourth back south again in the rowdy petroleum port of Tampico, where he would supposedly draw a crowd from the American oilfield roughnecks who labored there. Tampico was to be a charity exhibition, but the promoters cut corners and provided only beef cattle, not fighting stock—a situation guaranteed to make the *toreros* look foolish or inept when the animals would not charge. The exhibition was a disaster. It was going to be a long apprenticeship for the would-be American matador.

Sidney felt he needed to overcome the handicap of being a Yankee in a Latin discipline by knowing more than the competition, by pushing himself harder. To understand the anatomy of his future adversary, the bull, he worked at a large slaughterhouse in Paralvillo, where he arrived at four a.m. after a one-hour bus ride. There he slaughtered beef cattle with a short double-edged knife, one after the other assembly line fashion, plunging the *puntilla* into the animal at the base of the skull and cutting the spinal cord. While he was learning to kill matter-of-factly, he also became knowledgeable about the dressing out of the animal as the carcasses were prepared for the market or the meat locker. As an American who believed in the value of hard work and scientific study, Sidney was literally learning this bull business from the inside out. Whether his work at the slaughterhouse was purely educational or manual labor to make ends meet, Sidney does not clarify. For an artistic boy, this was hard, brutal, and bloody work, nothing "feministic" about it.

He does admit to becoming a regular at the city's pawnshops, hocking his watch, his cufflinks, a fountain pen, any of the emblems that marked the big city dude, the man about town of the early twentieth century. That too was hard for Sidney as another part of his urban identity passed over the counter in exchange for enough cash to see him through. Instead of dining at the Gallo de Oro or the Fénix, he was getting by with half of a ten-centavo *torta* and a glass of water for lunch. He was saving the other half *torta* for his dinner. American hobo slang of the era referred to something called a Mexican Breakfast: a glass of water and a cigarette. Sidney was not so far from such circumstances. No money for shoe shines then, or presumably, for shoeshine boys. Every morning he was out of the slaughterhouse by seven to hoof it across town to the Plaza de Chapultepec, where he joined the other aspirants for more and more practice. Now, like many a young Mexican or Spanish boy with dreams of bullring fame, poverty drove him. Stripped of his material goods, his discipline became his most valued possession. In June of 1924, Sidney would finally appear in the great Mexico City bullring El Toreo, but not on the regular program, only in an exhibition, an event that did not pique the interest of big-time promoters. His Chapultepec debut had been covered by such publications as *Excelsior, El Universal,* and *El Demócrata,* and subsequent appearances were eventually written up with pictures as well, but the reviews were not great. As Sidney's friends had warned, the bullfighting establishment did not easily embrace the concept of a foreigner. The novelty of the awkward Norteamericano was wearing off.

It was finally a regional impresario, one señor Badillo from the southernmost state of Tabasco, who booked Sidney for low-end engagements in Villahermosa and the surrounding hamlets during a winter tour. The circumstances in this jungle state were hard, the accommodations often mosquito, scorpion, and reptile infested, the arenas often swamps after the tropical rains, the promoters too often crooks, the animals frequently of poor quality, but Sidney was able to work at his trade for three straight months. He made a little money, gained more experience, acquired some friends among his profession—matadors with colorful names such as "El Arequipeño," "El Canario," "Faíco," and "La Rata"—and did not for a moment give up on himself. He seems actually to have had a wonderful time.

After becoming involved in an altercation that landed him in a small-town jail, Sidney says he was befriended by a fabulously wealthy expatriate American stranger, Nicolas Browne, who bailed him out of the hoosegow and placated the authorities. Grandson of a confederate officer whose family possessed huge landholdings in Tabasco, the handsome young Browne then took Sidney on all-male hunting trips up the Tenosique River on one of his paddlewheel steamers manned exclusively by his "native crew." Sidney describes Browne as "twenty-eight and unmarried . . . and as regular as they come." Fair enough. It was during one of these paddleboat excursions into the jungle, when Sidney and Nicholas were apparently the only Europeans in the group, that Sidney made his amazing claim about being absconded with by a local chieftain. Evidently, the chieftain wanted the young redhead to impregnate all the woman of his village — at least the young and pretty ones — so he could have a tribe of flame-haired young warriors. Sidney claims that he did exactly as the chief demanded, servicing a baker's dozen tribal teens, both married and unmarried, the very first night. His return to Veracruz after three months in Tabasco was described in equally fantastic terms. Sidney tells of a gulf passage marked by hurricane and shipwreck, part *Robinson Crusoe*, part *Lord Jim*, with the boy from Brooklyn barely surviving on his wits alone after being stranded on a desolate stretch of jungle coast. In the autobiography written a quarter century after these "facts," his account of this winter tour takes on an almost epic tone — the Rabelaisian adventures and triumphs of a plucky naïf in a mythical, if seedy, Eden. The bullfighting, however, was real.

With such steady experience behind him, Sidney began a period of life on the Mexican bullfighting circuit that was to last several more years, setting him in a slow, steady trajectory that would eventually land him in Spain. His first fight after the long winter in Tabasco was on February 22, 1924, at the other end of the country in the town of Nuevo Laredo, just across the Rio Grande from Laredo, Texas. For the first time, Sidney asked for, and then received, more than his usual starvation wages. The press in the United States began to cover this American who found himself engaged in such a novel occupation. He finally made the pages of his hometown paper, the *Brooklyn Eagle*. A photo of Sid contained the caption, "Brooklyn Boy Wins Fame as Mexican Bullfighter, Acclaimed One of the Most Popular of Mexican Matadors." Before this, his family had been so clueless about the bullfighting world that when Sidney had sent them clippings from Mexican papers,

they had assumed from his odd outfit that Sidney had been photographed at a costume ball. Unable to read Spanish, they had no
idea of either the status or the danger involved in his new pursuit.
Once enlightened, Officer Frumpkin demanded that his son quit
this foolishness and come home or he would sail down to Mexico
and haul him back to Park Slope himself. Unfazed, Sidney stuck
to his plan. He would show his father and the rest of his family
that he was his own man — a *real* man in a dangerous occupation.
Then, he again took his act on the road.

Sidney continued to learn his trade in small-town bullrings
across Mexico throughout the mid-1920s. His days were full
of travel, from the dusty towns on the American border where
his countrymen came to see him, back south again to the jungle
hamlets of Tabasco, then across endless plateaus past distant vol-
canoes under cobalt skies to beautiful colonial towns. (Despite
Sidney's claims, however, he never appeared in the lovely city of
Guadalajara, the boyhood home of Harper B. Lee. Lee was the
Texas-born, but Mexican-raised, American bullfighter early in the
century who, before Sidney's arrival on the scene, was considered
the first American matador, taking his *alternativa* in Monterrey in
1910. However, after several serious gorings, plus the disruption
caused by the Mexican Revolution, Lee retired without having his
alternativa confirmed in Madrid, thus giving Sidney the distinction
of being the first American to do so.)

Sid appeared as far away as Tijuana, in the upper northwest
corner of the country, where weekending Hollywood stars who
would later befriend him could sit to watch this redheaded novelty
in the old downtown arena within sight of San Diego, just across
the Otay Mesa. Sometimes, Sidney traveled by coastal steamers
and pilot boats, where he had to huddle next to livestock or ma-
chinery lashed to the deck. Often, he crossed the country by bus

or automobile and endured horrible roads as he shivered over the mountain passes of the Sierra Madre, or was swarmed by insects along the tropical coasts where the mosquito netting in the inns was necessarily thick, and one could be kept awake at night by the scurrying of lizards and roaches on the walls or the dripping of bat guano on the bedclothes. When he was able to travel by train, it was more often than not on the hard wooden benches of the third-class coach. His fellow passengers crowded in with the smells of the cooking they carried and the animals they tended. Sidney got to know well these smells of the Mexican earth and the people who clawed their living from it.

At every arrival in each new town was the anticipation of the next performance. Sidney loved being greeted as a person of importance. There were the afternoons before the *corrida* as the crowds trouped to the bullring along adobe walls covered in bougainvillea the color of a matador's magenta *capote*. There were the cries of the street vendors, the shady sidewalks and small-town plazas smelling of orange blossom and orchids, tree trunks painted white and water splashing in stone fountains in the parks, the streets filled with big-hatted *charros* — both the working cowboys and their ceremonial counterparts — packing their revolvers, rattling their heavy Chihuahua spurs, proud to show off their horsemanship and rope spinning for the crowds. Then there were the nights at the *ganaderías* with guitar music and clear voices singing songs of the revolution and of love, with bonfires in tiled patios, laughter and wine and *pulque*, the shy glances of lovers meeting in the shadows, the smell of roasting meat, the clatter of shod hooves on cobblestones. Mexico would always be a touchstone to Sidney, a haven, no matter how much of the world he would see. But Sidney was only going so far as a bullfighter in Mexico. He stopped appearing for a while in the late 1920s and went back to the breeding ranches to work on his technique. As always with Sidney, even his setbacks were good for a story with him as the star. One hacienda had him teaching all the peons to read. At another, he supposedly organized them into baseball leagues and created a mini Ebbets Field among the rattlesnakes and maguey. But whether or not he wanted to admit it, his career had stalled. Perhaps for a *novillero* he demanded too much money. Perhaps he was not as good as he fancied he was. Friends such as señor Guerrero of the Xajay told him what he already knew: for an American to join the ranks of the greats, he would have to go to the cradle of the bullfighting world to make his name and become the first American in history to take the *alternativa* there. He would have to go to Spain.

5

Thanks, Ma

AS WITH EVERYTHING IN SIDNEY'S life, the path was never straight. Now he found that the road to Spain led up Flatbush Avenue. In January 1929 Sidney caught the SS *Monterrey*, the same ship that brought him to Mexico almost seven years before, and sailed from Veracruz to New York. He had learned of an international exposition to be held in Spain that spring and figured correctly that such an event would be the best place to introduce the Spanish bullfight audience to the idea of an American matador. Although he had been a professional *novillero* in Mexico for five years, Sidney was broke. Plans with a promoter to bankroll an assault on the home turf of the bullfighting world fell through — more unrealistic hopes with nothing to back them up. Sidney had put together enough money for his passage home, but had not one Spanish peseta to launch his career in the old world.

His reception in Brooklyn was as he expected. Although somewhat curious about this exotic avocation that Sidney professed to practice, his mother, sisters, and brothers were glad and relieved to see their one wandering boy. His father was gruff, distant, and silently contemptuous of his son's accomplishments. He was still a bum, only now a bum in a funny suit. "It was just hello and goodbye with him," Sidney would say later. Without money for the trans-Atlantic passage, money to invest in quality swords, capes, suits of lights, and living expenses, Sidney was stuck back at his father's kitchen table as though he had never left. Once again, his view of the wide, beckoning world was reduced to the same two narrow windows in the gloomy front room through which he had watched the world go by on Jackson Place since he was a child. He was stranded just as he had been in high school, but now more of a stranger than when he had left, his dream going nowhere. After years of steeping himself in the Spanish language, he found the incessant whine of the accented English of the old neighborhood guttural, grating, and foreign.

Lubba Frumpkin had changed visibly in the seven years since Sidney had left her. Her auburn hair had turned gray, her fair skin had aged, but she was still the family peacemaker, the buffer between Abram and his children. As good as it was to again be with her long-absent son, the boy whose own red hair and fair skin had reflected her own, Lubba found it hard to see Sidney back at his father's mercy, his dreams thwarted. Lubba then did what some moms have always done for the happiness of their children. She went behind her husband's back to defy his wishes. She secretly decided to bankroll Sidney's Spanish adventure. Like many immigrant women, Lubba had acquired money of her own, money squirreled away over the years from the Frumpkin's working-class tenants, from careful shopping with the butcher, the produce man, from pinching pennies here to save a few there. Using this rainy-day money cached in bank accounts in her own name, Lubba staked Sidney to a five-thousand-dollar loan — everything he would need to get a start in Spain. She drew up a contract that made her his manager, probably the most reliable one he had yet run across. His father would never know. Now Sidney could go to Spain. In February he boarded the liner *Rochambeau* in New York and sailed for Europe.

What Sidney found when he arrived in Madrid was not what he had expected. The Spanish bullfight was different from the world in which he had apprenticed in Mexico for two very different reasons. The first was that the *corrida* was imported to Mexico from a colonial *patria*, a fatherland, and no matter how passionate the Mexicans became about it, bullfighting was not an outgrowth of their own indigenous culture, of their own soil. In Spain, however, the festival of the bull had roots deep in the Iberian Peninsula and went back into prehistory, permeating every level of the culture and psyche; so in that fatherland, bullfighting *was* Spain.

The reason for this is foremost the animal itself. The fighting bull — the *toro bravo* — is not a domestic beast that is poked or prodded into a rage for the purpose of the ring. They are their own species indigenous to Iberia, *Bos taurus ibericus*. Their herds ranged at will over the land south of the Pyrenees, terrorizing the inhabitants since before recorded civilization. They were believed to have descended from the now extinct Aurochs, the prehistoric ox of Europe, *Bos primigenius*. Paleolithic cave paintings in Altamira, in the Spanish north, depict charging bulls. (They also display a stylized use of line that seems positively Picasso.) These dangerous bovines inhabited the dreams of the Mediterranean peoples of the south just as the wolf once haunted the dreams and folklore of the hunters of the deep forests of northern Europe. A Spanish shepherd tending his flock in the Carthaginian era would know the hair-on-end terror at the sound of the snort and rustle in the brush from the wild bull, the fear for a child caught out in the open, exposed to hoof and horn.

These too were the bulls of the Minoan culture, which flourished on the Greek island of Crete fifteen hundred years before Christ. (Tauromachy, the art of bullfighting, has as its root the Greek word *tauromachía*.) Mosaics in the city of Knossos show bull baiting by near-naked young men and women who vaulted over the horns in public ceremonies. The myth of the half man, half bull, the Minotaur, is rooted in the fear, awe, and sexual power inspired by these Minoan bulls. The myth carried into the Roman culture, including the early Christian church, which attributed taurine qualities to the Prince of Darkness. The councils of Toledo must have been thinking of their homegrown beast when in 447 AD it said the Devil was not only huge and black with horns on its head and cloven hoofs, but that it smelled of sulfur and possessed a huge phallus as well.

The Hellenistic mystery cult of the god Mithras, with roots in the Zoroastrian religion of Persia, also became popular in the early Roman Empire before Christianity gained a toehold. As the Mithraic myth recounts this god's vanquishing of a bull, the cult's acting out the event in a ritual sacrifice of the animal was a common practice across the empire. Reliefs or mosaics of this savior figure and the dying bull were common, invariably showing Mithras wearing a cape. The slaying of the bull as the ultimate act of bravery by gods and heroes east of the Mediterranean goes back in ancient Mesopotamia to the earliest recorded epic, *Gilgamesh*. This Sumerian saga contains a fight between the "Bull of Heaven," sent to destroy the hero, and Enkidu, the hero's best friend and defender. With the exception of the tail twisting (itself recognizable to any buckaroo who ever worked cattle in a squeeze chute), the moment of truth would be familiar to every modern matador:

> . . . he lunged from side to side
> Watching for his chance to seize the horns.

The bull frothed in its rage at this dance
And suddenly Enkidu seized its tail
And twisted it around, until the bull
Stood still, bewildered, out of breath,
And then Enkidu plunged his sword behind its horns
Into the nape of the bull's neck, and it fell dead.

Olé, matador. *Gilgamesh* was written on cuneiform tablets four thousand years ago. Remnants of these tablets were discovered in the ruins of Nineveh in the mid-nineteenth century by a pair of explorers from the British Museum. Some scholars now believe that these were copies of originals, or perhaps of an oral epic, dating a full thousand years before that.

Two millennia after *Gilgamesh*, bulls were herded into traps in Iberia, crated, and then shipped by galley to Rome to be used in the blood spectacles in the Coliseum, and in the empire's similar arenas, which sprung up throughout the Roman world. Contemporary bullrings in Spain and Mexico reflect this gladiator past, employing the same basic design of Roman amphitheaters still standing in cities like Nîmes and Arles, where bulls today continue to be fought. The *toril* gate from which the modern bull charges into the ring is little changed from the entrance through which the lions sauntered into the arena to feast on the Christians.

Spain had the bulls and the Romans had bequeathed to them their arenas, but it would be another several hundred years until the two came together in anything resembling the *corrida de toros*. The seeds of Spanish bullfighting first had to take root out in the wild Iberian countryside with the arrival of the Arabs and their Berber allies, the Moors. The invaders brought two essentials to the equation: the Arabian horse, and a dandy little invention that the Arab horsemen had borrowed from East Asia via Persia and

India—the stirrup. True, the Romans had possessed fine horses, but for centuries these plumed conquerors bounced up and down the length of their empire on horseback with their feet dangling, their manhood crunched with every stride. Talk about hard traveling. Half of these fellows could not even get mounted without standing on the back of a willing slave. Once aboard with helmets and breastplates, even a good rider could easily be put off balance and unhorsed during battle. The Vandals, Visigoths, and other tribes that picked apart the empire came mounted from the north and east, and later invaders such as the Avars were beginning to ride with the stirrup. This simple addition to a saddle, which supported and balanced a rider's weight through his legs and feet, was most likely developed in northeast Asia by the Hsiung-nu (Xiongnu) and other Mongol tribes who roamed the dry grasslands north of China. Legend says emperor Shih Huang Ti of the Ch'in (Qin) Dynasty built the Great Wall in part to keep out such well-mounted horsemen as the Hsiung-nu, who would later go on to terrorize the West under their European name, the Huns. The stirrup revolutionized warfare fifteen hundred years ago, much as the longbow or gunpowder would later. A warrior could brace himself in his stirrups as he swung his sword, or put the weight and velocity of the animal behind the thrust of a lance, as jousting knights would soon learn to do. In today's bullring, the white painted step that circles the base of the *barrera* about sixteen inches off the ground to aid the *torero* who must vault the fence in a hurry is called the *estribo*, or stirrup board.

So, in the 700s when the Arabs swept across North Africa then, along with their recently conquered Moorish armies, took Iberia from the Germanic Visigoths, they brought Islam, architecture, and ancient learning on the backs of the Arabian horse. Fast and hardy, these nimble animals were perfect for light cavalry—and for sport. The Arabs were soon running down the exciting but unfamiliar wild Spanish bulls and killing them with lances — that is, when the bulls did not turn the tables on the horsemen. (To be fair, the Iberian Peninsula was already known for fine equines. The Iberian horse, ancestor of today's Spanish Andalusian and Portuguese Lusitano breeds, had been prized as a cavalry mount since the time of Xenophon in the fourth century BC. Partisans of these breeds today — especially in America — downplay the influence of the Arabian horse on Spain and its colonies. Still, the horseback hunting of native bulls seems not to have caught on until the conquering Arabs, as an extension of their skills in mounted warfare.)

Whatever the origins, this became a sport of the new Moslem ruling class. As they rode out in search of herds of *Bos taurus ibericus,* their vassals ran along on foot, flushing the prey from thickets, then hazing the dangerous critters toward the horsemen with blankets, animal skins, or cloaks — the roots of the capework of modern bullfighting. (The stirrup allowed Northern European nobles of the Middle Ages to hunt wild boar in much the same way, although their horses were heavier and less agile.)

Spanish legend has the great warrior El Cid starring in the first duel in an old Roman arena between bull and horseman. This would have been at the end of the eleventh century, when the great Cid was selling his services to both Christians and Moslems in turn as they scrapped for control of the peninsula. From then on, the Spaniards went bullfight crazy. It remained however the pastime of the nobility of both religions, with the peons continuing to haze the animals on foot. For the Christians in Spain, bullfighting became entwined with saints' days; the feast day celebration or *fiesta* soon became *fiesta brava.* It remains so today, from Lenten celebrations at Castellón de la Plana for Mary Magdalene in March, or the three-day festival of St. Joseph in Valencia, to the festival of Our Lady of the Pillar of Saragossa in mid-October. As most Spanish towns did not possess Roman amphitheaters, these early festivals were conducted in the town squares and plazas, where the streets were barricaded with carts, wagons, tables, and whatever was handy to form an enclosed space. Bulls were run through the streets to the city center for the event much as bulls are run today in cities such as Pamplona, and the term *corrida de toros* literally means a running of the bulls. Aficionados speculate that the poorer towns with plazas of dirt, not cobblestones, were more suited to the *corrida* as they provided better footing for both animals and men, thus allowing even the rudest hamlet a share of the action, which in turn increased the popularity of the pastime throughout the region. Today's bullrings are still of course called the *plaza de toros*.

Once the Moslems and Jews were finally driven from Iberia in 1492 by the very Catholic Ferdinand and Isabella in what was called the Reconquista, this intertwining of the pagan and the Christian — and the resulting carnage to both man and beast — was a cause of much concern to the church. Pope Pius V, a Lombardy Italian with no *afición* — no passion for the bulls — thought he could end the bloody business by declaring in 1567 that all those killed in the *plazas de toros* would simply be excommunicated. (This spoilsport excommunicated Elizabeth I of England three years later as well, but not, one assumes, for bullfighting.) The Spaniards largely ignored the most Holy Father. To make sure that there would be no shortage of Spanish souls on high, the papal ban was soon rescinded. The Spanish crown was more concerned that there be no shortage of the aristocracy here on earth, as so many were losing their lives to the bulls. Young Philip V was the first Spanish king of the French Bourbon line, and in the early 1700s he needed every member of the nobility he could get to support him in the War of the Spanish Succession. Being a grandson of Louis XIV — a fellow who knew how to cut to the chase — Philip simply banned horseback bullfighting by the nobility.

By this time a family of carpenters from Ronda, the Romeros, were refining the plebian practice of bullfighting on foot with capes by inventing the *muleta*, by killing the first bull on foot, and by starting an actual school to practice this new art. This style of facing the bull dismounted became more popular than the horseback ritual of the nobility — especially among those who were themselves neither noble nor horsemen. Bullfighting as practiced by the Romeros was becoming a populist pastime to which the lowliest could aspire. In Portugal, which half a century before had gained its independence from Spain, the nobility were beyond the reach of Philip's edict, and thus free to fight bulls from the backs of well-bred and well-trained horses, a practice that continues to the present day with the art of *rejoneo*, the Portuguese bullfight.

This passion for blood and death was not limited to the Iberians. Blood sports were common throughout the world. During the Middle Ages and Renaissance, the English ancestors of the early Americans enjoyed bull baiting, where dogs set on bulls in a confined space would grab the bovine by the lower lip until the animal was brought down for the pleasure of the crowd. The English bulldog is a relic of this practice. The foxhunt continues to be popular with country people of all classes in Britain despite attempts by urban animal activists to root it out. North America was no exception. In Spanish California, vaqueros — America's first cowboys — armed with nothing but their braided rawhide riatas, would hunt the grizzly bears that roamed the oak-dotted coastal hills. Several vaqueros had to dab their loops over the animal in quick succession, then take their wraps around the saddle horn with the *riata* to secure their prey, as the bear would tend to run up the rope to kill both horse and rider if snagged by only one man. Then, the vaqueros would drag the bear to a small arena, or "bull pen," where a *toro bravo*, a Spanish bull was waiting. In old Los Angeles, betting on the outcome of a fight to the death between these two captives was a regular and popular Sunday afternoon pastime that continued through the 1850s, well into the American era. It has also been said that President Lincoln got his moniker "honest Abe" from being a fair and reliable referee at cockfights in backwoods Illinois during the Black Hawk War. While these practices have either fallen out of favor or been banned outright in the non-Latin world, in Spain the *corrida* continues to flourish as an essential part of the national identity.

The second reason that Sidney Franklin found the Spanish bull-fighting scene markedly different from the Mexican world from which he had matriculated was a man named Hemingway. While still an unknown writer fresh from Oak Park, Illinois, Ernest Hemingway was urged by his Paris friend Gertrude Stein to visit the Festival of San Fermín in the town of Pamplona in Navarre, and to attend the bullfights there. His inaugural trip to Pamplona in 1923 made enough of an impression on the young man that when his first child arrived shortly after, he convinced his wife that they should give the boy the middle name Nicanor after the bullfighter Nicanor Villalta. A subsequent trip with a volatile mix of friends was the inspiration for Hemingway's breakthrough novel in 1926, *The Sun Also Rises*. For the next several decades, the Spanish bull-fight meant Ernest Hemingway to American audiences. Even now, the running of the bulls in Pamplona conjures up the world of his novel.

Hemingway not only made bullfighting interesting, he made

it chic. It is not quite so today. When contemporary Americans consider bullfighting at all, many tend to think it is unnecessarily brutal and cruel. In a popular culture where glib facetiousness passes for irony, the matador's cool disdain, his very un-ironic posturing in the face of danger, looks to many as an exercise in the decidedly unfashionable machismo of the Latin male, or worse yet, as merely ridiculous. The pose is simply too foreign. It is hard today to watch Irish-American pretty-boy Tyrone Power puff up as a poor Spanish waif who makes good in the bullring, then gets to chose between Rita Hayworth and Linda Darnell in Rouben Mamoulian's 1940 film version of Vincente Blasco Ibáñez's *Blood And Sand*. The persona of the future film producer, New York Jewish pretty-boy Robert Evans, as Hemingway's matador "Pedro Romero," who is seduced by Ava Gardner in the 1957 film of *The Sun Also Rises*, is almost unbearably campy.

There is another problem in the American perception of bullfighting as well. Because it takes place in a stadium with grandstands, paid admissions, a defined season, and cold drinks, American audiences associate the experience with sport, and find it a needlessly barbaric one. Bullfighting however is not a sport. It has been called a pastime, a passion, an art, or a tragedy. It is certainly bloody, perhaps cruel. Even in its golden age of Belmonte, Joselito, and Gaona, the bullfight was considered a symptom of the Spanish "problem," a residual cultural backwardness stemming from Catholic Spain's rejection of the Enlightenment. So bullfighting survives as a national ritual with deep roots in that premodern Spanish culture, just as the baseball of Barry Bonds, corporate naming rights for ballparks, and luxury boxes still have psychic roots in the lazy summer days of small town America of the nineteenth century and the immigrant eastern cities of the early twentieth.

It is difficult for a contemporary audience to grasp just how stylish the *corrida* was for a certain strain of Americans abroad. Tourists, socialites, bohemians, movie stars, literature students on sabbatical, and various other expatriates steeped themselves in Hemingway, spoke knowledgably about *verónicas* or the *pase de muerte* as they passed their *botas* full of wine back and forth, and argued who was the greater matador, Manolete or Arruza in the 1940s, Dominguín or his brother-in-law Antonio Ordóñez a decade later. When life imitated art, and Ava Gardner took Dominguín to bed in Madrid's Hotel Wellington, it was, if not commendable, certainly understandable and fitting. He was, after all, more of a star in Spain than she.

Americans of all stripes went to the bullfights, but they developed a certain café society allure from the 1920s through the 1960s that has since gone the way of café society itself. For a time during the last quarter of the twentieth century, the only thing less fashionable than the bullfighters' mystique was the pose of the gruff but knowledgeable male observer — the Hemingway mystique. In 1929, however, the Americans' passion for the festival and for Ernest Hemingway was on the rise. As far as the Americans were concerned, there could not have been a better time for an American bullfighter to come to Spain.

6

Yanqui Flamenco

THE SPANISH BULLFIGHT PROMOTERS naturally felt differently. They had little enough interest in Mexican *toreros*, much less Yanqui Mexicans. Sidney had made enough friends in the bullfight world that at least some of his fellow matadors greeted him with support. He soon caught up with two friends from Mexico, the Espinosa brothers, Juan and Fermín. They were both full matadors who fought under the names "Armillita" and "Armillita Chico." Like Sidney they had come to Spain to confirm their careers, Fermín taking his *alternativa* in Madrid just the year before. The Espinosas introduced him to the bullfighting community in Madrid and he soon was spending his mornings with fellow Mexican *toreros*, practicing capework at an inn outside the city where the patrons enjoyed the serious *toreo de salón* of the foreigners. In the evenings they hit the jai alai frontons or the cafés along the Gran Vía. Sidney grew to love Madrid, a city where he would experience much joy and pain both in and out of the bullring in the following years. He prepared for his debut by using his mother's money to order expensive suits of lights and accessories, right down to a bullfighter's special underwear. From Valencia he commissioned a set of *estoques*, custom killing swords that came in tooled leather cases. After the lilting Mexican Spanish in which he had become proficient, Sidney picked up the lisping Castilian of the capitol, at which he would soon excel. Through the Espinosas he met Luis Crovetto, a tiny bald sword handler who had worked briefly for Gaona years before. Luis became Sidney's *mozo de estoques*, his confidant, and his companion. Sidney would sometimes refer to him simply as his valet. As Sidney practiced with his friends, a young American woman took home movies of them so that the *toreros* could study their moves and improve both their performance and their pose. It was an optimistic time. Sidney had everything going for him except an engagement in the ring.

He was determined that the first time he appeared be something special, the introduction of the new American *novillero* to the people of Spain. Before his first meeting with the country's top promoter don Eduardo Pagés at a posh Madrid restaurant, an event arranged by the manager of Armillita Chico, Sidney was nervous. By his own admission, he obsessed much of the afternoon on just what to wear. He was disappointed when Pagés offered only second-rate fights in small cities for what Sidney considered insultingly low fees. He turned don Eduardo down. He did not feel he should be grateful for such offers. Sidney had a large sense of himself and an innate feeling for the dramatic and commercial possibilities that an American such as he could bring to the audience, especially the Americans in Spain.

Acquaintances at the American Embassy in Madrid again suggested the possibility of the American week at the International Exposition in Sevilla, but time was running out. The ambassador put Sidney in touch with former Arizona governor Tom Campbell, who had been appointed by outgoing president Coolidge to be the United States representative to the exposition. Sidney immediately caught a plane to Sevilla. There, Campbell told him that although he liked the idea of an American performing in a bullfight during the American week, the bullring in Sevilla was, as to be expected, supposedly booked for the duration. The truth was that the promoters were cool to the idea of the stunt booking of an American novelty act in such a serious venue. According to bullfight historians, at that time no American had ever set foot in a Spanish ring.

Sidney was disappointed, but he understood. A debut in Sevilla would have been more than he could have realistically hoped for. Madrid was the Spanish capitol, and its old bullring was famous, but the bullring in Sevilla was the Lourdes, the Mecca, the Yankee Stadium of the taurine world. Sidney compared the city's importance to bullfighting to that of Milan's to opera. He spent a few days knocking around the exposition, and then he met a young man. His name was F. Ross Dennison, an American engineer working on a reclamation project. He and Sidney began a friendship that would last for many years. It would finally take money, not friendship, to open the door to the bullring in Sevilla. Dennison was able to secure a fight in June for Sidney by raising a large amount of cash from the American community as a guarantee to the promoters that their expenses for such a risky performance would be covered. The money would also augment the meager fee to be paid Sidney—a fee he only agreed to for the chance to be showcased in the Sevilla arena. The American community was eager to see one of their own in the ring mastering the Spanish pastime. "Ross came to the rescue," Sidney said. Once again he was to benefit from the kindness of strangers.

Sevilla is a beautiful city on the Guadalquivir River in the southern province of Andalucía some sixty miles inland from the Atlantic port of Cádiz, itself one of most ancient cities in Europe. After the fall of Rome, the region became part of the old Germanic Vandal kingdom, Vandalusia. Sevilla was later developed as a walled town by the conquering Moslems. The Giralda, a minaret from their mosque, still looms over the Catholic cathedral not begun until 1402. In its current incarnation as a bell tower, the Giralda remains a visual symbol of the entire city. In the old neighborhoods, the narrow, winding streets are often entirely covered with awnings to protect from the blistering afternoon sun of the summer — bullfight season. To the passerby, the overhanging balconies seem almost to touch one another overhead. The Plaza de Toros de la Real Maestranza — the Bullring of the Royal Patronage — sits just across a tree-lined boulevard from the river. The fans of Sevilla were said to be the most rabid in Spain, because as Mexican matador Carlos Arruza would claim, 80 percent of the males in the stands had themselves tried their hand with the bulls and thought they could not be fooled. Aficionados say that the sand of La Maestranza is not a dull tan like other arenas, but a rich gold color. On this they are correct. The whole place is enchanted. The gypsies, in a slang known as Caló — a language Sidney would also soon master — call the city Servalavari, a word so musical it sounds almost Italian to an American ear. The city has spawned its own style of bullfighting, a flashy more adorned approach than the stripped-down classical style from the town of Ronda. This Sevillano style is also popular with the *toreros* of Latin America. To a Sevillano, an American *novillero* was a questionable proposition. He had better be good. Anything less would be an insult, a blasphemy.

At five in the afternoon on June 9, 1929, Sidney Franklin was more than just good. He was brilliant. Even if he said so himself. He entered La Maestranza after first visiting the bullfighter's chapel under the stands and lighting a few candles and saying prayers to the Blessed Virgin. This was not something of which his pop or his rabbi in Brooklyn would have approved, but hey, when in Rome. Sidney always adapted well to his surroundings, and figured that this afternoon he needed all the help he could get. He enjoyed saying later that after leaving the chapel he seriously considered getting the hell out of there and catching a cab all the way back to Madrid, then only reluctantly decided against it. "My decision is history," he said grandly. No matter how terrified he was, he entered the ring carrying his dress cape during the opening *paseo* not with false modesty, but in an act of pure Brooklyn chutzpah, mimicking the distinctive stride of twentieth-century Spain's most revered dead matador, Joselito (or so he says). He wore one of his new and quite expensive suits of lights, a twenty-five-pound tobacco-brown satin number that he bragged was heavy with twice the gold lamé adornment as normal, a suit that "fitted as though painted on me." Everything in Spain was different from what he was used to. Not only did the crowd feel that they were more knowledgeable, the bulls from the ranch of don José Rufino Moreno Santamaría were bigger as well. Even the music was different—the trumpets playing not the "Virgen de la Macarena" or "Cielo Andaluz" during the *paseo* as they did throughout Mexico, but some piece unfamiliar to Sidney, such as "La Morena de Mi Copla." Sidney was third on the program behind two *toreros* he felt were hacks, "Camará II" and "Echevarría." He was determined that his performance must set him apart from them.

Sidney did not immediately distinguish himself as he took his turn performing *quites* on the bulls of the other two matadors, drawing them away from the picadors' horses. With the third bull of the afternoon—Sidney's bull—his capework was again unspectacular, his timing just off. But when it came time for the kill, Sidney's sword thrust was, by his own admission, perfect. When the bull brushed passed the new American hopeful, the animal was already dead. As the bull hit the ground, the crowd erupted. Sidney knew he had them.

His second bull was huge, its charges airborne and fast. Spanish bullfight slang would say that the animal was "as big as a cathedral," and it would charge as if "on rails." Sidney had to bring the animal back to earth with slow deliberate *verónicas*. He spent the first act going back to the basics of his training with the Great Indian six years before. All that rote work was justified. Every move that Gaona drilled into Sidney in those first weeks of training now became second nature. He gripped his *capote* in both hands, drawing the bull's nose into the cape, keeping it low. Sidney's size and the strength of his hands made the repeated passes with the heavy cape look effortless and graceful. This low capework became, although he could not know it at the time, the beginning of what he would claim later as his signature style. He had heard the shout of "*olé!*" many times in Mexico, but these shouts now seemed to shake the bricks. This was *Spain*. He took his time and began to take chances, to show off. He held the cape behind his back, exposing himself with passes the knowledgeable fans would recognize, passes with names like the *gaonera*, invented by his mentor, the *mariposa*, a favorite of Joselito, and the *serpentina*, a hallmark of Marcial Lalanda. His performance was bold and showy, and the crowd loved it. They had not expected such a display from the American, such knowledge of their art. This was a Sevillano's style of bullfighting.

For the *faena* — the third act, the killing act — Sidney remained in control of the tiring animal. There is another florid bullfighting metaphor that the matador is the conductor and the bull is his orchestra. It is a concept that Sidney could understand after that day. However, it is not just the bull who is the matador's orchestra, but the crowd as well. Much is said of the distinct visuals of a bullfight — the bright pinks, golds, greens, or blues of the suit of lights, the magenta and yellow of the cape, the multicolored wraps on the *banderillas*, the bull's slick red blood on his silky black hide. But there is also the sound of a bullfight, over which a matador on a good day has much control. If one were to close one's eyes in the middle of an outstanding performance, there would be silence for a moment as the matador, once in the position he thinks most advantageous, *cites* the bull, inciting it to charge. One would barely hear the rush of sound as the animal galloped across the soft sand, then a sudden "ohhh" from a thousand voices, then silence. Then another rush and an "ahhh," then silence, then a louder "Ahhh!" and perhaps an *"olé!"* as the bull passed closely by. In those moments, when the matador has complete mastery over the animal and the bull turns and charges, then charges again and again, the "ohs" and "OHs!" come one after the other, thousands of voices united in an outpouring of group surprise, delight, fear, and appreciation that sounds downright sexual, the matador in control of each gasp like a skilled old roué. It is not surprising that Sidney said bullfighting gave him a feeling of sensual pleasure. He certainly understood the nature of that pleasure his first afternoon in Sevilla.

Again, he killed the bull cleanly and expertly. After that performance, the paper *La Union* of Sevilla said that Sidney was a born bullfighter. When the crowd carried an exhausted Sidney from La Maestranza, it was about seven in the evening on June 9, seven years to the day that he had sailed out of his family's life.

Back at his inexpensive *pension* off the Plaza de Cádiz, happy fans crowded into his room. Sidney claims that strangers even stripped naked and joined him as he took a shower, because, as he bragged later, the fans said that anyone who fought as he did must have *cojones* as big as melons. "All the sexes throw themselves at you," he said of his brand new notoriety. He did not seem to be complaining. He was about to experience a level of attention that far exceeded that which he had known in Mexico. Ross Dennison, the young man who had helped make it all possible, pushed his way into the room, embraced little Luis the sword handler to celebrate Sidney's triumph, then did his best to get Sidney out of the grasp of the rowdy fans and get him dressed. It took him a long time. After more delays, during which Sidney claims he stood on the balcony tossing coins to the adoring crowd waiting in the street below, Dennison herded him through the fans to a car and drove him in the middle of the night far from Sevilla to a country house near his reclamation project on the Guadalquivir Basin where his friends were waiting. The Americans had prepared a celebratory dinner for Spain's new bullfighting sensation. Dennison's soiree turned into a three-day bash. Sidney does not specify whether "all the sexes" attended. "I wondered as I ate the magnificent banquet what would have happened if my debut had turned out to be a dud."

This was the beginning of the most wonderful year of Sidney's experience, the Spanish chapter of his three remarkable lives. He became an instant celebrity, a condition that he felt only natural for a young man destined for greatness. Dennison accompanied Sidney and Luis Crovetto to the big promoters to help him negotiate his contracts, first in Sevilla, then in Madrid. Hemingway would write two years later that, although Sidney was quite proud of his business sense, his business sense was actually rather dreadful. Although Sidney's financial demands were outrageous, he clearly understood his value as a draw. Spanish crowds wanted to see this phenomenon. His debut performance in the Spanish capitol was on July 25 where he appeared with Manuel Agüero and "Maera II." Hemingway wrote that Sidney in that first season filled every seat of the Madrid bullring three times; only the first time was because of his novelty. The second and third times the most knowledgeable aficionados in the capitol came to see a true matador. Tickets sold out as soon as the bullfight was announced, and scalpers did a fine business. Spanish papers said that Sidney fought like one born in Spain, and joked that it was the Spaniards performing with him who performed as if they were from America. (Barnaby Conrad wrote that the Sevilla headlines said after his debut there that the fans went to see a Yanqui and instead saw a *torero*. Following a second, less successful *corrida* in the same city, the papers joked that fans went to see a *torero* — and saw a Yanqui.) The saying among the bullfighting community was that Sidney performed well in his Madrid debut because he was a *bullfighter*.

As he appeared in city after city that season, he began to be called the "Yanqui Flamenco." Lillian Ross translated this as "Yankee Real McCoy" for her *New Yorker* readers. For better or worse, as the defining posture of a certain type of Latin male exemplified by the bullfighter, "Flamenco" has a deeper meaning for the Spaniards. Barnaby Conrad states that flamenco literally means Flemish, and that *un tipo flamenco*

> is a term of encomium used to describe a man as an irresponsible bohemian with dash, flair, and arrogance. It is said that the term came from the Spanish soldiers who returned from the occupation of the Lowlands in the 16th century and, finding it difficult to adjust to civilian life, became gay and colorful wastrels.

Sidney Franklin could ask for no more glowing — or apt — description.

He soaked up the culture of this new country as assiduously as he bathed in the attention. He picked up regional languages and dialects with ease, and could soon speak to a hotel clerk in Barcelona in flawless Catalán or swap jokes in Caló with a gypsy cabdriver in Córdoba. Never bashful, this new star enjoyed holding forth with authority on any subject, whether or not he knew of what he spoke. He became an expert in the food of Spain, and grew to be quite a good cook. Although still just a *novillero*, he was able to secure the high fees that he demanded, and showed an ability to spend it as fast as he earned it. Always chatty and outgoing, he enjoyed the new friends and hangers-on who made up his ever-changing entourage and basked in his fame as they enjoyed his money. It was good to have all the sexes throwing themselves at you. As Hemingway would remind him later, a bullfighter is never alone. At the age of twenty-six, as he traveled from city to city, province to province in that summer of 1929, Sidney was just where he felt he should be — on top of the world.

7

Death in the Afternoon — with Drinks and Dinner to Follow

AT THE END OF THE SUMMER of his first season in Spain, Sidney sat at a sidewalk table at Madrid's Café Gran Vía having a pre-lunch drink with a dozen friends. He had now been famous for all of three months, and his regular entourage included, among others, a Spanish duke. While holding forth for his admirers, Sidney noticed a big American in rumpled tweeds and bedroom slippers talking to their waiter as the man looked and gestured in Sidney's direction. The American seemed to want something. Sidney was by now used to fellow Americans down on their luck putting the touch on him for a little cash, so he was not surprised when the waiter brought the seedy looking bruiser over to his table. Sidney was already reaching into his pocket.

Instead of a handout, the American claimed only a desire to meet the new American phenomenon. He said that his name was Ernest Hemingway, and that he was a writer. Sidney replied that he had never heard of him. Hemingway told Sidney that the Paris correspondent for the *Brooklyn Eagle*, Guy Hickock, was supposed to have contacted Sidney on his behalf. Sidney and the newcomer began sparring as to who would pay for the next round of drinks. Sidney wanted to pay to spare this fellow embarrassment; the newcomer wanted to order Pernod, the most expensive drink in the house, but only if he were allowed to get the round. They jockeyed back and forth until it was finally time to eat. Hemingway invited Sidney to lunch, but again Sidney doubted that Hemingway could afford it. Instead, he invited the man to his apartment where his cook, Mercédes, would prepare the meal, as was Sidney's custom. Hemingway agreed, stopping at a wine shop on the way to purchase several bottles for each course. The two men then ate, drank, and talked bullfighting until well into the evening.

The purpose of Hemingway's visit was to ask if he could accompany Sidney on his next tour. Although he had been following the bulls for half a decade, he wanted the firsthand experience that traveling with an American matador could give him. Sidney was at first concerned that such a trip would be financially out of reach for this scruffy fellow, as Sidney only stayed in the "swankiest" hotels. After Hemingway's assurances that cost was not a factor, plus being charmed by his new friend and impressed by the man's knowledge of bullfighting and its arcane vocabulary, Sidney eventually agreed.

At the point in Sidney's life where his story joins with Ernest Hemingway's, the telling becomes complicated and often contradictory. It would not be unkind to either man to acknowledge that both were accomplished bullshit artists. But these are also the same crossroads where the Hemingway biographers intersect and often collide. Hemingway himself told a different story to Lillian Ross, "I met Sidney by speaking to him over the *barrera*, after he had killed his second bull on August 15, 1929, in the old ring in Madrid. I made an appointment to meet him at a café the next day." Hemingway said he saw no reason to mention that he was a writer, and that when Sidney found out much later that he was a successful novelist, he at first did not believe it was true. It seems hard now to buy that Sidney could have been so self-absorbed, but recall that this was the same man who said that he was the sun, the moon and stars to himself.

Still, Hemingway's renown was hardly a secret. *The Sun Also Rises* had established Hemingway as a respected American writer in 1926, and as said earlier, made him well known among the English speakers who followed the bullfight in Spain. His next novel, *A Farewell to Arms*, would be published in the United States on September 27, 1929, roughly a month after Sidney met him. (As a teenager during Word War I, Hemingway had volunteered as an ambulance driver and became wounded on the Italian front; he then fell for his nurse, and later turned his story into an archetypal novel of love and war for modern Americans.) *A Farewell to Arms* would make Hemingway a unique legend — the writer who supposedly lived what he wrote. But then Sidney claimed to read only the *Saturday Evening Post*. One telling detail of Sidney's account was, however, dead-on — the bedroom slippers. Hemingway, who suffered self-inflicted wounds his whole life, had recently cut his foot severely.

Hemingway and his second wife, Pauline Pfeiffer, had been following the *corridas* since July, when they drove down to Pamplona from Paris for the five days of the Festival of San Fermín in a new Ford coupe purchased for them by Pauline's Uncle Gus, a patent medicine tycoon from Piggott, Arkansas. The long afternoons in the scalding heat of the Spanish summer, the big meals at midnight and copious consumption of red wine had taken as much out of the couple as the bad Spanish roads had thrashed the Ford. Pauline was a small dark-haired, stylish woman who was four years her husband's senior, but who often was emotionally overpowered by him. In Sidney's eyes she had class — she had written on fashion for *Vogue* in Paris while still in her twenties — and she had money. She was a Catholic, and also, according to several Hemingway biographers, bisexual. She and Sidney were destined to become close friends whose mutual devotion would become first a convenience and then an annoyance to the author. However, when Hemingway's Ford joined Sidney's auto caravan in the first two weeks of September, he was traveling solo if hardly alone.

The caravan itself was no small thing. In addition to the friends who drove along in their own vehicles, Sidney had to provide transportation for himself and his *cuadrilla* — his crew — which at a minimum consisted of three *banderilleros*, two picadors, his sword handler Luis, and all their costumes and equipment. It would not be unusual for Sidney to have employed more handlers as well. He claimed that his schedule was so full that his *cuadrilla* had trouble keeping up with him, and after wearing his out, he had to employ what was essentially a team of second stringers. A successful matador had to look — and act — like a successful matador.

The two men hit it off immediately. Their friendship was symbiotic and genuine. Sidney loved to have a fellow American who understood what it was to be a bullfighter, and with whom he could share the stories of his life as it had unfolded so far. Hemingway in turn savored this new ability to look at bullfighting from the inside out, to mentally take it apart and put it back together again in a way that allowed both the physical moves and the emotional and artistic content to be seen in a new way with total clarity. Sidney gave Hemingway unparalleled access to accomplish this. For the first time the writer was able to see the fights daily from the circular passage between the first row of seats and the arena, the *callejón*, where the matadors and *banderilleros* await their turn on the sand. He could prowl among the pros and their sword handlers, the ring servants, doctors and managers, watching, talking when it was appropriate, taking it all in through his writer's skin. This was better than having the best seats in the house. This was like going on the road with the 1927 Yankees, watching game after game from the dugout, kibitzing with Gehrig, Ruth, and Tony Lazzeri, then playing pinochle and drinking bootleg Scotch with the boys on the night train to Cleveland. Sidney and Hemingway would talk and drink in the cafés after the *corrida*, then yak halfway 'til dawn in Sidney's hotel room until one of them passed out. Sidney says that to keep the conversation going, he often had a cot brought into his room for Hemingway — ostensibly to save this supposedly down-at-the-heels friend from the expense of renting his own room. If a cot were not available, Sidney said they would simply share his double bed. Before searching for literary antecedents such as Ishmael and Queequeg, Huck and Jim, Jake Barnes and . . . whomever, such sharing of sparse accommodations was actually common enough in the boarding houses of an earlier era. Thus, if Sidney's claim is true, perhaps not so much should be inferred from such an arrangement.

Notwithstanding, they were certainly the odd couple. Sidney was fastidious. Hemingway was a slob. "Sidney always took a long time to dress in the morning," he said of his friend's fussiness with his wardrobe. Hemingway by contrast would simply pull his trousers over the sweaty underwear in which he had just slept, scratch here and there, and be ready to greet the day. "I always had to wait for him," Hemingway said. "I don't like a man who takes a long time to dress in the morning."

Sidney generously claims that Hemingway schooled him in the techniques of the great matadors of the past, of whom Hemingway had only read, and suggested that Sidney incorporate their anachronistic but classical passes into his repertoire. As Sidney's profile grew that first season, there were those in Spain who felt that he must actually be of Spanish blood to have mastered such technique. "This direction from him was the cause of my meteoric rise," he said. Hemingway modestly discounts all of this. He simply claims that he encouraged Sidney to not make his killing look too easy. "He'd just go in and wham!" He suggested that his new friend work on the drama of the thing.

Hemingway also critiqued Sidney's physique with the eye of a boxing trainer, focusing on what he felt was his prominent rump. "Sidney has no grace because he has a terrific behind," he said. "I used to make him do special exercises to reduce his behind." He does not specify what such exercises might include.

They also discussed the arc of Sidney's career. Hemingway felt that Sidney could take his *alternativa* at any time, but both men agreed that waiting until the following season would be the best. As Sidney was able to earn good money, waiting was of no financial impact. Hemingway felt that although Sidney was a master with the *capote de brega*, waiting another year as a *novillero* would allow him to improve his work with the *muleta*, perhaps increasing the drama of his *faena*—the killing act.

Sidney describes this tour with Hemingway as lasting a month and a half. It was probably much shorter. According to one biographer, Hemingway and Pauline saw Sidney fight in Madrid on August 30, presumably before the road trip. According to another, by September 12 the Hemingways were driving to the beach resort at Hendaye, from which they returned by car to Paris by the twentieth. So, Sidney's idyll with Hemingway perhaps lasted less than a fortnight. This short period in their lives was for Sidney the defining motif of their friendship, a relationship of equals. Sidney was at that moment the center of attention, a young man full of promise, and Hemingway was content for it to be so. There was no rivalry, no competition for the spotlight. Each was a rising star in his own world. There is a wonderful photograph taken about this time of the two new friends grinning at the camera, arms around each other's shoulders, a medieval castle in the background. It would never be quite this simple between them again.

Hemingway was of course doing his research on the bullfighting opus that would become *Death in the Afternoon*, his first nonfiction book. No matter how long this first excursion into the Spanish countryside and the strange terrain of their new friendship lasted, it made a lifelong impression on both men. Hemingway was genuinely impressed by his new pal, and was not stingy with his praise in print. "Franklin is brave with a cold, serene and intelligent valor," he wrote in a frequently quoted passage from *Death in the Afternoon*, "but instead of being awkward and ignorant he is one of the most skillful, graceful, and slow manipulators of a cape fighting today."

As Gaona had instructed Sidney during those first days of practice, the capework, the footwork, the repetition of the *verónica* was the foundation for everything that would come later. Hemingway proved to be as astute a student of the *corrida* as he claimed to be. He correctly points out that Sidney's style with the cape was a product of Gaona's instruction. He noted the variety of passes in Sidney's repertoire, but recognized the *verónica* at its most classical as the basis of his image as a matador. When he refers to Sidney as a "slow manipulator," he refers to this unique style — flatfooted rather than rising on tiptoe as the bull passes by — and of his practice of keeping his hands so low as he performed his *verónicas* that the cape dragged on the ground, giving a particularly American insouciance to his performance. "I just figured, 'Hell, the bull has more energy than me, so let the bull do the cavorting,'" Sidney told Lillian Ross. "I put oomph into the business."

Hemingway also enjoyed Sidney's company for its own sake, and his description of his friend would easily fit what later, tritely, came to be called the "Hemingway hero." He said that Sidney

> has the ability in languages, the cold courage and the ability to command of the typical soldier of fortune, he is a charming companion, one of the best story tellers I have ever heard, has enormous and omnivorous curiosity about everything but gets his information through the eye and ear and reads only the *Saturday Evening Post*.

If Sidney had any lingering doubts about Hemingway's stature as a writer, they were dispelled by the end of September. The reviews for *A Farewell to Arms* were outstanding, and the novel became a lasting literary and popular success. Sidney's cousin, critic Clifton Fadiman, praised it as a highpoint in modernism. Sidney, although never suffering a lack of self-esteem, had valuable lessons to learn in the handling of fame and self-image from Hemingway, as Hemingway himself was learning. (Fadiman would soon perceptively codify the blurring of Hemingway's fiction and his public persona in an essay "Ernest Hemingway: An American Byron" in the *Nation*, claiming the author was "the unhappy warrior that men would like to be. About him has sprung up a real contemporary hero-myth.") Sidney could not help but be influenced and seduced by the level of celebrity Hemingway would achieve, so different from what even a matador could attain.

By his own count, Sidney performed in fifty-eight bullfights large and small in Spain and Portugal from his June debut in Sevilla to the end of the season in October. (Aficionados today dispute this number as excessive, saying it would place this novice on a seasonal pace with greats such as Belmonte, whose 109 *corridas* from March to October in 1919 was for years the record to beat, although matadors who were in a position to surpass him, such as Arruza, had the respect not to. The definitive Spanish bullfighting encyclopedia, José María de Cossío's *Los Toros* puts Sidney's 1929 total at 14. Hemingway himself guessed the figure to be 12. The Spanish press at the time commented that had his financial demands been less, Sidney could have made more appearances.) By this time Ernest and Pauline Hemingway had returned to their new home base, Key West. They were all sure that they would be together again for the next season, when Sidney was to take the *alternativa* and enter the ranks of the greats.

8

To the Ear

Sidney is a marvelous fighter. He is absolutely courageous and keenly intelligent. He knows what it's all about. He's better than many of those boys who grew up in the tradition. They learn to go through the motions gracefully, but they don't know how to use their heads, as Sidney does. He's a regular Christy Mathewson. | ERNEST HEMINGWAY, Paris edition of *New York Herald Tribune*, September 20, 1931

SIDNEY'S SECOND FIGHT OF THE 1930 season was in the old bullring in Madrid. It would be the last full season there before the opening of the new Plaza Monumental the following year. The *corrida* was the afternoon of March 16. Hemingway's novelist friend John Dos Passos and his new wife, Katy Smith—herself a childhood pal of Hemingway's—were supposedly in the stands. The bulls Sidney would be facing were from the Murube *ganadería*, their bloodlines pure Vistahermosa, one of the five foundation lines of the eighteenth century from which modern fighting bulls descend. Such esoteric information is of major import to the aficionado, especially when the fight ends especially well, or especially badly. (Bullfighting is as statistically obsessed as baseball.

The name of every animal killed a century ago in some obscure bullring from Spain to Peru is recorded, so a Spaniard who had the time and the passion could access the details of a *corrida* that happened in, say, the Málaga bullring on a Sunday afternoon in 1915, just as an American might recover stats on Ty Cobb's at-bats in some forgotten game against the White Sox at Comiskey Park on the same date.)

Sidney had fought the prior Sunday at the opening of the season during the festival honoring St. Joseph in Valencia, killing not only his own two bulls but also the four bulls of the other two matadors when each was gored. If nothing else, it was a remarkable display of stamina and concentration. Sidney was the third *espada*, or "sword," on the March 16 Madrid program. He fought his first bull adequately but not spectacularly. When it was time for the kill, Sidney cleanly dropped the animal with a single sword thrust. Then, as the ring servant known as the *puntillero* ran up with his short-bladed dagger to deliver the coup de grâce at the base of the skull (the move Sidney himself had perfected hundreds of times with the *puntilla* in the Mexico City slaughterhouse) Sidney did something uncharacteristic, almost fatal. He turned his back on the bull. He said in his autobiography that it was to deny respect to the breeder for supplying an inferior animal, claiming the bull was blind in the left eye. Such contempt was understandable, even expected, under the circumstances. But the bull, in a final spasm of life at the moment of death, jerked himself upright, hooking out and up with his left horn. The thrusting tip caught Sidney at the base of his tailbone, plunging into his abdominal cavity through the rectum, piercing the sphincter muscle and large intestine, the horn sinking "to the ear." The bull fell dead, and so, almost, did Sidney. Spectators saw the bull drop like a stone. They saw the animal's killer crumpled in a heap twenty feet away. Sidney awoke hours later in a Madrid infirmary.

The doctors had not expected Sidney to live. Neither had Luis, his distraught *mozo*, who stayed at the bedside for the next three weeks, watching Sidney trussed up in slings with drainage tubes evacuating the violated cavity. Even if the horn wound, the *cornada*, had not killed Sidney, there was always the chance of death from infection when a foreign body is introduced to the abdomen, especially in those days before penicillin, when the most effective antibiotics were the sulfa drugs used in the trenches of the Great War on both men and horses. In addition, he was administered a potent anti-tetanus serum with a warning not to repeat the dose for another two years. Sidney reckoned later that if his body had turned as the curved horn slid out, it would have jerked his intestines with it, dragging them out onto the arena like the guts of a picador's horse, sand clinging to the sticky pale, bluish-gray membrane as it had since the days of the gladiators. Sidney had been lucky. His intestines were still within him as he was jostled to the ambulance on a canvas four-handed stretcher. The famous one-time ambulance driver Ernest Hemingway was in Key West that month, doing his bullfighting in his head and on the manuscript page as he began work on *Death in the Afternoon*. The actual day of the goring, the sixteenth, he was stranded by a storm at the old civil war fort on Dry Tortugas with his editor Maxwell Perkins and some fishing pals. They would not be rescued for two weeks. The following month John and Katy Dos Passos would visit Key West with details of Sidney's wounding. Hemingway biographer Carlos Baker somewhat snidely said that although Hemingway felt horrible about the news, "he managed to assuage his sorrow with another trip to Tortugas."

The bull in question was dragged out of the arena by the team of three mules, headed for the butcher shop. Whether it had a bad eye is unknowable now. Sidney had told Lillian Ross seventeen years after the fact that he had turned his back on the bull simply to wipe his face. Perhaps he felt the more elaborate version of the bull's bad eye made a better story, at least one of greater import to him personally. Perhaps he was still trying to make sense of that split second, that blink of destiny's eye that irrevocably changed the course of his life. "I was gored by a dead bull," he said, putting a jocular spin on the tragedy.

Sidney, in his twenty-six plus years, had up to this point displayed fearlessness, resolution, recklessness, and determination. Now, stranded in that Madrid hospital with his career dangling as precariously as his body had been on the horn of that bull, he summoned all those traits in a truly crazy but courageous feat. Ignoring his doctor's advice, he left the hospital and within five weeks of the wounding was back in the ring for a bullfight in Jerez de la Frontera.

The operation to repair the horn damage was the first of nine that Sidney would undergo in the next decade and a half. When Sidney got back into the ring so soon, it was with a still-open and draining wound. Facing bull after bull in such shape took a certain kind of bravery. During a fight in North Africa he tried to vault the *barrera* from the stirrup board but could not even move his legs, the adhesions from the knitting wound inside had so incapacitated him. Again, it was back to the hospital. Sidney offhandedly claimed that he had to get back to work quickly because of all the money he would lose — he still had to support his *cuadrilla* and keep them together — but his own confidence and his standing with the public was on the line as well.

Although in pain and facing the end of what might have been a great career as a *torero*, Sidney remained attentive to his appearance. To give himself relief from lugging the twenty-five-pound gold-encrusted suit of lights on his back during his recuperation, he ordered a salmon-pink uniform embroidered only with ivory-colored silk with no brocade—taurine tradition up to that time dictated black silk trim only—a sort of *traje de luces* lite. New duds may have been Sidney's way of positive thinking, his insistence to himself that he indeed had a future in the bullring. Or it may simply have been his feeling that even when one is hobbling in pain and oozing from one's bottom, one can at least look one's best. He recounts that this radical fashion statement drew a cool, sometimes hostile response from the fans in Madrid when on August 17 he made his first appearance there since his goring. Actually, the fans, sticklers for tradition, pointed and booed at the pink *torero*. He made one more appearance that month in the town of Calahorra, then for him the season was over. Although he could not foresee it, his life as an in-demand Spanish bullfighter was over as well. He would not appear again in Madrid for another fifteen years. By October Sidney was back in the hospital for his fifth operation.

That fall he sailed for New York to visit his family before heading for Mexico for the 1930–1931 winter season. In Brooklyn he again felt like an outsider with his family, showing them film footage of his ring performances that drew laughs instead of respect, as if he were just a clown in a funny suit performing a dog-and-pony show instead of a serious professional engaging in a timeless and life-threatening ritual. Lillian Ross recounts that the visit ended well enough when, preceded by an incongruous cowboy marching band, Sidney was escorted from the Battery to city hall to be presented by his brother Milton to the mayor—well, actually, the acting mayor, as His Honor Jimmy Walker was out of town—as "the idol of Spain."

The Idol of Spain had not been to his old stomping grounds in Mexico for well over a year and found himself as out of place as was his new Castilian accent. Promoters were as cool as they had been before he left, and booking remained a struggle as he picked up fights when and where he could. He did appear in Mexico City's main bullring, El Toreo, where he fought six young bulls — *novillos — mano a mano* with David Liceaga. On Washington's Birthday, 1931, he was booked to appear in a *corrida mixta* — an event featuring both *novilleros* and *matadors de toros* — in Nuevo Laredo with Marcial Lalanda, the Spaniard who fought in the first bullfight that Sidney had ever witnessed. Sidney claimed that Lalanda was ill that season and required Sidney to carry more of the load than usual, a fact that Lalanda confirms in his own writing.

The pageantry of the bullfight as it was performed in the great rings of Spain lost some of its pomp and luster in its practice in the towns of the Mexican-American border, such as Nuevo Laredo, especially when seen up close from the *torero*'s vantage, even more so when such a *torero* had just come from triumphs in Spain itself. Compared to the iconic arches and golden sand of La Maestranza in Sevilla, such border-town arenas seemed rickety and shabby, like a minor league baseball park with splintered plank grandstands and sagging fences in some small American town a half century ago. As Sidney walked under the Nuevo Laredo grandstands before the opening procession, the *capilla*, the bullfighter's chapel, would look small and closetlike, lacking the solemnity and adornments of such altars in Spain. A picador's horse, which seemed at least somewhat impressive in its medieval armor and finery when seen from across the arena or from high in the stands, would look tired and old as Sidney walked closely past, the modified war saddle cheap and worn, the animal standing alone, tied not with a fine halter but with a bit of clothesline to an iron stanchion while the picador awaited his appearance in the ring, perhaps having stepped away for a shot of Fundador or a quick piss. In February the horse would still have a shaggy winter coat from the damp cold of nights along the Rio Bravo. Its feet would be unshod and chipped, ring-bone swelling its creaky pasterns, indicating that this would be the animal's last employment. And as Sidney stepped into the ring for the first time with Lalanda for the ceremonial *paseo*, he would have also noticed that the arena footing was thick and deep with new unpacked sand dangerously slowing every step.

Whether it was the sand or the unhealed Spanish wound or simply luck, while facing his first bull that afternoon, Sidney was gored a second time. The bull caught him with a horn in the calf of his leg, then jerked its head up. Sidney pinwheeled over the bull's body and was tossed in a heap. Lalanda, though ill, rushed out with his cape to draw the bull away. Sidney regained his feet and went on to finish both this animal and his second bull, and only then was rushed off in an ambulance. To add to the pain, the bulls Sidney faced that afternoon came from his old home-away-from-home, the Xajay ranch.

His devoted friend from Spain, Ross Dennison, was in town for the bullfight and stayed with Sidney in the hospital throughout the treatment. Although sympathetic, Hemingway wrote of the calf injury in *Death in the Afternoon* with the offhandedness of one who has never been gored, as an unimportant wound. It may have seemed so at the time. However, over Sidney's objections, the surgeon gave him injections of the anti-tetanus and anti-gangrene serums he had been administered in Spain. Although not immediate, these doses of the same powerful drugs less than a year after their first introduction to his system caused his left arm to swell horribly in a sort of boil, ending all hopes of bullfighting for the next season.

Although he could not know it then, nor would he face it any time soon, this was the beginning of a long, slow slide in Sidney's life from star matador to one-time bullfighter, from someone in his own right to no one in particular. "Before the horn wound, he had the real completely," Hemingway said to Lillian Ross of the rectal goring. "Because of his bad wound he lost the real in bullfighting."

9

Hard Times

AFICIONADOS HAVE A SAYING THAT bullfighters shed
the brave blood first. Courage displayed before ever experiencing
a major goring is quite different from the fear that must be overcome after a sharp horn has torn violently into muscle, bone, or
viscera, and before such an injury infects the *torero's* imagination
and haunts his dreams. Many *cornadas* are to the thigh and groin,
although men have died from even more grotesque wounds, such
as Manuel Granero, whose face was virtually destroyed in front of
the fans during his fatal Madrid goring in 1922. A common wound
is that suffered by Manolete, an injury to the femoral artery of the
inner thigh that keeps the matador conscious for a time as his life
literally pours out of him onto the sand in an unstoppable flow.
Sidney's first wound shed that brave blood, but his determination to continue showed that he had more where that came from.
The second goring and his reaction to the tetanus serum took
something different out of him. Always cocky and vain about his
dress and appearance, Sidney was now not only unemployable,
with his swollen arm he was now temporarily deformed as well.
His future, which had only the year before seemed limitless, was

now receding from his grasp. He returned to Spain in April but was at first physically unable to fight in the 1931 season, which was already under way. Then, when he felt he was able, the fight promoters and arena officials, from whom he had demanded and received high fees when he was the hot ticket the year before, took their retribution by stalling him with one excuse or another until all their dates were booked. The *alternativa*, which had so recently been his for the taking at a moment of his choosing, was now looking more and more like an impossibility. That his career could end before achieving its ultimate validation was a bitter thing to contemplate. There was nothing left to do but put on a brave face and have a good time.

Hemingway returned to Spain after an absence of a year and a half and brought those good times back with him. He was two chapters away from finishing the first draft of *Death in the Afternoon*, and planned to steep himself in the bullfight for yet another season. As a friend, he was generous with his time and his money. As he had in 1929, Sidney gave Hemingway an insider's access, although he was out of commission. Together they critiqued the action. Together they checked out the new phenoms. In his new manuscript Hemingway wrote of going with Sidney in May to a *corrida* in Aranjuez to assess the skills of a much-touted young matador named Domingo López Ortega, as one would today write of going to Florida to watch the new kids at spring training with a knowledgeable big leaguer who was on injured reserve. Hemingway pronounced the young man's performance "lousy" and said that Sidney, knowing he could have performed better himself, berated Ortega as he and Hemingway drove back to Madrid that night. (Contrary to both Americans' assessments, Ortega, after a spotty first season, went on to become both extremely popular and admired in Spain. Hemingway would later say that Ortega even modeled his style after Sidney's — so much for knowing how to pick 'em.) For the two friends, it was almost like those first few weeks on the road in 1929. Almost.

Sidney joined Hemingway and the writer's eldest son, seven-year-old John Hadley Nicanor or "Bumby," in Pamplona in July for the festival of San Fermín. Along with the running of the bulls in the street, the night and day drinking in the cafés, the parades of giant puppets and general madness of the weeklong fiesta, were the *corridas* themselves. Sidney was still a member of the club and could move among the other professionals with ease. He was now and would always be one of them. Recovering from a goring was just a part of the game.

Sidney tells that he had a tiny cape and sword made for Bumby so that he could teach his little pal the basic passes of the bull-fighter's repertoire, or at least let him play at the spectacle that his father had let him witness for real. Back in Madrid in the heat of midsummer, the two friends would often congregate with other bullfighters on a stretch of sand and trees on the banks of the shallow Manzanares River. There on the playa they would while away the afternoons with a *paella* pan over an open fire, drinking, joking, and arguing about bullfighting. Both Sidney and Hemingway write of this idyllic time, and as usual the difference is in the details. Sidney speaks of a river only six-inches deep, and describes a leisurely all-male afternoon. Hemingway writes of failed matadors swimming with cheap whores, saying "beggars can't be choosers." (A year or so later Madrid built a bathing pavilion on the site, so Hemingway's description of the river itself at least seems to be the more accurate.)

A series of photographs in the Hemingway collection of the John F. Kennedy Library show Hemingway, Sidney, Luis Crovetto, and four other bullfighters on the playa goofing for the camera. All but

Hemingway, who wears bathing trunks, and a man wearing underwear, are naked. In one photo, a laughing Ernest leans a hand on Sidney's shoulder. (The five-foot-eleven Sidney seems as tall or taller than the supposedly six-foot-plus Hemingway.) Smiling, Sidney holds a monarchist magazine over his crotch (probably the first thing at hand, but fraught with symbolism on so many levels). Another man holds a newspaper in front of himself. Little Luis, standing at Hemingway's right, covers himself for the camera by holding a bag of something over his privates in his left hand, while his right hand stretches around the shoulder of a fellow wearing an improvised loincloth. A seventh man squats as mischievously as Pan while he squirts wine from a *bota* bag into his mouth, his eye on the camera, wearing what looks to be a rolled up bit of paper over his member, exaggerating the organ like something from a risqué Commedia dell'Arte. If a woman, whore or otherwise, were present, she must have been manning the Rolleiflex, because she certainly was not in the shot. And Sidney, so prominent in the photographs, is not mentioned by Hemingway at all.

Biographer James Mellow, in *Hemingway: A Life without Consequences*, considers these photographs and speculates that Hemingway made up the presence of the whores in *Death in the Afternoon* to transform the all-male group in the photo into something more acceptable, more emphatically masculine. Mellow also feels that the pictures belie Hemingway's assertions that he was uncomfortable with the touch of another male, however innocuous. The author looks at ease in the photographs. On the page, his pose is more aggressive, more gruff. But then that was always the way with Hemingway. Most telling, however, is that Professor Mellow seems completely unaware of Sidney's sexual orientation. The tone of his discussion of these events and photographs would be quite different if he were.

The scene on the Manzanares is from the last chapter of *Death in the Afternoon*, a beautiful, impressionistic laundry list of what Hemingway said was not included in the text because he did not write "enough of a book." It contains the immediacy, the sensual detail, the rush of images that make Ernest Hemingway still matter because he is still the master of such writing. Sidney too is there, in both his generosity of spirit and his obsessive fastidiousness:

> And up in Sidney's rooms, the ones coming to ask for work when he was fighting, the ones to borrow money, the ones for an old shirt, a suit of clothes; all bullfighters, all well known somewhere at the hour of eating, all formally polite, all out of luck; the muletas folded and piled; the capes all folded flat; swords in the embossed leather case; all in the armoire; muleta sticks are in the bottom drawer, suits hung in the trunk, cloth covered to protect the gold; my whiskey in an earthen crock; Mercédes, bring the glasses . . .

The passage is a lovely picture of the writer's friend and his world. (Mercédes is Sidney's cook who prepared the lunch at his apartment the first day that the two men met in 1929.) Then, Hemingway tosses off a riff on the stoicism of Sidney Franklin a year after his goring when things were still bad and the infections were still plaguing him but Sidney refused to complain.

> She says he had a fever all night long and only went out an hour ago. So then he comes in. How do you feel? Great. She says you had a fever. But I feel great now. What do you say, Doctor, why not eat here? She can get something and make a salad. Mercédes oh Mercédes.

No wonder they were friends.

This chapter is a nine-page love-letter to Spain. It was also, although neither man knew it, a letter of goodbye. Hemingway would be back in the late summer of 1933 for one last partial season of bull-fights, but Sidney would soon learn a hard truth. Bullfighting was a passion for Ernest Hemingway, and for a time when first they met, Sidney was at the center of that passion. But it was not to be Ernest Hemingway's only passion. Both as a writer and a rest-less soul, Hemingway moved from interest to interest even more frequently than he moved from wife to wife. He had already dis-covered the lure of an odd role model — the writer of cowboy pulp fiction, Zane Grey — which was deep-sea fishing. (Hemingway en-vied Grey's leisure pursuits more than his prose.) Hemingway had just purchased — again with the generosity of his wife's uncle Gus Pfeiffer — a home on Whitehead Street in Key West. From there, then Havana and Bimini, Hemingway made such serious assault on the big fish of the Gulf Stream that manufacturers of tackle had to retool to keep up with the demands he put on their equipment.

Sidney was not a part of this world. Nor was he a part of the world of African big-game safaris, a passion of another role model of Hemingway's boyhood, Theodore Roosevelt. Hemingway had his eye on that new African horizon even as he wet his first line in the gulf. By the summer of 1932, as *Death in the Afternoon* was about to go the printers, he was making definite plans for a safari, although he would not get the financing for another year and a half — yet again from the generous Gus Pfeiffer.

Unlike bullfighting, which Hemingway could only experience secondhand through Sidney and the true Spaniards, big game fish-ing and hunting allowed Hemingway to be the hero of his own stories. In these outdoor pursuits of a writing man in his thirties, *he* could be the matador. He had no use of a Sidney Franklin, much less *the* Sidney Franklin. His image, when not writing, imprinted on the world for the last three-quarters of a century was that of the man with the rod or rifle (or cocktail) in his hand. At the bull-fights he had to stay in the bleachers. So, for the next several years, Hemingway was through with bullfighting.

> It's all been changed for me . . . We'll all be gone before it's changed too much . . . We never will ride back from Toledo in the dark, washing the dust out with Fundador, nor will there be that week of what happened in the night in that July in Madrid. We've seen it all go and we'll watch it go again.

With the promoters putting him off in 1931 and his health still dicey, Sidney took one last stab at keeping alive as a matador: he attempted a winter tour of South America (on that continent, bull-fighting, although actively practiced in countries such as Venezuela, Colombia, and Peru, was not universal); however, poor bookings and unscrupulous promoters made it clear that, for the time, his career was on ice.

Over the next few years, Sidney would try to cash in on his celebrity and his knowledge of bullfighting in any way he could. Perhaps inspired by his literary pal, Sidney turned twice to writing. In 1931 he co-wrote with veteran journalist and poet Arthur Chapman a piece for his favorite magazine, the *Saturday Evening Post*, called "Inside the Bullring." It is surprisingly informative with none of the over-the-top self-aggrandizement that would color Sidney's later public statements. Instead, he and his co-writer present a lucid, first-person picture of the bullfight world as an esoteric yet sensible multimillion-dollar industry to which sober-eyed American readers bogged down in the midst of the Depression could relate. (Thirty years older than Sidney, Chapman would seem an odd choice of collaborator. A western author, Chapman wrote a column for the *Denver Republican*, novels such as *Mystery Ranch*, and was an early hand at what is now called cowboy poetry, his most famous piece being the 1917 classic "Out Where the West Begins.")

As narrator, Sidney sets the scene for *Post* readers with a description of the inner legal and business workings within the Madrid headquarters of the Association of Matadors as a new season is scheduled. He corrects the misconception in the English-speaking world created by the term "bullfight" by clarifying that *corrida de toros* means "running of bulls," which he says is a more accurate description of what goes on in the ring. He explains that it is the bull that runs at the matador, not the matador who dodges the bull. He makes clear that it is the manipulation of the *capote* and *muleta* — both described in color, size, fabric, and function — that controls the animal's charge. To show that the men in the funny suits are not some effete Europeans engaged in a silly and pointless pursuit, he informs the *Post* readers that the purses won by heavyweight champs Jack Dempsey and Gene Tunney in the 1920s were chump change when compared to the fees commanded by bullring greats such as Belmonte. He states that Gaona made a slick four million in six years while breaking the rigid nationality barrier by becoming the first Mexican to fight regularly in Spain. He does not mention that the Great Indian had been his mentor, but his intimate knowledge of Gaona's stature in Mexico speaks for itself. Perhaps with Gaona in mind, Sidney does mention colorful superstitions of the bullfight world, such as the improper handling of hats or anything to do with snakes, by telling droll anecdotes at his own expense. The whole piece is a skillful insider's tale meant to show that Sidney Franklin was, although a no-nonsense Yankee with whom his audience could relate, a successful guy totally in the know. (It is unfortunate that he did not have the restraining influence of Chapman's cowboy reticence two decades later during the writing of *Bullfighter from Brooklyn*.) Sidney ends with several columns that lovingly describe the costume, the *traje de luces,* from the matador's false pigtail, or *coleta,* to the heelless slippers, the *zapatillas de torear,* with every laced-up garter and lace-trimmed linen shirt in between. He pays credit to the needlework of silent nuns in nameless convents who hand-stitch the delicate but resplendent embroidery. He describes the feeling of being poured into a costume so tight that one cannot negotiate stairs, only to have the clothing ease just so, "as a new glove adjusts itself to the hand." And he tells of the *estoques* — the killing swords — custom made only in Valencia by a famous firm of father and son, the blade hand drawn by hammer strokes across the anvil face as they had been since the days of the Arabs, and of course, double-edged.

In 1933 he used his Spanish language skills to translate a popular bullfighting novel, *Currito de la Cruz* by Alejandro Pérez Lugín, into English. As translator he was somewhat out of his depth and soon needed help, especially with the dialogue. Sidney was fortunate to receive the uncredited editing assistance of a famous American novelist who happened to be in Madrid at the time, and who presumably also brought the manuscript to his own New York publishing house. The English language version of Lugín's novel, called *Shadows of the Sun,* came out the following year under the Scribner's imprint. Hemingway found his work assisting Sidney wearying and the book "trash," but he dutifully did it for his friend. The hard times were beginning to show on Sidney. "He looks sort of shoddy in Spain sometimes," Hemingway said of him "but by god he looked awfully good in New York. I believe he is the best story teller I have ever known." When Sidney was hospitalized in Madrid that year, Hemingway stayed with him through the surgery, which cut three inches from his lower intestine. He also paid for the operation.

Death in the Afternoon, the most concrete record of Sidney's friendship with Ernest Hemingway, was published in the fall of 1932.

The reviews of his first nonfiction work were only so-so. This was something new for Hemingway. Sales were also unspectacular. Since the great success of *The Sun Also Rises*, this too was a first for him. The writer Max Eastman published an article in the *New Republic* called "Bull in the Afternoon," which a few years later prompted a fistfight between the two men in Maxwell Perkins's Scribner's office — but only after Hemingway had torn open his shirt to show that the hair on his chest was indeed real.

Hemingway should have been consoled by the Spanish reviews, which were uniformly better, although based on the original American edition from Scribner's. Amazingly, there would be no Spanish language version of *Death in the Afternoon* published until the mid-1960s. A thorough examination of these reviews in the Spanish press by Nancy Bredendick in *The Hemingway Review* in 2005 shows that Hemingway accomplished what he set out to do when he first met Sidney: present a knowledgeable and complete picture of the Spanish art for the non-Spaniard, and to acquit himself as both extremely knowledgeable and sympathetic to the bullfight and to Spain itself.

Bredendick concentrates on the review of one individual, the novelist and journalist Tomás Orts-Ramos, who had been writing respected bullfight criticism for decades under the name "Uno al Sesgo." In a two-part review for the weekly *La Fiesta Brava* of Barcelona, Orts-Ramos praises the book highly, referring to Hemingway as an apostle who is effectively spreading the happy word of the *corrida* to the non-Spanish world. When Orts-Ramos finds fault, however, it is directly related to Hemingway's reliance on Sidney Franklin as expert witness. Whether on boxing, horseracing, or hunting, Hemingway always trusted the knowledgeable insider, the guy with the straight dope, and liked to play that role himself whenever he could get away with it. The very reason he sought out

Sidney in 1929 was for Sidney to play that insider's role for him in the bullfighting world so that he could write *Death in the Afternoon* in the first place. Orts-Ramos felt that by relying heavily on the opinion of bullfighters themselves, Hemingway allowed the self-serving opinions of men still swinging the cape to become an "intrusive influence" on his narrative, resulting in a skewed view based on some very subjective observations that Hemingway had been told or had read elsewhere. The accusing finger inevitably points to Sidney, as Hemingway relied on the opinions of no other bullfighter as much in the writing of this book. Orts-Ramos felt that the bullfighter's perspective was only one part of the equation, and that the professionals were poorly suited to evaluate the effect of their performance on the audience, an essential element of any art. Hemingway's poor opinion of the young matador Domingo Ortega is one glaring example, in Orts-Ramos's view, of this blind spot.

As Bredendick sums up Orts-Ramos, bullfighters do not make good critics of their own work—a common problem in many pursuits. As for Hemingway's reliance on the writings of others in which inaccuracies become repeated and repeated until they take on the status of accepted truth, Orts-Ramos does not single Hemingway out. He finds this common throughout the world not just of Spanish bullfighting but of any writing on a foreign subject. Having gently called Hemingway to task in an otherwise glowing review, he proceeds to let his big catch off the hook. "In his own defense . . . Hemingway could well ask how, without consulting spoken and print sources, can one write a book like this? And he would be absolutely right." As far as that goes, without such sources, how could one write any nonfiction book at all?

Throughout these years in the early thirties, Sidney would catch up with Ernest Hemingway when and where he could, in Paris or

Madrid or more than once in New York when Ernest was passing through, visiting friends Gerald and Sara Murphy up at Saranac Lake, Dos Passos or Scott Fitzgerald for lunch or drinks in town, or Max Perkins at Scribner's. Sidney, now of more modest means, would normally be staying with family in Brooklyn. Bernice Kert in *The Hemingway Women* describes Hemingway returning to his wife in the Hotel Westbury in 1935 to find her having cocktails with her cousin and Sidney, who had just presented his friend Pauline with cheap off-the-rack dresses from his brother-in-law's Brooklyn shop as if they were straight from Chanel. (Sidney's niece Eve, however, scoffed at this detail of the dresses.)

As Sidney had once come to see himself as a master in the bull-ring, he now tried to position himself as a master *of* the bullring. That same grandiose sense of self prompted him to head down to Hemingway's new turf with a plan to introduce the *corrida* to Cuba, where it had not been practiced since the United States banned it after the Spanish-American War. Sidney would become a bullfight impresario, one of the very sort who had denied him opportunities in the past. It was his old sense of noblesse oblige once again. In the fall of 1934, Sidney, along with one of his sisters and her husband, sailed to Havana, supposedly to meet with the new dictator Batista, certainly to join up with Hemingway who had decamped to Cuba for the fishing (although the presence of a twenty-five-year-old married blond socialite in Havana was as big a lure for Hemingway as the marlin). Again, Sidney would go to his friend for help. In his memoir Sidney describes the Cuban bullfighting scheme as well advanced, supposedly to be financed, as always, by Pauline's Uncle Gus. A series of photographs taken on this trip show a subtle distance between Sidney and his friend Ernest. They stand on the dock in Havana with a group of Cubans. Hanging between them is a blue marlin. This is Ernest Hemingway in a happy moment, as the public would always remember him: grinning with his kill, his hair tousled, wearing fisherman's sandals, dirty pants and shirt. Posing stiffly alongside in a grey flannel suit and black Basque beret with a forced smile—hands clasped primly over his groin in one shot—is Sidney. The world of sport fishing was not Sidney's world. He looks a man clearly not in his element, a stranger among friends, a ghost from a passion and a past that Hemingway had left behind. The bullfight scheme never came to be, although Sidney would try once more within the next few years to make it so. But by the time Sidney would visit with Hemingway in Cuba again, there would be more hanging between the two men than just a dead fish.

Bullfighters have an expression that when they retire they "cut the pigtail." Whether the pigtail is real as it was going back to the eighteenth century, or a false one attached by a clip at the back of the neck just for the afternoon's performance, the symbolism is that of an irrevocable decision. Once the pigtail is cut, the matador moves on to the next chapter. But for Sidney there was nowhere left to move. There was no movie star waiting to marry. No bull ranch that he could afford to purchase so that he could live out his days in the grand manner of a *ganadero*. His moment in the sun had been too brief, the money accumulated inadequate to support such a life.

A lack of money, as much as a lack of stature and poor health, kept Sidney from a serious return to bullfighting. Earlier in 1934 he had planned a visit to Mexico City—with a stop at Key West to visit Hemingway—to get back into fighting shape. He hoped to travel to Spain by the following year, first to participate in some *tientas*, then in paid engagements in the ring. He told Hemingway in a June 27 letter that he planned to "shoot the works," putting all his energies into restarting his career. His mode of transportation for the New York–Key West–Mexico journey was an automobile borrowed from his sister. Forget owning a bull ranch—Sidney could not even afford a Buick. That the unnamed sister was willing to part with her car for many months to help her brother is testament to the devotion that the Frumpkin siblings showed Sidney his entire life, no matter how odd they found his calling—or Sidney himself. It is doubtful that Sidney actually accomplished the Mexican trip, which explains why he, his sister, and brother-in-law showed up in Havana just a few months afterward.

He complained to Hemingway a full year and a half later that he was still unable to raise the money to pay off his debts, thus making a Spanish campaign impossible. And he was crowded by the passing of time—seeing his future again drift away from his grasp. "If I don't get back in the ring this winter I may as well give up the ghost," he wrote Hemingway in September 1935. By then he had lowered his sights, planning to get back in shape by practicing on the ranches of friends, then picking up a few fights along the border in Mexico that winter. He hoped that this would give him enough new professional exposure to then close out his career with at least a season or two back in Spain before cutting the pigtail for good. His health from the rectal goring was still spotty as well. Sidney contacted the top bullring doctor in Madrid—a Dr. Segovia—for advice, and wrote Hemingway that "the old ash can still leaks."

After the success of the *Saturday Evening Post* article, Sidney again tried writing as a way to raise cash, but without success. New stories—written without Arthur Chapman's help—were rejected. He turned out eighty pages of an autobiography that planned to cover the events from his arrival in Mexico in 1922 to his Sevilla debut, but the work failed to meet even Sidney's own breezy standards. He admitted to Hemingway that to be honest, "it smelled bad."

The September 1935 letter to Hemingway reveals that they had obviously been discussing a book on his life for some time, and refers to "our agreement that someday you'd do it." Sidney then asks Hemingway to look at his unfinished manuscript, offering to "drop it cold" should it conflict with any plans Hemingway might have had to write such a book himself. He then admits he should have consulted Hemingway before ever sitting down at the typewriter, while at the same time fishing for clues that his pal might still be interested. He concludes, "I'm up against a stone wall." Remember Hemingway's comment in the afterward to *Death in the Afternoon*: "The story of those lives belongs to [Sidney] and I will not tell it to you." He sure wouldn't. By 1935, after the lukewarm reception to his own lovingly wrought work on bullfighting, Hemingway was obviously suffering a bit of what we would now call been-there, done-that. So *Bullfighter from Brooklyn* became a two-decade-long solo project that never overcame that smell factor. Like a leaky ash can, some things a guy just gets used to.

The tone of these letters to Hemingway is a bit sad: the plaintive words of an unsuccessful man with time heavy on his hands trying to get the attention of a successful friend who is too busy with his own life to respond. There is the false bravado that cannot hide the anxiety, the repeated greetings to the family, the pleading for a reply, the wondering if a Christmas card sent nine months earlier ever arrived. (What would his pa have said about his observance of *that* convention?) Even his letterhead in those years is telling. It simply states *Sidney Franklin — Matador De Toros*. First, not having taken his *alternativa*, he was still just a *novillero* and certainly *not* a *matador de toros* and would not become one for another decade. Secondly, there is no printed address indicating any permanent home. He would often type in the Brooklyn address of whichever sister he was staying with at the time.

Had he been able to pull it off, becoming a Cuban impresario would certainly have been better than nothing. Failing that, he would hang on to that symbolic pigtail for as long as he could (long after most of the real hair was gone), and long after it was obvious that the keeping of it was largely futile. Although an adopted life, the life of the bulls was who he was. He loved it too much, and he simply had nothing else to cling to. That *Matador De Toros* letterhead shows that for Sidney, the dream never died, the goal was always there, shimmering on the horizon. It was what kept him going, kept him sane. He admits that the idle life back in New York — besides adding twenty pounds — was hard on his mental health. There was no way he could stay in Brooklyn for good and settle for becoming an accountant like his brothers. His self-cultivated sense of noblesse oblige was too great. Still, he had to eat.

Sidney even tried the movies. He makes a claim, which is hard to verify now, that in the 1920s, when he was still only a minor celebrity in the towns of Mexico, he met Douglas Fairbanks during a trip to Los Angeles and was invited to appear in Fairbanks's 1926 film *The Black Pirate*. The film still exists, but it is impossible to tell if Sidney is among the brigands who romped in high boots and tight pantaloons with daggers in their teeth at the old Pickford-Fairbanks Studio at Formosa Avenue and Santa Monica Boulevard in Hollywood. (His name does not appear on the credits, but that would not be uncommon for small roles and extra players of the silent era.) He claims Fairbanks offered him a five-year contract as a "featured player," which Sidney admits had been a secret ambition of his youth. He says he turned "Doug" down to pursue the life of a bullfighter, and then blames his career slump in the late twenties on his absence from Mexico during the filming.

There does exist a film record of Sidney Franklin that was shot at the same studio a half decade later, when the lot was run by Samuel Goldwyn. Sidney plays himself in a cameo role in a bit of fluff for Goldwyn starring Eddie Cantor called *The Kid from Spain*. Sidney was also technical advisor on the project. In the 1932 film, Cantor plays a schlemiel who, during a trip south of the border, is mistaken for a famous bullfighter. Although silly, the film was no hack job. It was directed by Leo McCarey (*Going My Way*); the cinematographer was Gregg Toland (*The Grapes of Wrath* and *Citizen Kane*); and the sexy pre-Code musical numbers were designed by Busby Berkeley, featuring the unbilled and somewhat undressed Betty Grable, Paulette Goddard, and Jane Wyman. Bert Kalmar and Harry Ruby wrote all the songs and co-wrote the screenplay with William Anthony McGuire. A bullring set was constructed on the lot under Sidney's supervision. Watching the film now, a viewer can see a sprightly Sidney, who, after being introduced to the crowd by Noah Berry Sr., performs in the ring for several minutes. He has no dialogue, but his cool, detached style is evident even then, although the sequence is poorly edited considering the talent involved. With his career going nowhere, caping a tame bull in a fake ring on the Goldwyn back lot on Santa Monica Boulevard, the only schlemiel posing as a bullfighter was Sidney himself.

ACT THREE

*La Faena, or the Suerte de Matar
(literally, the kill).*
*Here the matador works closely with
the small cape, the* muleta, *preparing
the bull for the kill with the* estoque,
*or killing sword. This is the most
dangerous act, the moment when a
matador is in greatest danger of being
killed himself. For every player in
the ring, it is do or die —* la hora de
verdad *— the time of truth.*

10

The Big Parade

THE PHONE RANG.

"'Lo, kid," said Hemingway, "want to go to the war in Spain?"

"Sure, pop," Sidney Franklin claimed he replied, "Which side are we on?"

It probably did not happen exactly this way, but it should have.

In the last days of November 1936, Ernest Hemingway left Pauline at their Key West home and sailed his fishing boat over to Cuba, specifically to persuade their old friend Sidney to accompany him on a great new adventure—covering the civil war already boiling in Spain. Sidney was back in Havana for his second try at the scheme to promote the *corrida*. As with the previous attempt, this one was not to pan out. Since *The Kid from Spain*, the years had not been any easier. He had spent time in both Mexico and Spain, staying at the places and seeing the friends where he still had a name and a reputation, but since he was no longer regularly fighting bulls, there was a restless futility to his travels. Too often he found himself living back with his sisters and visiting his mother in Brooklyn. He was the thirty-three-year-old bachelor son when being a bachelor was not necessarily suspect or odd. He would often fill the empty months traveling with his sisters and their husbands; his family ties — except with his father, who did not relinquish this life until 1942 — still strong.

The mid-1930s were also years of change for Hemingway. *Death in the Afternoon* may have been his first book to earn spotty reviews and unspectacular sales, but it would not be his last. Hemingway's third collection of short stories, *Winner Take Nothing*, was published in 1933 to a far less enthusiastic reception than the first two volumes had received. (*Winner Take Nothing* was an uneven mix of classics and clunkers compared to the unity and understated power of his 1925 collection, *In Our Time*.) Old mentor Gertrude Stein made snide comments about Hemingway in *The Autobiography of Alice B. Toklas*. He had transformed from the hot new thing to a plump target in barely half a decade. The distinctive style that swept out the attic of American prose had already become an object of parody, as it remains three-quarters of a century later with annual "bad Hemingway" contests — a tribute, one can suppose, to the power of the original. His second nonfiction work, *Green Hills of Africa*, an account of his first African safari with barbed asides on life and literature, again provoked some antagonistic reviews. These career pressures would have a spillover effect on Sidney as Hemingway tried to get back in his groove.

Celebrity itself had inevitably changed Hemingway. No American writer so successfully managed his public image, and none would have that image so intertwined in his work. But by the early thirties, the public image seemed to overtake the work, and the more quarrelsome, pugnacious Hemingway of later caricature began to emerge. This temptation to pontificate began to manifest itself more in his nonfiction work, which served to loosen the wonderful control and discipline of his novels and short stories.

Biographer Jeffery Meyers attributes this partly to living in a place, such as Key West, where he had no intellectual peers, such as he had in Paris in the twenties, and where he was surrounded more and more by acolytes and hangers-on.

"He was a great listener before he moved to Key West," Meyers writes, "and a great talker afterwards."

Hemingway found joy in other things than writing. He even visited Brooklyn, not to call on the Frumpkins but to see firsthand the Wheeler Shipyard, where he ordered himself a brand-new boat he would christen the *Pilar*, a pet name for Pauline when their adulterous affair was still a secret. This was one Hemingway luxury that would *not* be paid for by Uncle Gus, but rather by advances from Arnold Gingrich of the startup magazine *Esquire*. Hemingway also began an intermittent affair with Jane Mason, a beautiful but dangerously unstable married socialite who was a decade younger than he. This relationship, which lasted into 1936, was a poorly kept secret that threatened more than just his marriage. In 1933 Mason was driving Patrick, who was Pauline and Ernest's five-year-old son, and Bumby when she rolled her car down an embankment. Amazingly, neither boy was badly hurt. Mason's back, however, was injured. (A few days later the unhappy woman jumped or fell from a two-story window, actually breaking her back.) This several-year dalliance was uncharacteristic for the serial monogamist Hemingway, whose adultery in the past had ended in a bright new marriage. He would be running back to type soon enough.

So by December 1936, Sidney would have been only too happy for the chance to return to Spain. It was there he and Ernest had shared their best times when Sidney was, if not Hemingway's equal, at least able to command his own share of fame and finance. Only after the apolitical Sidney agreed to accompany Ernest to Madrid did he stop to wonder just which side of the civil war they would be covering. To him, it really did not matter. Despite an affinity for the rich and titled, his loyalty was to Hemingway, not to any cause. A trip to Spain would be a chance to recapture the magic of 1929, when their friendship was as fresh as the day they stood grinning, arm in arm, in the snapshot with the castle behind them. And there was the added attraction that someone else would be footing the bill. The young man who had held up the Spanish promoters for top dollar when he was in demand in 1929 and '30 was now, as stated earlier, often short of funds, as he would be for the remainder of his life. Although Sidney bragged to Lillian Ross in the 1940s that wise investments gave him an income of eighteen thousand per year—a mountain of cash in the Truman years—when Hemingway returned from Havana to Key West after convincing Sidney to accompany him to Spain, he had just spotted his old pal fifty bucks.

So why Spain after all those years? By the end of 1936, Ernest Hemingway was truly restless. He had his recently remodeled house with a new saltwater pool, his new boat, his celebrity despite the critical rough spots, and he was working to finish a new novel that would be called *To Have and Have Not*. After two novels and the two nonfiction books set abroad, he finally, deep in the Depression, was using a major work to tackle themes of class and conflict in American society. He attempted this just as the attention of the writing world was turning away from domestic issues to the erupting war in Spain. Hemingway knew the world of factionalized Spanish political and ethnic conflict well. He spoke to Max Perkins about his frustration as early as 1931. "Wish there were some market for what I know about present Spanish situation. Have followed it as closely as though I were working for a paper." Big things were happening in the Spain he knew. Alfonso XIII would be the last Bourbon king of the country for four decades. He had been supported by the dictator Primo de Rivera, who was forced to give up power in 1930. Shorn of Primo de Rivera's support, Alfonso was forced to abdicate the following year after a republic was voted in. By 1936, because of the Republic's agrarian reforms and popular front leanings, the power centers of the right, such as the Catholic Church and a large portion of army officers, were soon aligned against the government. A little general, Francisco Franco, led a revolt against the elected government on July 18, 1936, and Catholics in the West could not hide their smiles. Ten years earlier, Franco, at age thirty-eight, had become Spain's youngest general. By 1935 he was serving as chief of staff. He inherited the support of the fascist Falange Party organized by Primo de Rivera's son, and soon made allies of Europe's new likeminded dictators, Benito Mussolini and Adolf Hitler. Mussolini sent Italian troops to support the rebellion. Hitler sent planes and German pilots of his Condor Legion. The struggle was pure fascist archetype: the old order—the church, the aristocracy, the landlords, the industrialists, and the monarchists—put their faith in hyper-nationalist lowborn militarists, dreamers, and thugs who promised a return to a nonexistent golden age of national purity while guaranteeing to vanquish the Bolsheviks, the trade unions, the intellectuals and artists, the syndicalists—in short, the entire modern world. Naturally, Hitler was interested.

The Republic soon attracted logistical and, more insidiously, organizational support from the Soviet Union, which was happy to fill the vacuum left when the western democracies decided to keep the leftist Spaniards at arm's length. Following the debacle in China in 1927—during which their support for the bourgeois revolution of Sun Yat-sen, and then his heir Chiang Kai-shek, blew up in their faces when Chiang turned on the communists and slaughtered them in the streets of Shanghai — Moscow was looking for a success story. And a communist victory in Western Europe under the noses of the great powers would be much sexier and potent than one in backward and unmanageable China anyway (that would have to wait another decade). So Stalin was *very* interested.

Spain's internal struggle for land reform and trade union rights immediately became the world's ideological battleground. What the Falangists thought would be a quick coup d'état turned into three years of grinding slaughter, the likes of which had not been seen in that country since Napoleon's peninsular campaign. Both sides of the ideological divide observed attentively. American progressives formed volunteer units such as the Abraham Lincoln Brigade, while many American Catholics supported Franco as the defender of the faith and a bulwark against socialism. By the winter of 1936, the Republic still held on to the region along the French border and the Mediterranean, with Valencia on the coast serving as provisional capitol. Meanwhile, Franco's rebel troops had reached the gates of Madrid. The world watched, and idealists and poets did what idealists and poets do: they went into the thick of it and got themselves killed.

For Hemingway, with a career that had plateaued at a level of celebrity as high as any American writer of the twentieth century, a trip back to the front lines was just what he felt he needed. In his mind, war had made him, both as the subject of *A Farewell to Arms* and as the subtext of the best of his early fiction, such as the short story "Big Two-Hearted River" or the novel *The Sun Also Rises*. He felt that his experience as a wounded teenage noncombatant on the Italian front had helped make him as a man as well. Hemingway itched to see the fighting first hand, and to re-establish his credentials — and his public image — as a cold-eyed observer of the worst the world had to offer. He had learned his craft as a correspondent for such papers as the *Toronto Star* as he taught himself to write fiction. But now writers Hemingway knew personally were already in Spain covering the war, covering his beat in a country he felt he knew as well as any American. Poets like Stephen Spender and W. H. Auden; journalists like Josephine Herbst and Sefton Delmer; novelists like his friend John Dos Passos — also an old Spanish hand — and Antoine de Saint-Exupery were all converging on Madrid. It was infuriating as hell. Even journalist Paul Mower, the new husband of Ernest's first wife, Hadley, was in Spain while Hemingway was idling his days on the *Pilar* and in Key West saloons as if intent on becoming the caricature his detractors claimed he was.

Hemingway complained to his friend Matthew Josephson that

I've got this nice house and boat in Key West — but they're both really Pauline's. I could stay on here forever, but it's a soft life. Nothing's really happening to me here and I've got to get out . . . In Spain maybe it's the big parade starting again.

It was obvious he wished it *were* the Big Parade. Hemingway soon signed a lucrative contract with the North American Newspaper Alliance to cover the Spanish war. But why would the author get his nonwriting friend Sidney Franklin credentialed with the NANA as well? The reason was domestic. Pauline Hemingway thought it a crazy idea for a well-to-do father of three to put himself in harm's way. "Pauline doesn't like the idea," Hemingway told Sidney one night in Havana. "She says I shouldn't go. But I know it would be alright with her if you came along with me." It was good to feel indispensable to someone so important. As close friend to both

Ernest and Pauline, Sidney was the one choice of traveling companion who would make the trip acceptable to the woman left behind.

"Sidney Franklin is going with me," Hemingway wrote to his Pfeiffer in-laws the week before leaving for Spain, "and he can talk us out of most sort [sic] of trouble. At least he's been successful at talking himself out for years."

But by the time Ernest and Sidney sailed for Europe, Sidney would find himself playing the unwitting role of beard for his married friend. For at age thirty-seven, Ernest Hemingway had a new girlfriend—a leggy blond he had met in Sloppy Joe's Bar in Key West just days after convincing Sidney to accompany him on the next big parade. And unknown to either Sidney or Pauline, he was meeting the blond in Spain.

The blond was Martha Gellhorn. When Hemingway first laid eyes on her in late December 1936, in his favorite bar where she was drinking with her mother and brother, she was already a published novelist and respected journalist. She had also recently ended a rather public affair with married French writer Bertrand de Jouvenel. He had some minor notoriety as the stepson and lover of novelist Colette, who had seduced him when he was seventeen and she forty-eight. Gellhorn's liaison with him was so intense and protracted that they both thought of it as a "marriage," an outcome Gellhorn had at one time sought, hoping de Jouvenel's wife would give him a divorce. This very European arrangement caused friction between Gellhorn and her disapproving physician father, who correctly identified his daughter's role as that of a Frenchman's mistress, nothing more. The affair resulted in two abortions and bad feelings all around.

Like Hemingway's first wife, Hadley, Gellhorn had been born in St. Louis and educated at Bryn Mawr. (Pauline had moved to St. Louis at the age of six and attended school and university there.

For Ernie, there was definitely something about those Saint Louie girls.)

Gellhorn was only twenty-eight when she met Hemingway, nine years younger than he, but she counted among her friends First Lady Eleanor Roosevelt and New Dealer Harry Hopkins. She had a knack of cultivating powerful and connected friends who could help her career. These included British novelist H. G. Wells (*The War of the Worlds* and *The Time Machine*), who wrote the introduction to her second book, a chronicle of the Depression in America called *The Trouble I've Seen*. According to Wells, a sixty-nine-year-old free-love advocate known for dalliances with many much younger women (years before, he had fathered a child with writer Rebecca West, a mere twenty-one years his junior), Gellhorn engineered a weeklong romantic idyll with him in Connecticut, if idyll is not too attractive a word for a romp with a man forty-two years one's senior. Gellhorn furiously denied Wells' claim for the rest of her life, protesting that she would not have gone to bed with such a portly old rascal when there were so many strapping young fellows available to her if she wanted sexual gratification. That Gellhorn confessed to disliking sex for its own sake — while at the same time providing it generously when partners expected it or when it gained her some advantage — complicates her denial.

She also denied knowing that the decidedly un-posh Key West hangout, Sloppy Joe's, was famous for a patron named Hemingway when she sauntered into that tropical dive eleven months later at midday wearing a little black dress and high heels. As was his habit, Hemingway was barefoot with a tee shirt and dirty shorts. When he sat down next to Miss Gellhorn, the bartender recalled it was like beauty and the beast.

Hemingway stayed so long with the young writer and her family that he missed dinner, prompting Pauline to send one of their guests to drag him home. Ernest refused to come. The guest explained to Pauline that her husband had been detained by "a beautiful blond in a black dress."

In the next few days, the novelist so often impatient with intrusions in his life acted as tour guide for the visiting family from St. Louis. One day Pauline was walking down a Key West street when her husband's automobile pulled alongside and he asked her to get in. Only then did she meet his two passengers, Martha Gellhorn and her brother, Alfred. Martha would later write that Pauline was "grumpy," and her husband "sharp."

Martha decided to stay over in Key West for a week after her mother and Alfred headed home. She saw Hemingway frequently, spending some of her time with Pauline and visiting their house at least once. After just a few days, she was impressed enough by Hemingway to drop a note to the first lady, describing him as "an odd bird, very lovable and full of fire." But Martha insisted that this was just friendship, the camaraderie extended by an established writer to a promising up-and-comer. After all, the scruffy celebrity and the long-legged blond had been linked even before that afternoon at Sloppy Joe's. Gellhorn's novel *What Mad Pursuit* had prompted one reviewer to compare her style with Hemingway's, and the book had even contained a Hemingway epigraph, "Nothing ever happens to the brave."

Despite Martha's denials in later years that she went cruising for Hemingway in the first place, one of her biographers, Carl Rollyson in *Beautiful Exile: The Life Of Martha Gellhorn*, quotes Pauline's friend Lorine Thompson saying:

> There was no question about it. You could see she was making a play for him . . . Pauline tried to ignore it. What she felt underneath nobody knew.

What Pauline did know was that Martha Gellhorn was some major competition, cultivating her looks and style as carefully as she cultivated her image as a serious writer worthy of joining Hemingway's professional circle. Pauline, almost forty-two, could not compete with Gellhorn on either the professional or the physical level, despite her work for *Vogue*, or having been quite sexually adventurous when she first met her husband in 1926. By the late 1930s, however, she had settled into the role of famous wife. A visitor Arnold Samuelson describes the slightly built Pauline greeting him in her home wearing pants and no makeup, with an extremely short haircut, and looking for all the world like a boy.

Ohio-born novelist Dawn Powell, well acquainted with both the Hemingways, sensed a problem in the marriage that went much deeper than simply age or physical appearance, and for which Pauline's quite public Catholicism was not enough to overcome.

Pauline seemed sharp-edged, too eager, brown and desperate. Her confessionals, her rosaries, that kept her head up during the bad years (so that she amazed everyone with her poise) do not after all fill the major gap in her life and give it a frittering quality that does not flatter. She should have a cause, beyond Saks Fifth Avenue.

As she had with the Jane Mason episode, Pauline had to bear up to public acknowledgement of her status as the woman betrayed. Rollyson quotes Hemingway's cook, Miriam Williams, who said that within those first few days of the meeting at Sloppy Joe's, she caught Hemingway and Gellhorn in the Hemingway's yard, "kissing and carrying on."

Pauline remarked of one of Hemingway's long absences squiring Gellhorn around the island, "I suppose Ernest is busy again helping Miss Gellhorn with her writing."

But it was not literature that would draw the two writers into a collision of sex and politics, it was Spain. As with his friendship with Sidney, Spain was the common passion between Hemingway and Gellhorn. Both writers were itching to witness the slaughter in person, although Martha Gellhorn's interest was the more overtly political — part of a long line of causes that extended from covering the suffering of victims of the Depression to Civil Rights to Vietnam. Unlike Pauline, Gellhorn at least *had* a cause. Hemingway's interest was in Spain itself. Both writers were astute enough to sense the obvious: that local war was the prelude to global conflict. In addition to his commission from the North American Newspaper Alliance, Hemingway had also agreed to collaborate on a film on the Spanish war with fellow writers Lillian Hellman, Archibald MacLeish, and John Dos Passos. The four created a corporation that they named, without irony, Contemporary Historians. They enlisted Dutch Marxist filmmaker Joris Ivens to direct and John Ferno as cinematographer. Martha Gellhorn still had no official credentials to allow her to enter Spain, but she now had a new booster with a mission.

Having known one another for a short two weeks of drinking, swimming, and conversing in Key West, Hemingway demonstrated that his interest in the young woman was more than social or even professional when she left for her St. Louis home on January 10. Whether prearranged or by surprise, he caught up with her train in Miami and rode with her as far as her connection in Jacksonville. They shared a steak and made plans. Martha wrote kind letters to Pauline from St. Louis, but did not confide her hopes for a Spanish trip. By the time Hemingway met Dos Passos in New York later that month to finalize their plans for the film, Martha was frequently around, her presence impossible to ignore. The Hemingways' old friends were beginning to talk. "I watched

Miss Gellhorn," Archibald MacLeish said, "conduct her amazing and quite shameless attack on their marriage." Martha did little to discourage such talk. At a Connecticut house party she spoke openly of her new man's barrel chest and his prowess in bed. At the same time, she was pushing Hemingway to show her fiction to his own editor, Max Perkins at Scribner's.

Martha was planning to rendezvous with Hemingway in Paris, but still did not have a way to get across the border into Spain. The British and French had signed a nonintervention pact, and the U.S. Congress had passed several neutrality acts, which made visas to Spain almost impossible to come by. Her letter to Hemingway written twelve days before he sailed shows her anxiety about catching up with him in France. It also shows that if Pauline did have any fears about where Martha's friendship with her husband was heading, the fears were entirely justified.

"Angel," Martha wrote, "I have so much to tell you, but suddenly I find that there is no time to even think straight . . . please, please leave word in Paris." She closed by asking that he send her love to Pauline, then added, "Please don't disappear. Are we or are we not members of the same union? Hemingstein, I am very fond of you. Marty." (Hemingstein was one of the author's boyhood nicknames.)

It would take more than Sidney Franklin as traveling companion to kill Pauline's fears about Ernest's new Spanish adventure. Whether or not she suspected the extent of his budding closeness to their new friend thirteen years her junior, Pauline was already aware of the dangers such closeness posed. She knew how fragile a celebrity marriage could be, and how susceptible her husband had been in the past to the flattering attentions of a pretty, young, single woman.

Pauline had only to remember the way in which she had ingratiated herself into the life, then the bed, of the then unknown

Hemingway and his wife, Hadley, in France a decade before. She had always used overtures of friendship to Hadley as her entree to Ernest, but by 1926, with their affair an open secret, she took closeness to a new level. In *Less Than a Treason*, the second volume of his Hemingway biography, Peter Griffin recounts a visit by Pauline to the Hemingways in Juan-les-Pins on the Riviera. In some audio tapes recorded in the last years of her life, Hadley told of a typical morning when Pauline would knock on the Hemingways' bedroom door, then pop in on the couple she referred to as her "two men" wearing her robe and pajamas. Ernest was a boyish twenty-six, Pauline a sleek and stylish thirty, while Hadley, still carrying some extra weight after the birth of their son, Bumby, two years earlier, felt matronly at thirty-four. Pauline would soon drop her pj bottoms to join Ernest and Hadley—who slept similarly bottomless—in bed, making herself the ultimate breakfast treat. Later Ernest and his "two girls" would skinny-dip at a secluded cove. Hadley described those weeks in the Hotel de la Pineda: "Here it was . . . that the three breakfast trays, three wet bathing suits on the line, three bicycles were to be found."

This *ménage a trois* was an arrangement Hadley Richardson Hemingway was willing to endure to try to keep her husband. It failed. During one day of nude swimming when Ernest was back at the hotel working, Pauline confessed to Hadley that she was as in love with her as with her husband. (The sexual and emotional confusion of this idyll is explored in Hemingway's posthumously published novel, *The Garden of Eden*.) If ever there were a wife who could spot trouble in a black dress, it was Pauline Pfeiffer Hemingway. Her good friend Sidney, she hoped, would keep an eye on her man. It was a task that would put Sidney in the middle of not only a country that was breaking apart but also a marriage that was about to be split down the middle in its own private civil war as well.

1. 14 Jackson Place, Brooklyn: Sidney Franklin's boyhood home as it looks today, 106 years after his birth. *Photo courtesy of Heidi Paul.*

2."I looked like a Christmas tree." Sidney posing for artist
Lillian Genth, New York, 1931. *AP Wide World Photos*.

3. Sidney Franklin was perfect in his triumphant Spanish
debut in Sevilla, June 9, 1929. *AP Wide World Photos.*

4. Sidney and friends at a Madrid café at the height of his fame, sometime between July 1929 and March 1930. It was at such a café while among the bull-fighter's entourage that Ernest Hemingway first introduced himself to Sidney. The little man with the possessive hand on Sidney's knee is his devoted sword handler and companion, Luis Crovetto. *Source unknown.*

5. Hemingway and Franklin—two pals in Spain—shortly after
they met in September 1929. *John F. Kennedy Library.*

6. "Sidney has no grace because he has a terrific behind.
I used to make him do special exercises to reduce his behind."
—Ernest Hemingway. *AP Wide World Photos.*

7. An afternoon with the boys: Hemingway (in bathing trunks),
Franklin (to his left, naked except for the magazine), Franklin's *mozo*
Luis Crovetto (on Hemingway's right), and their matador friends
on the playa of Madrid's Manzanares River, 1931. *John F. Kennedy Library.*

8. *above* Sidney, his career in tatters, puts on a brave face as he arrives alone in New York from Spain on the *Rex*, November 9, 1933. *AP Wide World Photos.*

9. *opposite top* The matador in the gray flannel suit. A stiff Sidney visiting Hemingway in Havana, 1934. *John F. Kennedy Library.*

10. *opposite bottom* Ernest watches Sidney perform *toreo de salón* with his overcoat for friends and the press during a going-away party thrown by Sidney's sisters in his stateroom aboard the ss *Paris*, February 27, 1937. *Corbis.*

11. Franklin and Hemingway somewhere in the mid-Atlantic as they head for the Spanish civil war on the *Paris*, February 1937. Their friendship would begin taking on water in less than eight weeks. *John F. Kennedy Library.*

12. "My beautiful girlfriend is coming," Hemingway told filmmaker Joris Ivens. "She has legs that begin at her shoulders." *John F. Kennedy Library.*

13. *opposite top* Serious filmmakers: John Dos Passos, director
Joris Ivens, Sidney Franklin, and Ernest Hemingway discuss their documentary,
The Spanish Earth, in Madrid during the spring of 1937. *Corbis.*

14. *opposite bottom* Hemingway and Joris Ivens as they film segments
of *The Spanish Earth* with loyalist troops outside Madrid in the spring of 1937. *John
F. Kennedy Library.*

15. *above* On the town! Hemingway shows off his new mistress,
Martha Gellhorn, to a gang of literary friends at the Stork Club while his
wife, Pauline, waits in Key West, May 1937. *John F. Kennedy Library.*

16. "For Barnaby Conrad—the best of everything." Sidney in
toupee and corset in Málaga around the time of his 1945 *alternativa*
in Madrid. *Photo courtesy of Barnaby Conrad.*

17. The *Alternativa:* twenty-two years after he first stepped into a bullring, Sidney finally becomes the first American *matador de toros* in Spain on July 18, 1945. *From the collection of Tony Brand.*

18. *Un tipo flamenco.* Barnaby Conrad's portrait of the
matador in middle age, as Conrad first knew him in Spain
in 1944. *Painting courtesy of Barnaby Conrad.*

11

A Fine Romance

CELEBRITIES DO NOT GO OFF to war quietly. Sidney was
again a celebrity — if a bit of an appendix one — and he was milk-
ing it for all it was worth. His sisters Bella, Helen, and the twins,
Charlotte and Rosalind, threw him a going-away party in his stateroom on the liner SS *Paris*, docked in New York harbor prior to
sailing for Le Havre, the first leg of the trip to Madrid. The cabin
was full of laughing, chatter, and drinking as Sidney held court
for a crowd of reporters, happy to be where he felt he belonged, in
the spotlight sharing his knowledge of Spain. As his editor Max
Perkins looked on, Ernest Hemingway tried to maintain a more
somber tone, telling a correspondent that his job was to inform
the American people of the nature of total war, which he felt would
be the inevitable result of the course Generalissimo Franco and
his fascist allies were willing to take. His warning was that in the
future the role of the noncombatant would disappear, an astute
observation since the first use of modern air power against civilians was still over two months away. Then as now, however, the
press was more interested in the celebrity persona than in the facts
of war. Biographer Carlos Baker describes one of the questioners

in the stateroom, a reporter named Wolfert, whose resulting story was more focused on the size of the writer's chest bulging through a tight sports coat than the accuracy of his observations. (Apparently, Martha was not the only one impressed by the Hemingway torso.) It is difficult to imagine anyone asking a contemporary American novelist for his or her take on world hotspots, then reporting the answers as newsworthy. The size of the chest, however, might still be fair game.

Sidney may have been heading to a combat zone, but he could not have been having a better time. He and Hemingway goofed for the cameras at the party, a smiling Ernest watching Sidney perform *verónicas* with his overcoat as their friends and family laughed. Sidney looks trim and happy in those photographs, and he had reason to be. After years of Sidney needing Hemingway—needing money, connections, friendship, and support—it was now Ernest who needed help from Sid. It was Sidney who in the preceding weeks had investigated the French Line schedules and booked their passage on the *Paris*. It was Sidney who planned their itinerary and saw to the details, discussed money for ambulances and acted as intermediary to the network of loyalist supporters. He also typed out a list of contacts for them within the Republican government and military—names, ranks, and addresses of old friends of his who would insure the success of their stay in Madrid and give them the preferred treatment that Hemingway wanted. As Hemingway had told Pauline, Sidney was the ideal choice to accompany him to Spain. This role of personal assistant was new to Sidney, but at least it was a part to play even if he was, as he said, just "tagging along." In a letter to Hemingway three weeks before they sailed, Sidney could not hide his enthusiasm. Still, after half a decade on the skids, he knew his place: "this is your party and . . . all you have to is give the orders for me to carry out. And everything will be as it should be."

The third member of the traveling party, poet Evan Shipman, was not a celebrity. He left the party and slipped off alone to the ship's bar. Shipman's intention was not to write about Spain but to help the cause. He intended to volunteer as an ambulance driver. When all the Frumpkin sisters, the reporters, and friends finally were sent ashore, the *Paris* sailed for Le Havre on February 27, 1937.

When they arrived in Paris, Hemingway checked into the Hotel Dinard; Sidney, into the more downscale Hotel Montana on the rue st-Benoît. They were soon meeting with Dos Passos, MacLeish, and their film director, Joris Ivens, at Hemingway's favorite cafés, such as the Deux Magots, to plan their documentary film, *The Spanish Earth*. Sidney was indifferent to the leftist sympathies of these loyalist friends of Ernest's. His own circle from his bullfighting days remained from the upper classes or those who aspired to them: the wealthy landowners who bred the bulls or on whose estates he relaxed to hunt, fish, and dine as an honored guest. Sidney always felt that he was destined to associate with the elite, the select. As a son of immigrants, Sidney had worked hard at a dangerous calling to surpass his parents' humble beginnings, and he had little use for idealizing the proletariat. As he often said, "I was destined to lead. It was always noblesse oblige with me."

Noblesse oblige cut no ice with the United States Department of State. Hemingway could fool his wife that Sidney was going along as a fellow reporter, but not the government, which was trying to maintain its neutrality. They refused to accredit Sidney with a visa as Hemingway's fellow correspondent, making his passport good only as far as France. The two men wasted ten days in Paris trying to obtain a visa. At first, Hemingway did not seem to mind, spending his days catching up with old friends, including lunching with *New Yorker* writer Janet Flanner and her romantic companion Solita Solano. Twenty-five years after the fact, Solano related how she, Flanner, Hemingway, and Sidney would frequently return to Sidney's room in the hotel Montana. According to Solano, Sidney had brought along much of his bullfighting wardrobe and equipment. As the others watched, Sidney would unpack and display his gold encrusted *trajes de luces*, his capes and *muletas*, even his swords and special underwear. Sidney would lay these treasures out on the double bed, the chairs, and table for the ladies' inspection, while Hemingway, who by this time knew all of Sidney's gear backward and forward, would fiddle with the killing swords. As if on cue, Sidney would grab a cape and yell "toro-huh-toro!" With a big grin, the ever-loyal Hemingway would jump for some maneuvering space in the small room, slap the back of his hands above his ears, and simulate horns with his fingers, then lower his head and charge. Sidney would perform his capework, trying to keep his *capote* from snagging on the bedpost as he worked his famous "bull," while Miss Flanner and Miss Solano watched from along the wall. The cavorting men described their bullfight as they acted it out, just as small boys playing catch might describe an imaginary World Series. Eventually, a sweating Hemingway would drag his two "guys" off for a drink while Sidney stayed behind, alone with memories of past glories, "carefully brushing, folding, and repacking his collection, down to the last white stocking." It is a fascinating image, both poignant and curious. As Sidney played *toreo de salón* to his famous friend's puffing pantomime bull while the women watched, the supposedly homophobic Hemingway was the only heterosexual in the room.

The State Department would still not budge on a visa for Sidney, so on March 14 Hemingway took the night train to Toulouse, where he caught an Air France flight to Valencia, where the Republican government provided him with a car and driver for the overland journey to Madrid. He was carrying in his pocket a homemade safe conduct pass, typed by Sid on his own *Matador De Toros* stationary, that claimed the bearer was indeed the famous writer who had done an excellent job in informing the world about their cause, and hoped that the civil and military authorities would assist him in his "mission." It was always good to know a famous bullfighter.

Sidney was left to negotiate a less formal — and less legal — border crossing. He describes a series of cloak-and-dagger meetings with various agents of loyalist Spain on the back streets of Paris to make arrangements to enter the country. The French border guards were continuing to stop individual reporters and observers from leaving their neutral sovereignty for the war zone, although the Italians had recently sent over ten thousand troops to aid General Franco.

By this time Martha Gellhorn had sailed for Europe on the *Ile de France*, a posh liner so well known it was immortalized in a bitter ditty from a Fred Astaire–Ginger Rogers musical. (This ship was also where, in the fall of 1931, Hemingway had met his previous blond temptation, twenty-two-year old Mrs. G. Grant Mason, while he and Pauline, then pregnant with their son, Gregory, were sailing back to America; and where, in 1934, he met Marlene Dietrich, who would become a close but platonic pal. Jane Mason, Marlene Dietrich, and Martha Gellhorn: if those bulkheads could talk.) Following Hemingway's lead, Gellhorn was making her way to Spain through Paris, finding, she claimed, that Hemingway had not only left without her, but without spelling out just how exactly she was to cross the border. While in Paris she eventually obtained a letter from a friend at *Collier's* magazine that gave her the status of special correspondent, at least on paper. Never shy of publicity, Gellhorn had already been spilling her plans to her hometown newspaper. The March 17 edition of the *St. Louis Post Dispatch* outlined her travel plans and named her companions. "She has made arrangements to join Ernest Hemingway and other Americans seeking entrance into that country." That certainly would have been news to Pauline waiting back in Key West.

Sidney claimed in his autobiography that he was instructed by Hemingway to meet Gellhorn at her Paris hotel, escort her to the Gare d'Orsay, and see that she made it safely on the Toulouse train. He describes his first meeting with an imperious and somewhat ditzy woman who treated the famous matador like a redcap, demanding that Sidney schlep her ten pieces of luggage up the sidewalk to her cab. In her book *The Hemingway Women*, Bernice Kert addresses Sidney's description of the event, saying that Gellhorn herself "pointed out the absurdity of such a tale." As to the bags, Kert says, "she had a knapsack and the clothes on her back — grey flannel trousers, sweater, warm windbreaker," and just fifty dollars in her pockets. She then crossed the border into Spain on foot from Andorra in the Pyrenees and made her way to Valencia from there.

One of her biographers, the somewhat unsympathetic Carl Rollyson, mentions that female writers in Spain, such as Josephine Herbst and Lillian Hellman, commented on Gellhorn's Saks Fifth Avenue duds. He also said that Diana Forbes-Robertson, the wife of veteran correspondent and old China hand Vincent Sheean, claimed that Gellhorn's clothes were too showy for a war correspondent. Rollyson then somewhat cattily wonders how Gellhorn fit such a chic wardrobe into that little knapsack. (For her part, Gellhorn fought the publication of Rollyson's book, calling it a "paean of hate.") A posthumous and more favorable biography,

Caroline Moorehead's 2003 *Gellhorn: A Twentieth-Century Life*, thickens the layers of legend by claiming that, in addition to the knapsack, Gellhorn crossed the Andorran-Spanish border lugging "a duffle bag full of canned food," an extra load that would have weighed more than she did. She would have needed a Sherpa to get out of Andorra.

If the eventual Hemingway-Gellhorn marriage and divorce produced definite dueling narratives of their time together, Sidney's dealings with the blond in the black dress generated their own subset of assertion and counter accusation. This specific moment in history, Hemingway's first six weeks in Spain in 1937, was shared by some of the world's finest writers and correspondents. Add personal rivalries, romantic entanglements, and differing politics, however nuanced, and the result was that everyone had a story to tell and every story was different. Many friendships would not withstand the telling.

It is true that Sidney could be accused of being the poster boy of unreliable narrators. He was certainly the source of many Martha Gellhorn stories that Carlos Baker put into *Ernest Hemingway: A Life Story*. Gellhorn had trouble enough when she read Baker's manuscript of matters *not* related to Sidney. She bristled at the assertion that she and Hemingway had been lovers before their rendezvous in Madrid, positioning herself as the thoughtful and dedicated aspirant hoping to share work and politics with the master, everything noble and aboveboard, and that she was her own woman, a politically astute journalist, not just a "luscious blond," and on and on. She objected to Baker's perspective as he described her initial relationship with Hemingway, specifically such phrases as "growing infatuation" and "soon to follow Hemingway." She wrote on the back of the manuscript "Carlos: This is wrong, in tone & implication, and injustice to us both." Martha Gellhorn considered herself a serious writer above all else. For the rest of her long life, she chafed at this brief role she had once so assiduously pursued as Hemingway's appendage, the famous man's sexy third wife, more clotheshorse than warhorse. What Mad Pursuit, indeed. That so much ink has been spent from 1937 to her death on her appearance was just another part of a lifelong frustration to which this discussion would only add were she around to hear it. "Honestly!" she complained to Baker, "Have you ever read *my* Spanish reporting?"

As the first biographer to dive into the depths of the contrary life of the most influential American writer of the twentieth century, Professor Baker took his shots in ways that many who followed did not. (When his name came up in conversation with Lillian Ross in 2003, she responded with typical humor, "Baker? Oh groan. *Groan!*")

Later in her life as she was still trying to maintain that image of herself as a woman independent of Hemingway—and perhaps tweaking the facts to that end—Martha Gellhorn found that the one witness who could constantly challenge her version of events was indeed Sidney. When she read the portions of Baker's manuscript based on Sidney's version of events, Gellhorn scribbled "Balls!" in the margins. Adding to the confusion, the correspondent Herbert Matthews, who spent much time in Madrid with Hemingway, Gellhorn, and Franklin, and looked at their three-way dynamic with a wary eye, said of Baker's manuscript, "You cannot trust Franklin *at all*." Matthews, however, apparently had a yen for Martha himself, so his perspective, despite being a journalist of impeccable credentials, was just as skewed as everyone else's.

You're just as hard to land as the Ile de France,
This is a fine romance.

(Dorothy Fields, "A Fine Romance" from *Swing Time*)

Sidney did finally leave Paris for Spain. The last conventional part of his journey was a train trip to Toulouse, where after a surreptitious rendezvous, he traveled by a series of buses in a circuitous route to the border. His companions at that point were men from many countries who had volunteered to fight for loyalist Spain. All they had to do was get past the armed French border guards to Republican-controlled Catalonia. Sidney recounts a night border crossing on foot, then stripping naked to cross an icy chin-deep river, carrying his bundled clothes on his head. He was also carrying an expensive surgical kit destined for the front lines, plus wound dressings for himself, as his now seven-year-old rectal wound was still draining from his most recent operation. Sidney made the crossing, but caught a cold that he would not shake for months. Once back in his beloved Spain for the first time since the outbreak of the civil war, Sidney found changes he did not like. He was in the company of rough men in filthy barracks who wanted to fight the war, not help a celebrity writer cover it. As usual, Sidney was a man out of place, even in a country he knew "like the palm of my hand." His lack of a Communist Party card made access to basic amenities harder and harder as he pursued the next leg from the border, catching a train down the coast to Barcelona. The Gothic coastal city he had known so well was now full of soldiers and party members. The influence of the Republic's new soviet advisors was as palpable as the March sunlight on the Mediterranean. Even the simple salutation *adios* (to God) was suspect in a struggle where the church was allied with the fascist rebels. Service as Sidney had come to know it — and love it, by the way — did not exist. Hotel rooms were not for the unconnected. He relied on a method more Brooklyn than Bolshevik — a fat roll of cash — to secure a hotel room at the "swank" Hotel Oriente on the Ramblas, the main boulevard, then obtain a third-class rail ticket to the provisional Republican capitol of Valencia, the jumping-off point for Madrid.

The train to Valencia was worse than the one to Barcelona. Sidney had known poverty and deprivation in Mexico when he was starting out, and he did not like it nor did he romanticize it. He felt through his bullfighting that he had earned the respect and adulation of Spain, from marquesas to bellhops, but now he was in a world where respect mattered for nothing, where hard won status was ignored and where, because no man should wait upon another in a workers' paradise, bellhops were unemployed. It was bad enough that the self-proclaimed Idol of Spain often went unrecognized among these new fighters for the Republic. That they took perverse pleasure in using the first class rail compartments as public toilets was more than he could bear. "There was utter disregard for property and order," he said. "That trip was a nightmare." Perhaps Sid should have had Ernest clarify what it meant to be on "their" side.

Valencia was a welcome relief. Although full of refugees, there was available food and, as Sidney said in cadences worthy of his pal, "here the old and good qualities of the Spanish character still held." He delivered the needed surgical kit he had brought from Paris to the general hospital. The nerve centers of the Republican cities during the civil war were the government offices of press and censorship. Running the Valencia office was an aristocratic leftist, Constancia de La Mora, whom some described as looking as austerely beautiful as a Modigliani painting. When Sidney visited her office, señora La Mora delivered to him letters from Hemingway, and graciously reminded him of a party they had attended together in Rome. She also put a government car and military driver at his disposal. (Although depicted by rightist historians as a doctrinaire Marxist whose husband as head of the Republican air force was complicit in soviet torture in his own basement, La Mora had many devoted friends among those who covered the war. When she wrote her own memoir of the period, *In Place of Splendor*, it contained an introduction by her friend Ernest Hemingway.)

Following the instructions in Ernest's letters, Sidney scoured the city for gourmet chow, as decent food of any sort had ceased to exist in Madrid. He assembled all that he thought his assigned car could carry: huge dried Spanish hams, a hundred kilos of jelly and marmalades, tins of butter, ten kilos of good coffee, two restaurant-sized cans of cooking lard, candies and caramels, and a bushel basket of citrus. Booze was not on his list, as Hemingway had already secured ample stores in the capitol. Alcohol was one of the few items in the besieged city that was not perishable, except perhaps in a roomful of war correspondents.

On the morning of March 30, Sidney and his driver pulled up in front of Valencia's Hotel Victoria in a Citroën packed to the roof with food. Sidney had been asked by his friend "Connie" de La Mora to pick up two passengers for Madrid, and he was in no position to refuse. The passengers were Martha Gellhorn and a young reporter for the Federated Press named Ted Allan. For señora La Mora, it made sense—they were all going to meet Hemingway. In her role as the head of the press and censorship office, she had asked Allan to give Gellhorn a background on the government's position on the political situation. (The assumption was that the new *Collier's* correspondent was a novice with no knowledge of Spain, a notion that again would have made Martha bristle had she known of the request.) When Allan balked, La Mora suggested that the young man would be glad to enlighten the newcomer once he laid eyes on her. She was not mistaken. "I absolutely flipped for her," Allan said of Gellhorn, "the wonderful smile, the hair, the great figure."

Sidney was forced to repack the car to make room for the new arrivals in the back seat, leaving the much-needed hundred kilos of fruit for Madrid on the sidewalk. Sidney watched with undisguised annoyance as Gellhorn and the young man piled in instead, and their overloaded car chugged away from the curb. With his lingering cold from the river crossing in the Pyrenees, and his still draining rectal wound leaving him literally on the edge of his seat, the long overland car ride put Sidney in a foul mood. Being stuck in the little car as Hemingway's new female friend snuggled in the back seat with this glib stranger did nothing to help his disposition. Allan, then only twenty-one, would later write that he and Gellhorn necked and fondled for much of the trip, a claim that if true would have really steamed Sidney. Here Gellhorn was cheating on "Ernie" before she even *got* to Madrid so they could cheat on Pauline. What a war. (Allan also asserted that once in the capitol, Sid, in a moment of totally conflicted loyalties, threatened to pound him if he ever came near Martha again, a threat Allan took quite seriously. Sidney was, after all, Hemingway's man, and a physically imposing one at that.) Sidney glared over his shoulder at the two giggling correspondents all the way from Valencia to Castile. His nagging feeling that he had slipped from being Ernest's companion to the mere transporter of his new sweetie was aggravated whenever Martha would insist that they stop along the way to stretch her long legs or find a decent café for a meal. After many such stops, they finally saw Madrid in the distance rising above the plain, the late afternoon sunlight beaming off the snowy peaks of the Sierra de Guadarrama. They hit the customs inspectors' station outside Madrid around dusk.

12

The Beard

BOTH SIDNEY AND MARTHA were to stay at the old Hotel Florida on the Plaza del Callao where Hemingway had already set up residence a week before. After checking in and stashing the food goods, Sidney pointed their driver up the Gran Vía to the hotel of the same name, located just across this main thoroughfare from the headquarters of the International Telephone and Telegraph Company, known in the city as the Telefónica. This white office building served a dual purpose for the Republic: as the tallest building in Madrid, it functioned as an observation post for the city's defenders; it also was the headquarters of the press and censorship offices, run by the frazzled couple Ilsa Kulcsar and Arturo Barea. When they met Martha Gellhorn the following day, their first impression was similar to that of Ted Allan, Constancia de La Mora, Lillian Hellman, and others; it focused on the physical presence and style of the "sleek woman with a halo of fair hair, who walked through the dark fusty office with a swaying movement," which reminded them of the sexy sashay of American film stars. Either the girl just couldn't help it, or when it came to the "luscious blond" business, Martha simply protested too much. Either way, Sidney had a rival who could compete for Hemingway's attention in ways that he could not.

Martha, for her part, found her role uncertain. Sidney's confident manner, his knowledge of every corner of Madrid, his glib patter and indifference to the nuance of the antifascist cause infuriated her. He at least *had* a job — assisting Ernest Hemingway in his writing and filing dispatches for the North American Newspaper Alliance, and helping in any way necessary the filming of *The Spanish Earth*. Martha's *Collier's* credentials were essentially bogus, a pretext from Kyle Crichton of the magazine to allow Martha passage into Spain, but hardly a specific assignment. Hemingway himself seemed less interested in her antifascist bona-fides or her abilities as a war correspondent than in other attributes. He told director Joris Ivens, "My beautiful girlfriend is coming. She has legs that begin at her shoulders." To others he referred to her simply as "La Rubia" — the Blond.

Gellhorn's exasperation came to a head that first night in Madrid when she followed Sidney into the makeshift basement dining room of the Hotel Gran Vía, where planks on sawhorses passed as tables and the fish was suspect. The regular ground floor dining room had been closed because of the danger from incoming artillery. Martha Gellhorn stated to Carlos Baker that Ernest Hemingway, the new man in her life whom she had not seen for three months, announced, "I knew you'd get here daughter, because I fixed it so you could." Gellhorn claimed that he rested his hand on the top of her head in a gesture of ownership when he said it. Supposedly, she publicly and emphatically set him straight: as a veteran world traveler she had made it on her own with absolutely no help from him. This exchange has since been repeated by biographer after biographer, a matter of anecdote becoming legend. It has also become exhibit A of Hemingway's clueless macho posturing. Oddly, Gellhorn's new biographer Caroline Moorehead downplays the specifics of Martha's response. To bring the competing narratives full circle, Stephen Koch, author of the 2005 history *The Breaking Point — Hemingway, Dos Passos, and the Murder of José Robles*, systematically demolishes Martha Gellhorn's version of these encounters. (Koch is a Dos Passos partisan who brings yet another lens through which to view these same, frequently described events, and quite understandably comes up with another image that is to him the probable truth. For openers, he found Martha quite unsympathetic.) Gellhorn based her depiction of herself as the independent globetrotter who arrived in Spain with no help from Hemingway — much less his man Sidney — on her assertion that she had no personal contact with Hemingway from the time they parted in Key West in December 1936 to the moment in March 1937 when she followed Sidney into the basement of the Hotel Gran Vía. Koch, relying partly on Moorehead's account (and her unprecedented access to Gellhorn's papers), shows that Hemingway and Gellhorn were in constant communication by letter and telephone, and that as others have noted, they were together in New York all through the last days of February before he sailed with Sidney on the *Paris*, socializing with his friends and incessantly discussing their plans for Spain. Koch makes a convincing case that when Hemingway told Gellhorn that he had "fixed it" so she could arrive, he was telling the truth, and that the agent of such fixing was of course Sidney Franklin himself. Koch completely vindicates Sidney's version of events, from picking up Martha at her Paris hotel — luggage and all — and putting her on the train to Toulouse to their arrival together at the Hotel Florida after the prescheduled drive up from Valencia in the car provided courtesy of Hemingway's friend and personal contact within the government, Constancia de La Mora. Hemingway's imminent conflict with Dos Passos would result in three strong-minded writers — those two and Gellhorn — spending the next several decades verbally blasting away at one another in a triangulated field of fire that inevitably hit the nonwriter Sid with the occasional stray round. With all three gone, their biographers are still firing away each on their own behalf, with more words written about the celebrity correspondents at the siege of Madrid than those correspondents ever wrote about the siege itself.

No matter the circumstances or the hint of friction between them, Ernest Hemingway and Martha Gellhorn were finally in Spain, and they were there together. The only hitch in this budding wartime romance was that they were in Spain under the disapproving eye of Mrs. Hemingway's devoted friend Sidney Franklin.

Sidney at first took a room on the fifth floor facing the Plaza del Callao. Early on his first morning in Madrid, as he was slipping into one of his natty turtlenecks, he heard the scream and explosion of an artillery shell as it landed down in the street below on the corner of the square. The concussion shattered all the glass in Sidney's room. When he rushed outside, he saw his first war dead at the edge of the artillery crater, a man whose head had been severed by the blast. The Madrid that Sidney had known from 1929 to 1934 was on the brink. The artillery of General Franco pounded the residents daily from Garabitas Hill just outside the city. Intersections were barricaded with sandbags, half-destroyed buildings remained next to those untouched by the shelling, whole streets stood empty except for a burned out auto or abandoned streetcar. With food scarce, the occasional dead draft horse or mule did not last long on the boulevards. In his chronicle of American volunteers in the Spanish civil war, *Between the Bullet and the Lie*, Cecil Eby describes wartime Madrid.

> Paintings in the Prado had been packed up for safekeeping
> and the façade boarded up. The famous Sybil and Neptune

fountains were hidden by a deep layer of bricks and sandbags. Republican snipers fired with impunity from the windows of the National Palace, which overlooked enemy trenches in the Casa de Campo, since they knew that monarchist officers of Franco's army were reluctant to damage such an august Bourbon shrine. The Retiro Gardens, having been converted into an artillery park, was decidedly no place to get away from it all. In the zoo, the carnivores were dead or were starving by degrees. (It is said that when the elephant died, strange cuts of meat appeared in the butcher stalls of Madrid — but this same story is told of Barcelona.) The fancy hotels like the Ritz and the Palace had been converted into hospitals . . . Under the gilt and glass chandeliers of the once-regal dining room of the former stretched rows of white cots filled with unshaven men . . . Many an American came to Spain, only to die at the Ritz.

This began one of the most remarkable five weeks of Sidney Franklin's life. He and Ernest moved into a two-room suite on the third floor on the side of the hotel farthest from the shelling. Martha Gellhorn was installed just down the hall. Josephine Herbst, the former wife of Hemingway's friend John Herrmann, who would later write of her experiences in *The Starched Blue Sky of Spain*, camped with her duffle and her typewriter in a room on the same floor as Sidney and Hemingway. She claims it was the fourth floor, but who's counting. The Florida, like its famous inhabitants, is long gone, existing only in the memories of the dead. The hotel was the favorite of correspondents, the place to be, to drink, to exchange gossip and war news during the siege. There was Herbert L. Matthews of the *New York Times*, the pro many others looked to, a man who became a firm Hemingway friend despite his eye for Martha. From the *New York Post* was George Seldes; Virginia Cowles wrote for King Features; Sefton "Tom" Delmer represented the *London Daily Express* (and proved invaluable for buying up a looted stash of 1904 Chateau d'Yquem pinched from the royal wine cellars); and Henry Buckley worked for the *Daily Telegraph*. Then there were the serious writers who were in Spain to support the Republic, who either resided in the Florida or came to meet and work. There were Hemingway's partners in Contemporary Historians, poet Archibald MacLeish, playwright Lillian Hellman, and of course John Dos Passos, whose friendship with Hemingway was already strained. There were the British poets W. H. Auden and Stephen Spender, the Chilean diplomat and poet Pablo Neruda, and French novelists André Malraux, a no-nonsense leftist and China veteran who had obtained French aircraft for the Republic and helped organize a volunteer flying unit in the city of Alcantarilla, and aviator Antoine de Saint-Exupery who would later write *The Little Prince*. A British visitor said the place was becoming another Bloomsbury. Saint-Exupery was, according to Delmer, hoarding grapefruit in his room at the Florida and using the scarce citrus as a come-on to nervous women during bombardments. He would stand at the foot of the staircase in his blue satin bathrobe, a grapefruit in his outstretched hand, and ask, "Voulez-vous une pamplemousse, Madame?"

The staircase of the Florida rose in a spiral around a soaring rotunda. The once-grand lobby, overseen by a fussy, stamp collecting desk clerk known as don Cristobal, now had its overstuffed chairs populated by correspondents just back from the front and covered with the ever present brick and plaster dust from the shelling, or by soldiers on leave cruising for a hot meal or for one of the prostitutes who worked the hotel. Hemingway jokingly referred to these women as "whores de combat." Despite the threat from

Franco's forces just fifteen hundred meters outside the city, the civil authorities still found the manpower to staff a vice squad to roust the whores from the Florida's lobby and guest rooms, even when they were ministering to the needs of the very men who were defending the city. To add to Martha Gellhorn's list of outrages suffered at the hands of the men in her life, she awoke from the thunder of a bombardment during her second night in the hotel to find that Hemingway had locked her in her room. His excuse was that he did not want her wandering around at night only to be bothered by men looking for whores. Perhaps he was not locking Martha in, but locking Ted Allan out.

On almost any morning in April 1937, one could sit with Josie Herbst or perhaps Tom Delmer in one of those fat chairs in the Florida's lobby under the travel poster that said "Visit Cuba!", drinking weak tea but smelling the rich percolating coffee and the frying ham and toasting bread as their smells drifted down into the rotunda from the Hemingway-Franklin suite. While waiting, one might observe, as Herbst did, Martha Gellhorn breezing across the lobby in "beautiful Saks Fifth Avenue pants, with a green chiffon scarf wound around her head", or Dos Passos, looking professorial in jacket and tie. Finally, one could hear Sidney's baritone call echoing down that chow was on. Soon, the suite was full of some of the most famous writers in the world rubbing elbows with kids from the Abraham Lincoln Brigade just back from the fighting as they lined up for the best breakfast in Madrid, whipped up by Sidney on an alcohol stove in his room. The suite became the unofficial headquarters of the correspondents. Hemingway not only had some of the best food, compliments of what Sidney brought from Valencia and scrounged daily in the shops and stalls and black market, but the most plentiful whiskey—Sidney claimed that they possessed all the Johnny Walker left in Madrid—and the best maps and intelligence as well.

They were all in Madrid to work, to film, to report. Hemingway enjoyed a special status with access to cars, safe conduct passes, and scarce gasoline through special petrol vouchers thanks in part to his friendship with Miss Kulcsar and Mr. Barea of the censorship office. (Barea, a Madrid native who would go on to become a respected writer, but whose lukewarm Marxism would get him exiled from the Republic, would marry Ilsa Kulcsar the following year.) Despite this status, Ernest and Sidney were not above lugging cameras and gear to the battle zones for Ivens and cameraman John Ferno, acting as big-name gofers on this little, but important, film. There was something surreal about being able to visit a war zone on the edge of the city by tram from your hotel, then return in the evening for a drink at Chicote's bar and hit clean sheets (solo or otherwise) while the soldiers one had covered that day hunkered down in the dirt. "No matter how often you do it," Gellhorn said, "it is surprising to walk to a war, easily, from your own bedroom where you have been reading a detective story or a life of Byron."

When the Republicans began a counterattack against Franco's forces who were dug in at the old royal game preserve called the Casa de Campo, the crew of *The Spanish Earth* hit the battle lines to film the action. The fascists had been shelling all night, keeping many in the Florida awake after their boozing, and Joris Ivens was eager to get an early start. After hiking over open country as close as they could to the action, Hemingway, Sidney, and the film crew lost too much altitude for good filming and found themselves in an open position exposed to rebel snipers. John Ferno found a safe observation post for his camera in a shelled-out row of apartments on the Paseo Rosales that overlooked the wooded preserve where all the hunting was now done by young men with machine guns. Hemingway christened the empty shell the "Old Homestead" after his grandfather's grandiose name for his house in suburban Chicago. The next day, the film crew was joined by Virginia Cowles, Herb Matthews, Sefton Delmer, and Martha Gellhorn, and Hemingway had to warn the others not to let camera lenses or binoculars catch the afternoon sun and draw fire from Franco's Moorish riflemen.

As both famous novelist and famously wounded veteran of the Great War, Hemingway often assumed the role of senior military authority with the other correspondents, occasionally to their annoyance, as his actual combat experience was slight. (In addition to driving an ambulance, his frontline role in 1918 included passing out candy bars and cigarettes to the Italian grunts who actually did the fighting.) Claud Cockburn of London's *Daily Worker*, the communist paper, wrote that one morning during one of Sidney's breakfasts in the suite, Hemingway had spread a large map out on the table and was explaining to visiting generals and politicians as well as his fellow writers why it was a ballistic impossibility for Franco's shells to reach the Florida. Then a shell actually *hit* the room above, dropping ceiling plaster down on his map. Rather than being embarrassed, Hemingway supposedly acted as if this proved rather than disproved his pontificating. He gravely asked the officials, "How do you like it now, gentlemen?" (This is the quote that Lillian Ross would, thirteen years later, take for the title of her *New Yorker* profile on Hemingway.) This is a great story. If it were correct in all its details, it would most likely have been repeated as a good joke at Hemingway's expense by others present as well, as so many other incidents of this well-covered period were repeated.

Despite some resentment of the access to information and commodities his celebrity afforded him, Hemingway was mostly well thought of by this hard-to-impress bunch. Herb Matthews — no pushover—wrote that his new friend "exemplifies . . . much that is brave and good and fine in a somewhat murky world." Rather than setting himself apart as a prima donna, Hemingway was considered more a first among equals, a man who was respected more for what he was doing at the moment than what he had accomplished up to that time. When they were alone, he confided to Stephen Spender that he had come to Spain to see if he had lost his nerve under fire. When others were around, Spender noticed, Hemingway drank and sang and "became the Hemingway character again."

Martha Gellhorn admits that during this brief moment Hemingway was at his best.

> I think it was the only time in his life when he was not the most important thing there was. He really cared about the Republic and he cared about that war. I believe I never would have gotten hooked otherwise.

That Gellhorn was getting hooked was obvious to all. Sefton Delmer tells of the night when rebel shells hit the Florida's hot water supply, revealing "all kinds of liaisons," including Ernest and Martha. George Seldes was even more specific.

> There was never any secret about Hemingway living with Martha Gellhorn at the Florida Hotel. . . . When the hotel was shelled our great fun Helen [Mrs. Seldes] and I, was to stand at the foot of the stairway to see who was running out of what room with what woman. I don't need to tell you who came out of Hemingway's room.

Even among longtime friends, Hemingway's public affair with Martha, and his assumption that all should share his happiness from an appropriate distance, seemed selfish and inappropriate in the middle of a city under siege, especially in the crowded halls of a hotel whose residents saw dying every day, even if only on the way to dinner. Josie Herbst said, regarding the romance, that each correspondent knew "the corks popping were not for you."

To have Ernest not only betraying his friend Pauline, but actually huffing and puffing with Miss Gellhorn in the adjacent room, only added to Sidney's discomfort. This frequent grappling went on under Sid's nose, although Gellhorn, by her own accounts, did not find Hemingway very attractive sexually. To be fair, it was not just him. Gellhorn did not really enjoy sex, despite having "more lovers than I can count or remember," both famous and otherwise, over the years. As their love affair devolved into marriage, Hemingway's hard drinking and, by her standards, lack of attention to hygiene — a matter Sidney himself had observed first hand as the two men bunked together on the road in 1929 — did nothing to boost Martha's ardor. She seems to have engaged in sex when necessary to keep a man interested or because it was expected at a certain moment in a relationship, not out of any carnal desire on her part. "I didn't like the sex at all," she wrote of her love life to a friend when she was in her sixties, "to enjoy it probably . . . seemed a defeat." Of the men in her life, at least a few of whom must have labored mightily to please her, she said, "that seemed to be their delight and all I got was a pleasure of being wanted." And what, as he covered his ears with his pillow in the Hotel Florida, would old Sidney have said about her self-assessment: "I daresay I was the worst bed partner in five continents." Amen, brother.

But Sidney was in Madrid to help his pal Hemingway, Martha or no Martha, and that is what he did with the same thoroughness with which he approached everything else in his life. Throughout these weeks, Sidney was everywhere, typing the first batch of the thirty dispatches Hemingway would write for the North American News Alliance, then filing them with Ilsa Kulcsar at the Telefónica, (while taking time to complain to her of Martha Gellhorn's unholy influence on Ernie). He might be seen driving Joris Ivens to the Jarama front, but pausing to offer a correspondent a ride. He could scavenge for food or booze or life-saving necessities for the troops. George Seldes recalled Hemingway shouting: "See if you can dig up some hypodermic needles, Sidney, Dr. Bethune's unit is desperate!" (The Montreal-based Dr. Norman Bethune was a renowned thoracic surgeon working for the Republic.) Hemingway himself remembers Sidney as the invaluable one "who bought us all our food, cooked us breakfasts, typed articles, wangled gasoline, wangled cars, wangled chauffeurs, and covered Madrid and all its gossip like a human Dictaphone." Sidney was the one everyone counted on to be cheerful when times were bad, the one to crack a joke and keep everyone's spirits up, to know where food could be had in a city where the shelves were bare. He possessed what Josie Herbst called, not entirely unkindly, "a kind of buoyant mindlessness." He would tell stories about his bullfighting triumphs, then bring them down to earth by confessing that after killing his first bull back in Mexico, he vomited from the experience. (This would be a detail left out of later interviews and memoirs, yet it was shared in the hallways of the Hotel Florida.) In fact, were it not for Gellhorn's presence, being in Madrid at Hemingway's elbow while history was being made would not be such a bad thing. As it was, Sidney began to feel that he was being used, but not for the work he was doing for Hemingway, or for the film, or even for the Spanish Republic itself. (He probably would have had just as good a time and performed just as admirably had they all been covering the Franco faction, as Sidney always said he had just as many friends on one side of the war as the other. He did, however, get with the loyalist program during the siege, once saying that a fascist victory would set the country back a thousand years.) Instead, he sensed that he was being used as an unwitting agent in the betrayal of Pauline, becoming little more than a valet for the adulterous pair, a *mozo*, a sword handler of a most unseemly sort. His very presence provided cover for them, just as the sandbags in the street provided cover for the Madrileños, his silence making him a knowing accomplice in the infidelity.

13

The Master Horn

THE JOURNALISTS PASSING THROUGH the Hotel Florida during Sidney's busy stay were well aware that what they were witnessing was nothing less than the opening chapter of a new world war. Hemingway was right. It *was* the Big Parade all over again. These men and women had illusions about many things, but not about that. From the beginning, the civil war was a mini world war with regular troops from fascist Italy and Germany fighting the volunteers from the International Brigades who descended on Spain to defend the Republic. The most well known to those watching from back in the United States was the Abraham Lincoln Brigade: young men from the streets of New York, the woods of Oregon, the steel mills of Pittsburgh, the colleges of the Big Ten, or the mines and smelters of Butte, Tonopah, and Coeur d'Alene who came to turn what they saw as the fascist tide. Hemingway enjoyed the company of these young bruisers and idealists, and Lincoln Brigadeers could be found soaking in his tub, drinking his whiskey, eating one of Sidney's breakfasts, or shooting craps on Hemingway's floor. It is true that not all of these committed volunteers enjoyed Sidney's cynical wisecracks or his assumption that all politics were suspect, but his performance for the cause was unquestioned. Still, the gulf between those covering the war, no matter how committed, and those fighting it was clear. When the correspondents went back to their rooms to write what they had seen, or flew off to Paris to talk passionately about *la causa* in the cafés as the saucers and the bill piled up and the talk got loud, the men of the brigade went back to the front to die.

One odd fashion sidebar to the chronicles of these American volunteers: when Martha Gellhorn left Madrid after her first trip in the spring of 1937, she had added to her wardrobe a lovely fox fur coat, a gift, she always claimed, from the boys of the Lincoln Brigade. Again, Dos Passos biographer Stephen Koch weighs in to question the truth of Gellhorn's account, first noting that such a bourgeois, if not elitist, affectation would be an odd gift from such hardscrabble and underpaid men who had come to Spain to die for justice and social equality, no matter how much they enjoyed basking in the presence of the blond correspondent. (The image of lean and hungry men stinking of sweat and cordite browsing the furrier shops of the Gran Vía for just the right wrap for Martha *is* a bit surreal.) Koch cites Gellhorn's own diary entries (first reported by Caroline Moorehead) to support his claim that she put in long hours shopping between the shelling—as admittedly did Sidney—hunting for bargains and inquiring as to the probable cost of a custom-made fox fur coat while the citizens of Madrid risked death queuing up for food. "With Ginny [Cowles], went and priced silver foxes and got desperately greedy wanting them . . . At three a shell ricocheted from the Telefónica and killed five women in front of the Gran Vía." She also ordered several pairs of handmade pumps, and chewed out the cobbler when she did not like the results. "Home, after a bitter séance with the shoe man. How those shoes have turned out, like gunboats for a clubfooted pregnant woman." War was a bitch after all.

Koch admits that it is impossible to know just where the Famous Fox got her famous fox, but he doubts it was obtained from what was left of her original fifty bucks.

Civil war represents not just the failure of politics but also the triumph in one of the factions of political passion fired past the point of reason, so that violent suppression of the opposition is the only result worth accepting: slaughter Pompeii's army; burn the Albigensians; behead the papists; quarter the Roundheads; fire on the Yankees, Mr. Beauregard. The presence of those who had only recently been one's neighbors suddenly becomes intolerable. Spain in 1937 was the new primer for this madness. The men of the Lincoln Brigades were of all sorts: liberals, union men, Jeffersonians, socialists, ex-Wobblies, and true communists. Some simply saw themselves as old-fashioned, bare-knuckled American workingmen who set sail for Spain because they felt that justice and the ballot box were more important than someone else's army or church, and who feared the dark cloud of reaction on the horizon. Milt Wolff, a Brooklyn boy who commanded the Lincoln Brigade while still in his early twenties after four previous commanders had been killed, stated that — although a communist — he felt he was preserving American democracy by fighting for democracy in Spain.

No matter the politics of the various participants, the defense of the Spanish Republic against the forces of fascism became one of the great liberal causes of the twentieth century. George Seldes remembers Hemingway in Paris a year after his first trip to cover the war. At the end of a long night of drinking, Hemingway said, "I had to go to Spain before you goddamned liberal bastards knew I was on your side."

The fight is still debated in America today. It retains its capacity to stir up both ugly emotions and memories of romantic youth for the simple reason that these culture wars used real bullets. A traveling California college grad fresh from Berkeley named Elsa Jaeger recalled being harassed by Franco's troops at a roadblock in 1937. Miss Jaeger, raised in Santa Barbara although born near Berlin, said she was detained for no other reason than the rebels found a leatherbound set of Pushkin's poems in her luggage. Seen as a threat to the czar in the 1830s, the poet's works were looked at as evidence of a pro-communist slant one hundred years later. What poet today would have such power? For that matter, what carbine-toting trooper leering at an attractive college girl would be so literate? (Jaeger was eventually sent safely on her way and went on to marry Hungarian refugee violinist André Ocskay after World War II.)

Joe Stalin finds few defenders outside the former Soviet Union anymore, but Franco still draws kind words from the American right. The men of the Lincoln Brigade remain romantic heroes to liberals and progressives who see them as the first wave of the U.S. war against fascism and the precursor to our men landing in Normandy to fight the same enemy. The arguments won't die: Franco was as bad as Hitler; the Lincoln Brigade volunteers were nothing but Stalinist stooges. Under the skin, the wound is still raw.

In Spain things are naturally worse. The dead of this war literally will not stay buried. The socialist government of Prime Minister José Luis Rodríguez Zapatero in 2007 passed a Law of Historical Memory condemning the atrocities of the Franco dictatorship, calling for the removal or modification of public monuments honoring the regime, granting posthumous justice to its victims, and demanding the exhumation of those victims buried in common graves for proper burial. Spanish conservatives were fiercely opposed. Just days before the legislation was introduced, the Vatican beatified 498 priests and nuns who were said to be true martyrs killed for their faith by Republican forces during the civil war. It was the largest ceremony of beatification — the first step on the road to sainthood — in the history of the Catholic Church, an act many in Zapatero's government saw as more political than religious. Seven decades after the war, deciding the true master horn of Spanish politics is still a dangerous business.

Although a substantial but unknowable percentage of the writers, intellectuals, and Lincoln Brigade troops supporting the Republic were not Communist Party members, and some, like John Dos Passos, became famously anticommunist after their experience in Spain, there is no disputing that the Communist Party and their soviet advisors controlled much of what happened on the ground on the Republican side once the bullets started flying. Sidney got his initial taste when he first crossed surreptitiously into Spain and found his credibility and movement impaired by not having party identification. (This need to prove up one's leftist credentials was nothing new, and had roots in this country as well. During the heyday of the Industrial Workers of the World — the Wobblies — in the early decades of the twentieth century, many itinerant workingmen got thrown off freight trains or out of hobo jungles for failure to produce the IWW's "Red Card.")

Hemingway's friend Stephen Spender was another liberal who became disturbed by the influence of the Communist Party in the day-to-day business of fighting Franco. Spender found disillusionment common among younger volunteers who viewed Republican Spain as a noble cause, only to find a hard jolt of reality when they arrived to fight and found that they would be serving under communist brigade leaders. Spender demanded in an article in the *New Statesman* that communist control of the International Brigades should be made clear to all new volunteers before they shipped out, not hidden from the public. He was chastised by party members safely back home for jeopardizing new recruitment.

For John Dos Passos, what began as unease with soviet influence in the loyalist cause cost him two of his closest friends. The first was a man he had known for twenty years, since they met in Spain as idealistic but radical students in 1916, José Robles Pazos. Robles had joined Dos Passos in America to become a professor of Spanish literature at Johns Hopkins, and had been Dos Passos's Spanish translator. Although from an aristocratic family, Robles had become a true Marxist and served as a Republican colonel after returning to Spain at the war's beginning. The second friend Dos Passos would lose was Ernest Hemingway.

There had always been an undercurrent of rivalry between Hemingway and Dos Passos—three years his elder—since they became friends as young aspiring writers in Paris. A Chicago boy like Hemingway, Dos Passos had been to Spain years before Ernest. He had gone to bullfights, including those in Pamplona, and had become an aficionado before Ernest. He was in print first with the 1921 publication of *Three Soldiers*, and famous with his novel *Manhattan Transfer* in 1925, a year before the appearance of *The Sun Also Rises*. He introduced Hemingway to Key West. Then in 1929 he in turn was introduced by Ernest to Katy Smith, his childhood friend. (Hemingway had always implied that Katy was an early sexual conquest, a claim she discounted, treating him with indulgence as one would a boisterous younger brother.) Katy Smith soon became Mrs. John Dos Passos. Whether because of this marriage or simply because of professional friction, Hemingway began to take swipes at Dos Passos in print, caricaturing him unpleasantly in the original manuscript of *To Have and Have Not*. It did not soothe Hemingway's professional jealousy when Dos Passos made the cover of *Time* magazine in the spring of '37, just as they all converged on Madrid. There was creative friction between them as well over the direction of *The Spanish Earth*. Hemingway's interest, in addition to covering the human cost, was in capturing the military angle so that the public could see the scope of the war, its effects on the country, and how warfare in general had changed since 1918. Dos Passos wanted to focus more on the devastation of the fighting at the village level, showing the personal toll on a country and a people he loved in a cinematic way that would be otherwise indescribable. The friction over Robles was more serious.

Robles had enemies within his own Republican cause, specifically the soviets, who would prove more deadly to him than the fascists. He was warned in the fall of 1936 to leave the country, but refused. In December of that year, just when Hemingway was checking out Martha Gellhorn in Sloppy Joe's, Robles was arrested by government forces in Valencia. Dos Passos worked for several months to find out what the charges were and what had happened to his friend. By March 1937, just as Ernest, Sidney, and Martha were arriving in Madrid, Dos Passos received word from Republican sources in Valencia that Robles was not in real danger, and that the charges against him were minor. Hemingway, supposedly on Dos Passos's behalf, contacted the government's head of counterespionage, a man named Pepe Quintanilla, the brother of Hemingway's good friend, the artist Luis Quintanilla (whose 1939 painting of Sidney graces the front cover of this book). Hemingway then told Dos Passos that he had Quintanilla's personal assurance that Robles was fine and that his trial would be fair. Hemingway as usual liked to think of himself as the insider, the man with the contacts, the guy with the built-in bullshit detector. He told Dos Passos not to worry. He also wanted Dos Passos to drop the whole Robles business, as it was casting suspicion on all involved with *The Spanish Earth*. Questioning Quintanilla's word was jeopardizing their situation, despite the fact that the man had a reputation as an executioner. On the day Dos Passos returned to Madrid, he was met by Sidney and escorted to Hemingway's suite in the Hotel Florida. Martha Gellhorn, sitting imperiously on Hemingway's bed, complained that Dos Passos's persistence on the Robles matter "caused us embarrassment." Dos Passos, like Sidney, seethed at Gellhorn's appropriation of Hemingway. "Us," indeed.

By this time, however, it did not really matter. José Robles was past embarrassing anyone. He was already dead. He had been executed, most likely by the NKVD — the precursor to the KGB — after a secret court-marshal, supposedly for spying for the fascists. He was dead even before Dos Passos had arrived in Spain. Josephine Herbst had found this out from government sources in Valencia who swore her to secrecy, and who only told her because of her friendship with Dos Passos. After some anguish over leaving Dos Passos in the dark any longer, she spilled the news to Hemingway so that the leak of information could not be traced directly to her. It then fell to Hemingway to tell Dos Passos, which, incredibly, he did at a festive correspondents' lunch with a group of Russian officers at a castle outside Madrid. Dos Passos had to swallow the painful information along with his meal while keeping up cheerful conversation with a soviet division commander in a great hall under eyes of the portraits of ancestors of the castle's previous owner, the Duke of Tovar. To press for more information in front of the Russians would paint Dos Passos as the dupe, or worse, the protector, of a fascist spy.

Rather than feel he had been lied to by Pepe Quintanilla, who he still felt was a great guy, Hemingway chose without question to assume Robles's guilt, confident that his execution was justified. He took the position that Dos Passos's belief in his friend showed nothing more than typical liberal naiveté. For a man who adopted a skeptical pose toward all politics, this was an uncharacteristic buying into the party line by Hemingway, hardly a communist by anyone's stretch of the imagination. Dos Passos was devastated. He never believed the charges, first because of his closeness to Robles and more importantly because of his friend's lifelong rejection of all that the fascists stood for. He knew Robles had been murdered by the communists and was dismayed at Hemingway's attitude, which in today's terms was simply, "get over it." This tore open a rift between the two men that became a fatal wound. The breakup of their friendship would become bitter, public, and final. As Sidney would find out, it would not be the only friendship to not survive those five weeks in Madrid.

14

The Sword

ALTHOUGH ROMANCE AND INTRIGUE stalked the halls of the Hotel Florida, the reality of violence was never far away. It was more than just the occasional shell that hit the old landmark after missing the Telefónica. The war was sometimes in the streets, right in front of the correspondents, so that the horror and the banality of life existed side by side. There was the headless man that Sidney found next to the smoking shell crater his first morning in Madrid. There were the women who refused to relinquish their place in line for scarce supplies outside food stores even when shells were hitting close, the risk of a mother's death balanced with the risk of a child's hunger. And there was the entire grocery queue of women near the Plaza Mayor hit by a single shell from Franco's batteries, or the little girl killed in the street by shrapnel. When the artillery barrages got heavy, the correspondents could do nothing but huddle together in their rooms in the Florida or better yet in the basement of the Gran Vía as the buildings shook and loose plaster rattled within the walls, bumming tobacco and rolling papers from the Spanish waiters when their own cigarettes ran out, keeping off the empty streets, which filled with dust, puddles of blood, and flying stones.

By late April, when they had been in the city about a month, Hemingway did what Hemingway was known for: he disappeared early one morning, then brought back to his hungry crew at the hotel a partridge, a duck, and four rabbits bagged with a borrowed shotgun. He thought he had a woodcock in his sights but blasted a fellow hunter, an owl, instead. It would not be the last time that his aim would be more accurate than his judgment. Such diversions aside, much of the correspondents' time was actually spent going where the war was fought.

During her first weeks in Madrid, Martha Gellhorn filed no stories herself. She followed behind the professionals "who had serious work to do," but did none of her own. That did not mean that her presence went unnoticed. Cecil Eby describes her striding through the American volunteers at the Jarama front who were sunning themselves during a lull in the fighting. The men were stunned to see a tall blond from back home, and Martha found herself quite naturally the center of attention. Sidney claims that her presence was so distracting that the men abandoned their positions to follow her around, and that women were banned from visiting the front lines after that — a doubtful proposition, as Martha would continue to visit various scenes of combat in the next few weeks, as did many of the women journalists both accredited and otherwise, such as Virginia Cowles and Josephine Herbst. In Herbst's case, after casting about to find a subject and an approach to the conflict that would be uniquely her own, she established herself as a serious correspondent by living alone in the village of Murata with loyalist troops, immersing herself personally in the war in a way that Gellhorn never would. Observing the fighting first hand, Herbst covered the story while ministering to the boys of the International Brigades — Polish, French, German, American, Czech, Cuban, and Romanian, as well as the Spanish, who being a proud people were both grateful but somewhat embarrassed by this help from strangers. And the person who had suggested that she visit this specific frontline hamlet, and who had then driven her there himself on one of his filmmaking forays with Joris Ivens? It was Sidney Franklin. He had much to teach a newcomer about Spain.

From Hemingway, Martha Gellhorn learned the sounds of war: to differentiate between machine gun and rifle fire, to tell in an instant by the sound which shell would harmlessly sail overhead and which had your name on it. Hemingway felt that Martha was very brave, more so than he, although he was happy to acknowledge that by the age of eighteen in Italy, he had already shed the brave blood first. (He also said a few years before that Pauline—remember Pauline?—had been the bravest person he had met for not dying on the operating table during a gruesomely difficult childbirth.)

Finally at Hemingway's urging (so much for him stifling her career) Gellhorn wrote her first piece about the hardship of daily life for the citizens of Madrid and cabled it to *Collier's* with surprisingly low hopes for its acceptance, considering that she was a published author who kept company with both Ernest Hemingway and Eleanor Roosevelt. Despite the doubts, her first byline appeared under the title "Only the Shells Whine," a quite fitting one, all things considered. Martha Gellhorn was finally one of the boys. She would be known primarily as a war correspondent for the rest of her life.

Gellhorn got more surprises when she, Ernest, and Sidney would arrive at small villages on their travels from one skirmish to another. What she saw would not have surprised Hemingway because he had seen it all before: the townspeople would point and murmur among themselves, small children would run after them, and adults would press forward bashfully to put themselves in the presence of greatness. Often the mayor would come out to greet the little group, honored to shake the hand of one so famous. Were they awed by the presence of the author of *A Farewell to Arms*, or by the tall blond in the slacks from Saks? No, the villagers came out to swarm around the unforgotten man who had triumphed in the bullrings of Spain only a few short years before, the Yanqui Flamenco, maestro Sidney Franklin. *That* must have really galled Martha Gellhorn.

Once back in Spain, even with his beloved Madrid shelled, sandbagged, starved, and overrun with celebrities, bullfighting was never far from Sidney's mind. He still had time to haunt the shops of his old hometown (Madrid was just one of half a dozen hometowns such as Brooklyn, Mexico City, and Sevilla that Sidney could claim in his lifetime) for bargains on used bullfighting costumes and equipment. As with everything else during the civil war, bullfighting suffered. The new Plaza Monumental was temporarily shuttered. The old traditions were strained by partisanship and hate. Barnaby Conrad tells a story of a particularly noble bull named Civilón that had been inadvertently gentled by an employee of the *ganadería* where it was raised. The young bull became a media sensation, and even youngsters were photographed with it, so unusual was it for an animal bred for killing to respond like Ferdinand the Bull in the children's story. Then, on the eve of the outbreak of hostilities in the summer of 1936, Civilón was booked by the impresario of the Barcelona ring to be fought by Sidney Franklin's good friend (and later his patron when he would take the *alternativa*) El Estudiante. The tamed bull performed true to his breeding, fiercely charging both El Estudiante and the picadors' horses, putting on such a great show of bravery that the crowd demanded the bull be spared. Then, the man who had gentled Civilón was coaxed into the bullring. The fellow entered timidly holding a fistful of hay. As the silent crowd watched, the bull, breathing like a locomotive, his tongue out, foaming at the nostrils and bleeding at the shoulders from the picadors' lances, walked up to the man and nuzzled him, following him out of the ring like a pet to great applause. The breeder bought the animal back from the impresario, intending to take it back to his ranch once the wounds of the picador's *vara* healed. Then, on the night of July 18, Franco's rebels entered Barcelona, marking the kickoff of the civil war. Needing meat to feed the new army, the rebels swarmed the stock pens at the bullring where Civilón was recuperating. There, the gentle giant was shot and butchered on the spot, one of the first, but hardly the last, victims of the dark wind unleashed by Franco. Most of the victims would at first be the soldiers and politicians, but the violence would quickly spread to civilians, with atrocities both committed and denied by both sides. Unlike Civilón, some of them could at least shoot back.

On the morning of April 22, Ernest and Martha left Sidney in Madrid and took a tour of the Jarama front. Ernest left behind a news dispatch — his first in many days — for Sidney to type and file with Ilsa Kulcsar. But it was Martha who left behind a breezy "Dear Sidney" note that seems, in retrospect, curious. In the note, Martha says she proofread the article by "E" but goes on to explain to Sidney which room in the Telefónica is Ilsa's, who gets each of the copies, where to find extra envelopes, the location of the pressroom, and the fastest means — by way of the diplomatic pouch — to get the story out. She is telling Sidney how to do the duties he had been performing meticulously for Hemingway for a month. So, either Martha was so self-absorbed that she was completely oblivious to Sidney's command of the situation, or she was trying to show off her own knowledge of the process — in short, writing for posterity. She ends by leaving instructions for the feeding of a sick commissar, Hemingway's friend Gustav Regler ("has had bad fever again, and Bethune still thinks it is typhoid"), apparently also a duty of Sidney's. She ends with a friendly "Gracias, Marty."

Ernest and Martha were gone ten days, traveling far into the Sierra de Guadarrama. Once, they were driving on a mountain road in an armored car when it was sprayed four times by rebel machine gun fire, the bullets pinging off the steel plates as they hunkered down. For part of the journey, they traveled on horseback where there were no roads, going high through the Scots pines and granite outcroppings to hidden loyalist positions — experiences and locales that Hemingway would use for his hugely successful novel of the war, *For Whom the Bell Tolls*, which came out three years later. They were still in the field on April 26 when modern warfare took an ugly turn, the bombing of the Basque town of Guernica on market day. Guernica was old and stone walled, situated inland from where the Oka River flowed into the Atlantic through an estuary named for the town. It had been a center of Basque tradition for centuries, and under an ancient oak, laws and leaders had long been affirmed. The Basques' ferocity and independence were well established. They held out against the Visigoths; they held out against the Umayyad Caliphate; they held out against Castille; and they held out against Franco. For that matter, they still hold out today. On that April afternoon, the population of the town was swollen with refugees from the fascist advance who had fled from other villages of the Basque provinces. As the people crowded the market stalls, Junkers from Hitler's Condor Legion droned in the sky, dropping wave after wave of incendiary and shrapnel bombs on the farmers and their cows and sheep and chickens, and on the citizens of the town who, with their children, were out to shop. The surprise assault thundered on for over two hours. Those who fled from the town were caught out in the open by Hinkle fighter planes, which strafed them with machine guns, cutting them down as they ran. It was just a town. There were no soldiers, no antiaircraft defenses. Such a thing was never considered. Casualties — total killed and wounded — equaled one third of the population of Guernica, with a death toll alone estimated over fifteen hundred. The oak of Guernica, however, survived the attack — for a time. While the slaughter by bombing of civilians and attendant "collateral damage" is today an accepted part of not just war but of the most routine skirmishes, police actions, and "surgical strikes," back in the spring of 1937, it was a fresh horror and the world took notice. The mixed carnage of children, livestock, farmers, and other civilians made up the hell captured by Pablo Picasso in his huge painting that best captures the madness of the twentieth century. The painting "Guernica" seems what Cubism was meant for, more real than realism itself. One can almost hear the screams.

Hemingway filed no story on Guernica, perhaps out of a reluctance to comment on that which he did not observe first hand. He did later attack the denials of the fascist forces, who stated that they had not been responsible for the carnage, and who instead blamed Basque separatists.

"I was not in Guernica, but I was in Mora del Ebro, Tortosa, Reus, Sagunto and many other towns," Hemingway said, "when Franco did exactly what he denies having done in Guernica."

While Ernest and Martha were out of Madrid, Sidney had much to do. In his memoir he mentions his role in one of the more curious episodes of the celebrity side of the war, the visit to the besieged city by the actor, adventurer, and supposed sexual omnivore

Errol Flynn. According to Sidney, Flynn came to Spain with two separate collections of relief funds solicited from the motion picture community in California, one for the loyalists and one for the fascists, so that Hollywood's neutrality could not be questioned. (How one went about raising dollars for dictators, even among hard-nosed studio heads, is anyone's guess.) Sidney claimed that, as he was a friend of Flynn's wife, the actress Lili Damita, he was the one chosen to escort Flynn through the lines at night to the rebel forces. Sidney pointed out that this would probably get them both killed if he tried it, and convinced him to backtrack through Valencia, take a boat to Gibraltar, and approach the fascists by sea. Flynn agreed, and then he, Sidney, and some friends partied until 2:00 a.m. in the actor's suite at the Hotel Gran Vía. Finally, Sidney saw Flynn to his hired car and set him off on the road to Valencia. There have subsequently been other less charitable and more questionable versions in print of what Errol Flynn was doing behind Franco's lines, but they do not involve Sidney Franklin.

In Hemingway's absence, Joris Ivens wrote to Sidney and cameraman John Ferno that they were to proceed to the village of Fuentidueña on the twenty-eighth of April and finish the last two days of shooting *The Spanish Earth* there. Ivens was on his way to New York, but he had hoped that Ernest could join Sidney and Ferno for those final scenes before Ernest flew to France on May 6. When the bullfighter was asked to play the role of assistant director, he took the request in stride, as he did every other chore that spring, and delivered the goods without fuss or pretension. Apparently, Hemingway never did catch up with them, but Sidney and Ferno performed as instructed and shot the needed footage. Once Ivens had this last bit of film, and with Hemingway bound for Paris, this whole heady scene in Sidney's life was about to wrap.

15

Separate Trails

"ABOUT SEVEN MONTHS AFTER I got to Madrid, the war situation went into one of its critical phases." Such is the way Sidney concludes not only his chapter on the Spanish civil war, but his entire autobiography. He had been in Madrid less than seven weeks, not the seven months he claimed, and Hemingway did not stay behind, but left even before Sidney did, to return without Sidney on three more occasions during the duration of the fighting. Sidney was in bad physical shape with the old horn wound and the cold that would not go away, plus there had been his poor diet due to food shortages in Madrid once the carload of supplies he brought in March was consumed. Sidney writes that, after reaching the safety of France, he sailed up to Scotland to recuperate, perhaps not the best place to shake a lingering bronchial condition. Then, after two pages covering a bloodless bullfighting exhibition that he put on for the 1939 New York World's Fair, and one sentence telling his readers that he took the *alternativa* in 1945, Sidney's autobiography is finished. It is as if, like that other freckle-faced boy Huckleberry Finn, he felt that there was nothing more to write. As usual with Sidney, the life he leaves out is often more interesting than the yarns he puts in. His choice of destinations in the summer of 1937 after he and Hemingway parted company is particularly telling when compared to Hemingway's own restless travels, and does much to explain what happened to their friendship.

For Hemingway, first it was Paris, where he landed on March 9. There, over four days, he spoke to the press about the situation in Spain, met with loyalists friends about the specific needs of those fighters still left in Madrid, and made public appearances. One such event was in a supportive locale from his twenties, Sylvia Beech's bookstore, Shakespeare and Company, which was attended by Hemingway's old friend James Joyce. Both Hemingway and Stephen Spender gave readings for the bookshop audience, Spender of his poetry, and Hemingway from the unfinished manuscript of *To Have and Have Not*. His time in Spain had rejuvenated him and put him more in the spotlight than ever. By March 18 his liner docked in New York and he headed straight down to Key West to domestic life with his wife, Pauline, as if he had not just spent forty-five days as one half of the new star couple of the literary world. His plan was to take the *Pilar* to Bimini and see to those big fish he had been neglecting while filing his dispatches for the North American Newspaper Alliance, but he was never with Pauline for long. After just a week, he caught a milk run for Newark, then was rushed from the airport to a sweltering Carnegie Hall, where that night he had agreed to address the second American Writer's Conference. The event was put on by the League of American Writers, whose president was Hemingway's old friend Donald Ogden Stewart. The master of ceremonies was fellow Contemporary Historian Archibald MacLeish. Joris Ivens was to speak and show part of the rough cut of *The Spanish Earth*. A second speaker was the secretary of the American Communist Party, Earl Browder. The star of the evening was, however, Ernest Hemingway. Hemingway was nervous, overweight, and sweating in a tweed jacket, a poor choice for the hot evening. (How a man having just spent six weeks in a besieged city where food was scarce could put on extra pounds when the surrounding populace would risk death to stand in a grocery line was perhaps a tribute to the scavenging and cooking skills of Sidney Franklin, plus Hemingway's copious consumption of alcohol.) When it was his turn to speak, the standing-room-only crowd of thirty-five hundred roared approval at this rare public statement from Hemingway on the need to take a stand in a dangerous world. "Fascism," he said, "is a lie told by bullies," a statement no one in the audience could dispute. He went on to say that there would be years of undeclared wars in the world's future, war enough for any writer to study if he or she chose. He was certainly right about that, too. Fellow producers and crewmembers of *The Spanish Earth*, John Dos Passos and Sidney Franklin, were conspicuously not in the audience or on stage at Carnegie Hall that night. Hemingway and Dos Passos's mutual friend, Dawn Powell, wrote a consoling letter to Dos Passos afterward, playfully summarizing Hemingway's remarks about the war being

pretty nice and a lot better than sitting around in a hot hall and that writers all ought to go away and get killed and if they didn't they were a great big sissy.

Powell also caught the celebrity quotient of the evening with her unsparing eye.

The foreign correspondents marched on each one with his private blond led by Ernest and Miss Gellhorn, who had been through hell in Spain and came shivering on in a silver fox chin-up.

But Martha Gellhorn was no longer Hemingway's "private blond" — especially in that infamous fox jacket. It was one thing to carry on an open affair in a foreign city in wartime, far from home in an era when gossip traveled at the speed of steamship, surrounded by colleagues who, even if they disapproved, would be constrained by Hemingway's fame and temper. It was something else to parade his infidelity among longtime friends like MacLeish in Manhattan nightspots, as Powell noted:

> Then he went over to the Stork Club, followed by a pack of foxes.

There would be no escaping the public humiliation for Pauline when café society and literary gossip were as close as Winchell's column in the next morning's newspaper. If she did not find out in that fashion, there were confidants such as Katy Dos Passos and Josephine Herbst, whose loyalties were now more to her than to Ernest and who would be glad to set her straight. It is not known if Sidney, complicit in the deceit and in a thankless position between two close friends, told Pauline anything about the affair. (A desire to avoid the inevitable conflict, much less be the one who spilled the beans, makes his story of hightailing it to Scotland from France almost ring true. The braes around Glasgow were about as far from the Stork Club or Whitehead Street as a guy could hide and still get room service.) It would be obvious soon enough that Sidney and Pauline were in contact and making plans. Back in the spotlight, Hemingway had no need for a trusted friend to cook his breakfasts, scrounge for food, or keep a secret that he had already exposed himself.

While in New York, Hemingway took time to visit with Scott Fitzgerald, who was recovering from his darkest days and was on his way to Hollywood and a lucrative contract with MGM. Hemingway returned to New York — and Martha — a few weeks later to record Orson Welles's reading of Hemingway's narration for *The Spanish Earth*. At the urging of Lillian Hellman and Fredric March,

Welles's reading was soon discarded as too theatrical and replaced, at Joris Ivens's suggestion, with Ernest's own gruff but sincere voice. This replacement would cause friction between Hemingway and Welles for years.

Hemingway flew alone to New York for a third time on July 5 for the premier of *The Spanish Earth*. Three days later, at an event arranged by Martha Gellhorn, he, Gellhorn, and Ivens flew down to Washington DC for dinner at the White House with the Roosevelts and Gellhorn's friend, presidential advisor Harry Hopkins. There they suffered through an inedible meal and screened *The Spanish Earth* for the first couple. (It is hard to imagine presidential handlers today allowing a Marxist propagandist like Ivens within ten blocks of the president, no matter how inclined he — or she — might be to see the film in question, and no matter how famous the filmmaker's friends were. In 1937, however, Eleanor Roosevelt was still capable of determining her husband's dinner guests.)

Having missed the once-in-a-lifetime presidential dinner — to which of course she was not invited — Pauline caught up with her husband in New York two days later, on July 10. That same day Ernest and Joris Ivens hopped a plane for the coast, landing in Los Angeles with a copy of the film for a fundraising screening. (Whether accompanied this time by Pauline or not, the evidence is contradictory, so it may have been a short reunion. Baker says that only Ernest and Ivens flew west. Reynolds states Pauline wrote to Sara Murphy that the purpose of her trip to New York was so that she could join the two men on their trip to the coast. Sidney wired Hemingway in Hollywood from Brooklyn on July 15, 1937, closing with "Salud Pauline Joris," so it would seem that Pauline was indeed included in her husband's star tour.) This event for a select group of famous Hollywood supporters of the Republic was organized by Fredric March and his wife, Florence Eldridge, to raise money to buy ambulances for the loyalist cause, and was held at the couple's brand-new home. (Hardly proletarian digs, even this house, designed by architect Wallace Neff, would become famous.) But for that one night in 1937, Ernest Hemingway was the biggest star in town. He was the only major novelist of his generation who never had to support himself by writing for the movies. Fitzgerald and William Faulkner were the most obvious cases of those who had, and even Dos Passos had tried his hand. Hemingway could thus afford to be dismissive of the films made from his novels, going out of his way to skip the premiere a few years earlier of the Gary Cooper–Helen Hays version of *A Farewell to Arms*, which had been arranged for his convenience in the Arkansas hometown of his in-laws whom he was visiting. (He did become a lifelong hunting, drinking, and skiing pal of Cooper's, and supposedly had the actor in mind as he wrote the character of Robert Jordan in *For Whom the Bell Tolls*, which Cooper went on to play in the 1943 film.) His professed indifference to Hollywood glamour and money, plus his obvious passion for the Spanish cause and the studied high-mindedness of his political mission, put Ernest Hemingway in a class by himself. He labored for freedom in Spain. His contemporaries schlepped for Harry Cohn, Jack Warner, and Louis B. Meyer.

Scott Fitzgerald, who had begun schlepping for Meyer by that time, was with Hemingway at March's home that night. Fitzgerald was not invited as a committed loyalist, however, but only as a friend of Hemingway. "The picture was beyond praise," he wired Ernest the following day, "and so was your attitude."

Enough money was raised in Hollywood that night for a multitude of Spanish ambulances. The actress Sylvia Sidney supposedly donated one of the thousand-dollar bills she normally threw away at the illegal gambling joints on the Sunset Strip.

Hemingway then returned to Bimini for a last few weeks of fishing. He also proofread, with Pauline's invaluable assistance, the manuscript of *To Have and Have Not*. By the first week in August, he sailed his boat back to Key West, and the couple made plans to head off in different directions. As before, Sidney Franklin would accompany only one of them.

Pauline's attempt to make a writer's paradise for her wandering husband in the Key West house purchased for that very purpose had been a bust. (Biographer Michael Reynolds calculated that over a thirteen-month period, from late 1936 to the end of 1937, Ernest Hemingway spent a total of three weeks in Key West.) On August 17 he sailed from New York on the *Champlain* for France; his final destination was again to be Madrid. Two days later Martha Gellhorn discretely followed, sailing on the *Normandie*. They would again set up residence in the Hotel Florida, but this time without the companionship and prying eyes of Sidney. It would take more than separate trans-Atlantic liners to hide that arrangement. Inspired by their second stay, Hemingway even wrote a play, *The Fifth Column*, about an American agent for the Republic and his leggy blond correspondent lover. His fictional riff on Martha Gellhorn in the play is staggeringly uncomplimentary, describing the character obviously based on her, although beautiful, as "lazy," "on the make," a "bitch," and worst of all, "stupid." (If intended as humor, it was cruel at best. If it betrayed inner feelings, one can only wonder why she married him after reading it.) So for Pauline, her husband's affair was now a painful open secret among not just their friends but the general public.

Throughout much of the 1930s, the Hemingways had made summer visits to the Nordquist ranch in Wyoming. With Ernest and Martha going back to Spain, Pauline took another ranch vacation in August 1937, but this time she aimed south, not north. She headed for Mexico with her husband's son Jack (Bumby, by then a teenager), Ernest and Pauline's own eldest boy, Patrick, then eight, and her friend Lorine Thompson. They motored around the gulf coast, then down to Mexico City, where Pauline visited friends. Later, they drove out to a large bull-breeding ranch where they stayed as guests on the hacienda for several days and the boys caped some calves. Driving the big Lincoln was their traveling companion and guide for this vacation, Sidney Franklin. "Franklin was a fascinating fellow with a lot of bullshit and a tremendous amount of self-esteem," Jack remembered years later. Whether Sidney's role in this excursion as what Michael Reynolds called a "dubious father figure" was Pauline's idea, or whether Sidney was performing one last chore for Hemingway before their friendship vanished under the onslaught of the Gellhorn relationship, it is hard to know. "Franklin was a pleasant fellow to be around as long as you paid him a certain amount of homage," Jack said. Perhaps considering the destination, and the reliance on the hospitality of his friends on the *ganaderías*, the decision to escort Pauline to Mexico might have been Sidney's own — the taking of an emotionally wounded friend under the protection of his own irrepressible personality — but it is equally likely that he was diverting Pauline on Hemingway's behalf. (On July 15, when Hemingway was still in Hollywood, Sidney was again greasing the skids for Ernest and Martha's relationship. He wired Hemingway from Brooklyn, advising that a new Ford could be delivered to Portbou on the French-Spanish border more quickly than a Chevy. Obviously, Sidney was still stuck in the role of fixer and facilitator.) Either way, such a short time after the intensity of their shared Madrid experience — the close quarters far from home with physical danger always a possibility — Sidney and Ernest were now, for the first time since their meeting in 1929, heading off permanently on separate paths. As Pauline's friend and confidant, Sidney's presence was intolerable to Martha, dooming his place in the inner circle of Hemingway's short third marriage. For the rest of their lives, he and Ernest would meet only rarely, and then mostly by chance. A fatal space had been allowed between them. Only time and bitterness would fill it.

16

Hemingway's Gay Blade

THE PROBLEM WITH HEMINGWAY, Sidney told his new
friend Barnaby Conrad in Sevilla in the late spring of 1944, was
that for his whole life Ernest was concerned about the size of his
penis. It had been seven years since the intense times during the
city's siege, and Sidney was taking public swipes at his old friend
and confidant in the most personal way. It had been probably a
year or two since the two friends had last crossed paths, and that
had been in Mexico.

"His *picha*," Sidney told Conrad that day in Sevilla, "was like
this." He held up the end of his little finger, pinching the base
with the thumb and forefinger of his other hand. "About the size
of a .30-30 shell." Conrad seems to have been a bit skeptical at the
time, and says that he only included this story in his 1969 memoir,
Fun While It Lasted, in response to what he felt were Hemingway's
uncalled-for comments on the size of the departed Scott Fitzgerald's *picha* in Hemingway's memoir of his Paris years, *A Moveable
Feast*. At the time, Conrad was the United States vice-consul in
Spain at the startlingly young age of twenty-one. He had been
raised in the leafy, stuccoed gentility of Hillsborough, California,

on the San Francisco peninsula. His future was assumed to be bridge, golf, and amateur theatricals at the country club, then the Southern Pacific commuter train steaming north from the Burlingame station to some investment bank in San Francisco's financial district. The neighbor occupying the estate next door was the author and naturalist Stewart Edward White, through whom young Barnaby got his first glimpse of the worlds of both literature and exotic animals. With that, plus the boy's raging appetite for adventure, investment banking never had a chance. Conrad had gone off east to college, but during a summer trip to Mexico City to study art, he had done what many a young bullfight spectator had before him—succumbed to the twin lures of tequila and the *corrida*. Looking very Ivy League in his seersucker jacket and tie, he worked his way down the grandstands, then leapt the barrier to cape a *toro* during a bullfight already in progress. In the bullfight world such bold dreamers and fools are called *espontáneos*, and for their trouble usually get jail time ("ten days in the shade" as Conrad said) unless pardoned by the ring authorities at the insistence of the crowd. While Conrad was executing *verónicas* with his Brooks Brothers raincoat, he was infected by a bullfighting passion that would define the rest of his life. He decided to learn the art. He, like Sidney almost two decades before, trained with young novices, then faced his first bull in a private performance on a ranch. It did not go well. A previously injured right knee was smashed and three fingers were broken. Two years later the bum knee would end an extremely short career as an officer in the U.S. Navy. Almost by default Conrad landed in the Foreign Service as a way to serve his country in wartime. By then he was a tall, lanky, talented professional artist, Yale grad, and handy cocktail party pianist who made—and, more important, kept—friends easily, so his posting to Spain was a perfect job for the young aficionado.

By early 1944, the U.S. Fifth Army under General Mark Clark was pinned down at Anzio, the Nazis still controlled France, and from the east, Marshal Zhukov was leading the Red Army counterattack from Ukraine into Poland. But in Spain, which was forced by circumstance and self-interest to sit out the war that it had helped ignite, bullfighting was back, and Sidney Franklin was there in Sevilla to see it. He had returned for the first time since he had parted company with Hemingway in 1937. In wartime with Nazi U-boats prowling the shipping lanes, booking passage from New York to neutral Spain was not a simple thing. The voyage itself — often via Portugal — could take over two weeks due to the evasive measures necessary to avoid the submarine wolf packs. As an American, Sidney was Barnaby Conrad's entree to Spain's taurine world. He seemed to know everyone, and everyone in the bullfighting life knew Sidney. After a mutual acquaintance in the consular office had arranged an introduction, Sidney offered to meet Conrad at an outdoor café. Sidney soon introduced the new vice-consul as a fellow *torero* to his old friend Marcial Lalanda, to the gypsy matador Joaquín Rodríguez — "Cagancho" — and to the new sensation, Manolete. (Manolete made such an impression on him that Conrad went on to fictionalize the last day of Manolete's life in his best-selling 1951 novel, *Matador.*) Two weeks later, Cagancho would in turn introduce Conrad to the legendary Juan Belmonte, who also became a lifelong friend.

Sidney was gracious and charming to Conrad, taking him to Manolete's first fight of the season on the first afternoon they met. Sidney was well connected and had the tickets hand delivered to his hotel by Manolete's own *mozo*. At the *corrida* Sidney correctly appraised Manolete's first bull and explained the particulars of the melancholy matador's audacious style. Conrad remarked that even Sidney was caught up in the mastery of the performance. In his memoir he paid Sidney the compliment that seeing Manolete in Sevilla with the Brooklyn matador was like a little leaguer being taken to his first World Series by Joe DiMaggio. That evening Sidney dragged Barnaby to Manolete's crowded hotel suite, where the new maestro shared his precious, hard-to-get Scotch with the two Yanquis and no one else. By the end of the evening, Manolete had invited Conrad to dine with him a few weeks later. At forty-one Sidney may have been out of the spotlight, but he was still in the center of the world he loved.

Their friendship grew during Conrad's service in both Sevilla and then Málaga. When asked years later if there was at this time any indication of Sidney's sexual orientation, Conrad said absolutely no, even during a road trip when they shared hotel accommodations. As others have, he remarked on Sidney's strong physical presence, his baritone voice, his jaunty, aggressive masculinity. The only hint may have been Sidney's lack of interest in the beautiful women of Spain — always of interest to Conrad — who crossed the two Americans' path as they socialized at the bullfights and elsewhere. "There was nothing swishy about him at all," he said. Any rumor of homosexuality would have ruined him in Spain.

Even with his new friend the young vice-consul, for Sidney the ghost of Hemingway was never far away. Conrad, like many other Americans, first heard of Sidney Franklin in the pages of *Death in the Afternoon*. Meeting Sidney, Lalanda, Cagancho, and the rest was, he said, like the pages of that book coming to life for him on the streets of Spain. When Sidney had only known Barnaby for an hour or so, Sid volunteered that he had lost respect for "Ernie" during the shelling of the Hotel Florida, claiming he had to pull a whimpering, terrified Hemingway out from under his bed. He also claimed to have written much of *Death in the Afternoon* for Hemingway.

Barnaby Conrad's *picha* story would not be worth dwelling on — except for its amusement value — were it not part of a larger picture of Sidney Franklin slamming Ernest Hemingway in ways that he knew would hurt: calling into question Hemingway's courage and his masculinity. It was obvious that from Sidney's side, by 1944 the friendship was on the rocks, although the luster of that friendship would continue to illuminate Sidney's legend and self-image for the rest of his life. The few times the paths of the two men had crossed since 1937 had been mostly unplanned encounters, usually — but not always — with other acquaintances, and with one known exception, without Martha. There did not seem to be any public animosity, particularly from Hemingway's side. He was always gracious and full of praise. As far as the world knew, Sidney Franklin was still a pal.

There was the time in mid-December 1940 when Sidney was in New York staying with one of his married sisters. One morning he walked into George Brown's gym on West Fifty-seventh Street for a workout and saw two men sparring in the ring. "Hey," he shouted, greeting the boxers who stopped punching mid-round. One man was Brown, a former trainer. The other, wearing trunks and a sweatshirt over long underwear to work up a sweat, was Hemingway. A reporter conducting an on-the-fly interview with the writer was the only spectator. As Brown and the reporter watched, Sidney and Hemingway hugged fiercely, pounding each other on the back. Hemingway introduced Sid to the reporter, then went back to throwing punches at Brown. Chatting up his tenacious pursuit of his career, Sidney told the reporter that he had just returned from Mexico, where he had been fighting. Hemingway told the reporter that after Christmas he was off to San Francisco, then China, where Martha would cover the fight against the Japanese as a war correspondent for *Collier's*. Having only married the month before, the China trip would be a bit of a dangerous honeymoon for them. Hemingway's initial role would be that of observer and loyal husband while his bride filed dispatches.

After six one-minute rounds, Hemingway hit the showers and the rubdown table. Later, Sidney and the reporter followed Hemingway into the massage room. Sid observed that Ernest always kept himself fit and trim, although the man sprawled out on the table like a dressed-out steer had just weighed in at a solid 219. The reporter left as Ernest reminisced with Sidney about sailing on the *Paris* to cover the war in Spain.

That first afternoon in Sevilla with Conrad, Sidney began his Hemingway critique by describing a bizarre incident that happened in that city, but whether it was 1929, 1937, or some time in between, he did not make clear. In response to Conrad asking what Hemingway was like, Sidney became uncomfortable. What follows is Sidney's voice as recollected in *Fun While It Lasted*:

> He's changed. Something's changed. See that street over there? He and I were walking down it one day and we see a Nancy-boy walking along on the other sidewalk—a real hair-dyed, limp-wristed type, but just minding his business. "Watch this," says Ernie. He crosses the street and knocks the poor maricón down, hurts him, with no warning. That sort of tells one about Ernie, doesn't it?

It also perhaps tells one about Sidney as well. In recounting such a tale to a new friend, it is clear that Sidney felt Hemingway possessed a loathing, a hostility, and perhaps a fear of men such as he, and that such hostility reflected poorly on Hemingway. Sidney also seems to be expressing a fear that if Ernest knew his true nature that he might be in for the same fate as the Nancy-boy—if not the violence, at least the contempt. Whether either the *picha* or the *maricón* stories are true exactly as Sidney told them is almost beside the point. Sexual anxiety is at the root of both. Such a precarious place cannot have been an easy one to occupy for Sidney, who, one hopes, was more self-aware than the swaggering façade he presented to the world. That Hemingway had discovered Sidney's secret by 1937 — or perhaps had known all along — is another possibility to be discussed later. When asked in 2004 what happened to the Franklin-Hemingway friendship, Barnaby Conrad looked over his glasses with a little smile at the obviousness of the question and said, "He probably found out he was a [homosexual]." In any case, sex, homosexuality, courage, masculinity, marital betrayal, and respect all seemed to have reared their heads to complicate and eventually corrode the once-solid bond. These issues would only become more problematic for the two men as the years went on.

About two years before the negative jibes to Conrad, Sidney had briefly rejoined Ernest and Martha in Mexico. The particulars of this last wartime rendezvous remain unexamined by most Hemingway biographers. There is no record of whether things went well or badly between the three, but like their journey to Madrid in 1937, Hemingway had his own agenda and kept his own counsel. It had been almost a year since Ernest and Martha's return in the spring of 1941 from their China trip, during which Hemingway did his best to turn his role as supportive husband into everything from geopolitical expert to military advisor. To give himself professional standing alongside Martha, he had arranged to write a few pieces for a new current affairs newspaper, *PM*, on the economic and political aspect of the Japanese war and occupation. (On that trip he had met another Jewish soldier of fortune, the Cockney-born boxer, bodyguard to the late Sun Yat-sen, gunrunner, and sometime Chinese General, Morris "Two-Gun" Cohen. While Hemingway held court at the Repulse Bay Hotel in Hong Kong, Cohen introduced him to Sun's widow, Soong Ch'ing-ling, the most beloved woman in modern Chinese history, and advised him of the liveliest war zones for Martha to cover. Once again, Hemingway had found his insider, the guy with the straight dope.)

In the months after Pearl Harbor, with China still fresh in his mind, Hemingway was anxious to participate in America's war effort. His offer to John Wheeler of the North American Newspaper Alliance to cover the war as he had in Spain five years before had been turned down, not because of any problem with Hemingway's work, but because Wheeler felt that firsthand unfiltered accounts of America's fledgling attempts to regroup so soon after the Japanese attack would be bad for home-front morale. Hemingway then dreamed up a more active role for himself than correspondent, which was becoming more of his wife's gig after all. He conceived of a Havana-based counterespionage unit to keep track of Nazi agents in Cuba, where pro-Franco and thus pro-Hitler sentiment was popular among many of the ruling class. Fearing that he was too conspicuous a figure in Cuba, where he had purchased a home known as the Finca Vigía shortly after his new marriage, he was leery of sitting down with U.S. officials in Havana. According to musician, *aficionado práctico*, and author Anthony "Tony" Brand, who lived in Mexico, Spain, and South America for many years, Hemingway arranged a meeting with American government personnel not in Havana at all, but in Mexico City. The cover for this visit was a week of socializing with a Hemingway friend and fan, wealthy art collector Nathan "Bill" Davis, who served as the Hemingways' host during their stay. In that 1942 season, Sidney was back in Mexico picking up occasional fights—mostly along the border. Whether Hemingway asked Sidney to join them for show or for old times' sake, or whether Sidney simply got a hint of the trip and elbowed his way along, is impossible to know. But it was there, in Sidney's familiar territory and far from the intrigues of Havana, that Hemingway could slip away for meetings with State Department underlings to pitch his idea.

Bill Davis was a large, thick-featured, balding man with a lot of money but no apparent vocation, and with what Hemingway's last secretary and eventual daughter-in-law, Valerie Danby-Smith Hemingway, sensed was a cruel streak. Although outwardly just a camp follower of the famous author, Bill Davis had some interesting political connections of his own. Earlier in Mexico City, he had become acquainted with and interviewed Leon Trotsky (shortly before the day in 1940 when one of Stalin's assassins swung an ice axe at the exiled soviet leader, driving the point deep into his skull). Davis moved to Spain in 1953, renovating an estate outside Málaga that became an expatriate haven and literary salon. In the summer of 1959 when Hemingway was covering the bullfights for *Life* magazine, Davis offered him and his entourage the hospitality of the estate, where Hemingway and his friends then celebrated his sixtieth birthday. Davis remained devoted to Hemingway until the end, even when Hemingway, in his last, sad visit to Spain in 1960, was convinced Davis was trying to kill him. There was some talk among fellow expatriates in Spain's bullfighting community that Bill Davis had OSS connections during the war, but this could be said of many Americans living in neutral capitols during the early 1940s. If true it might explain the trip to Mexico City and its subsequent success, but it probably would not have been essential, as key American officials were openly behind Hemingway's outlandish scheme.

Supported first by Bob Joyce and Ellis Briggs at the American embassy, then by the new ambassador to Cuba, Montana-born

Spruille Braden, Hemingway received official U.S. approval for his spy plan. Braden was particularly enthusiastic. (The FBI agents attached to the embassy were apparently less impressed with such amateur sleuthing. Director J. Edgar Hoover himself requested that any information regarding defects in Hemingway's performance as an informant be relayed directly to Braden, and claimed that his information about German submarine activity in the Caribbean "proved unreliable.") Back in Cuba Hemingway did for a short time head a loosely affiliated web of friends — exiled Basques, barflies, jai-alai players, fishermen, waiters, and aristocrats — to keep tabs on suspected Nazis in Havana. He called this cadre the Crook Factory. Although there at its inception in Mexico, Sidney was not part of this new adventure, probably because he was more interested in reviving his bullfighting career, and possibly because he was not asked. (The only person who would have been more conspicuous than a celebrity writer snooping on fascist spies in the cafés or pastel alleys of Havana would have been a redheaded matador. And as he always said, Sidney had many friends among the pro-Franco elite.) For her part, Martha Gellhorn did not have much use for these cloak-and-dagger shenanigans either. Within a few months, Hemingway had dreamed up an even more exciting job for himself: outfitting the *Pilar* as a submarine hunter. Armed with government-supplied grenades, machine guns, bazookas, and a radio (as well as privately supplied cases of Scotch and rum), Hemingway intended that his crew pose as harmless fishermen along the Cuban coast, hoping to get close enough to surfaced German U-boats to attack the unsuspecting Nazis with guns blazing and perhaps lob a grenade or two down an open hatch — a natural job for the jai-alai players. Although he was deadly serious about this, his wife found such plans at best a distraction from the war reporting she felt he could be doing, and at worst childish thrill-seeking and an excuse for excessive secrecy, gun-toting, and heavy drinking. By this time Sidney was actively planning his own return to Spain. When it came to pursuing his bullfighting, he had no use for distractions, even war.

Within a year or two of these events, for Sidney to deride Hemingway to someone such as Barnaby Conrad who was at the time still almost a stranger, seems a reckless act, a Rubicon crossed. He obviously recognized the profound change in Hemingway from the serious correspondent of 1937 to the would-be spymaster and one-man navy of 1942, but the bitterness of his comments speak to a more serious rift. So, it would be Sidney who first lobbed a grenade across his friend's bow. He knew that Hemingway was not a man who took perceived insults easily. Ernest was a counterpuncher and held long grudges. He savaged Dos Passos quite publicly in print after the Robles affair, treating his old rival with contempt for the rest of his life. During his troubled time with Dos Passos and Sidney, Hemingway had a falling out with Archibald MacLeish that, although not permanent, was also public. His brawl in Maxwell Perkin's office with Max Eastman came several years after Eastman had written the article chiding Hemingway for false machismo. Yet Sidney persisted in prodding the legend. In his interviews with Lillian Ross, he continued in the same vein as he had with Barnaby Conrad three years earlier.

"I weighed Ernest in the balance and found him wanting," he told her, "when he began coloring his dispatches about the war."

"Obscenity!" Ross has Hemingway reply, in a clever nod to the mannered speech of his fictional loyalist guerilas in *For Whom the Bell Tolls*. Despite Ross's jocular presentation — perhaps an intentional ploy to take the sting off Sidney's remarks — Sidney must have known that comments made in the pages of the *New Yorker* would get back to Hemingway and cause him annoyance, if not embarrassment or hurt. But Ernest Hemingway did not counter-punch. He never landed a glove, and never publicly tried to until toward the end of his life. For the time being he left Sidney alone. He even defended his old friend in a letter to Lillian Ross from Cuba in 1948, saying how adversity reveals character "when the heat is on. That is why never re-negged [sic] on Sidney because really saw him good and it would be a crime to deny it."

A final frivolous note on the *pichas* of both Hemingway and Fitzgerald to set the record straight: *Esquire* magazine founder and editor Arnold Gingrich was asked about Sidney's comment years later by Denis Brian, who recounted his reply in *The True Gen*. Gingrich told Brian that, having traveled, shared accommodations, and gone swimming with both writers, he could vouch that they were both adequately and normally equipped. He felt that Sidney's crack about Ernest was, as Conrad had suspected, just cattiness—a low blow at an old friend who had let him down. Both writers were important to Gingrich, and he to them. He had persuaded Hemingway to write for *Esquire's* premiere issue in 1933. That first piece lent the publication a literary credibility that it maintained for several decades. Hemingway continued to contribute short stories and articles on hunting and fishing during the magazine's early years, and Gingrich gratefully published and paid for whatever was submitted. John Dos Passos, when he was still speaking to Hemingway, felt that his friend played Gingrich like a hooked marlin.

Conversely, at the end of Fitzgerald's life when his lucrative MGM contract was over and he was living precariously on oc-casional script-writing assignments while trying to meet the fi-nancial demands of maintaining his wife, Zelda, in an institution in North Carolina, his daughter, Scotty, at Vassar, and himself in a modest West Hollywood apartment, Gingrich accepted and published new short stories of Fitzgerald's, which appeared in an astounding seventeen straight issues of *Esquire*. These stories about a hack screenwriter, collected as *The Pat Hobby Stories*, were still coming out in the magazine after Scott's death in December 1940. Gingrich could only pay about two-hundred fifty dollars per story — less than a tenth of what Fitzgerald commanded from top magazines like the *Saturday Evening Post* during his heyday in the 1920s — but it was steady money and allowed him to work on his final but unfinished novel, *The Last Tycoon*.

Arnold Gingrich had one last, somewhat intimate, and certainly complicated connection to Hemingway that may have made him as unreliable a witness about Ernest as Sidney had been: Gingrich eventually married Hemingway's former mistress, the beautiful but troubled Jane Mason. Talk about basking in reflected glory. He had been introduced to Jane by Pauline in a defensive ploy to derail her husband's activities with the married socialite. Gingrich soon began seeing Mason himself, arranging adulterous trysts with her in New York shortly after the affair with Hemingway ended sometime in 1936. They were not married, however, until several divorces later in 1955, an event that after all those years still galled Hemingway and ended his association with the magazine. If Gingrich had any personal questions of his own about Ernest's attributes, he could by then, presumably, get the information straight from the horse's mouth.

17

The Alternativa

BACK IN SPAIN FOR THE first time since the civil war, and caught up in the excitement generated by Manolete, Sidney was again thinking seriously about reentering the Spanish bullfighting world and finally taking his *alternativa*. It would still take him another year, but it is remarkable that he was able to do it at all. At forty-one he was no Manolete. The truth be told, he was no Manolete at thirty-one either. Watching that first *corrida* with Conrad, he blurted out that Manolete was as good as he himself had been in Sevilla that amazing day of his debut back in 1929. Then, perhaps realizing how self-aggrandizing that sounded — even for him — Sidney admitted that Manolete was indeed better than he had been on his best day.

It is worth repeating the context during which all this took place: the northern part of the continent was still firmly in Nazi hands; the monastery at Monte Cassino had just been bombed into a pile of rocks; D-Day was still over two months away; and the Warsaw uprising would not begin until a good four months into the 1944 Spanish bullfighting season. But with the bullrings open and Manolete with his sad, gaunt face filling the arenas, and Carlos

Arruza with his dazzling smile on the scene from Mexico to excite the battle-weary Spaniards, the war was a long way off. For Sidney, the greatest enemy was the calendar. There is something grandly tenacious about a man who has watched his fortieth birthday come and go without realizing his dreams and who nonetheless decides that he will not be deterred. This had been his world before he had ever heard of Ernest Hemingway, and it would be his world long after Martha Gellhorn and Hemingway parted ways, but he had to get moving. And then there was the matter of the death of his father, the irascible but unreconciled Abram Frumpkin, who had finally passed two years before. Sidney would no longer have to suffer the old man's disapproval, but at the same time he could no longer hold on to the illusion of some future peace with the patriarch either. Whether the removal of this negative force in Sidney's life was the final push he needed is again unknowable, but should not be ignored.

Bullfighting may have its timeless quality, but time is the adversary for all whose art depends on physical grace, not to mention timing. Sports reporters may speak of a veteran NFL cornerback who has lost a step when he is beaten on a pass route. The result may be six points, benching, or retirement. Bleeding to death from a horn wound is almost never a worry. But Sidney *was* forty-one, still a *novillero*, and an infrequently active one at that, despite fighting as often as he could in Mexico since 1937. His career had started late and ended early. Sidney said that for most bullfighters the career arc was about six years: two years to achieve greatness, two years at the top of one's game, then two years of decline — and that is if they avoid serious injury or death. Only the true greats such as Belmonte or Gaona could beat those odds. Even Joselito and Manolete could not. At the age when Sidney saw that first *corrida* in Mexico City, most young men who would go on to become matadors had been performing for years. Carlos Arruza was a professional at an age when Sidney was still a junior high show-off singing with two girls on a Brooklyn stage. In the early 1930s, Hemingway joked about Sid's delayed start in a consoling letter to Scott Fitzgerald, whose wife's most recent nervous breakdown had been exacerbated by her anxiety at failing to make it professionally as a ballet dancer, an unrealistic goal that she only began pursuing as an adult. "She wouldn't have wanted to start late and be the Sidney Franklin of the ballet, would she?"

Now at forty-one, Sidney was not only not as good as Manolete, he was obviously nowhere close to where he had himself been at twenty-six. The excitement generated by the new sensation also made the early 1940s no time for a matador to coast along on established technique. Manolete did not so much invent new passes as refine a cold and classic style. Elegance was his attitude. He took incredible chances, such as looking off at the crowd during his work with the *muleta* as the bull charged. Juan Belmonte Jr., by then a matador and contemporary, said that Manolete was driving the others in the profession to suicide trying to keep up with him. Even his habit of holding the collar of the *capote* in his teeth as he adjusted the location of his hands was soon copied, as Sidney predicted to Conrad, by many young matadors.

In those first days of his return after the seven-year absence, Sidney got a good look at the ravages of time on a bullfighting friend from the 1920s. Sidney was sipping sherry with Barnaby Conrad one afternoon in his Madrid hotel room as he was being interviewed by a reporter about his plans. Luis Crovetto, Sidney's *mozo* from a decade before, was tending to his duties just as if no time had passed: sharpening Sidney's swords, shining Sidney's boots, and fluffing Sidney's toupee, which perched on a stand on the dresser. (Sidney only wore his rugs for ceremonial occasions, bullfights, and formal photographs. He had three: two parted on the left, one parted on the right.) All the evidence in his room pointed to a maestro who was back in business. As the interview ended, a thick-waisted, bald, and slumping Spaniard knocked on the door. Sidney introduced him to Conrad as Cayetano Ordóñez, the matador known as "Niño de la Palma," who had been Hemingway's model for the character Pedro Romero in *The Sun Also Rises*. The bullfighter at twenty with his raven black hair had been described in the novel as incredibly handsome. The youth's beauty had not been lost on Sidney, who called him an Adonis. "Niño had a marvelous figure," he said. "All the sexes were wild about him." There was no trace of that dazzling twenty-year-old boy in the nondescript man now standing before Sidney in a well-worn suit nervously tossing down a glass of sherry. Ordóñez and Sidney had known one another for many years. During the 1931 season when Sidney had tried to keep his dying career alive with a South American tour after his goring in Nuevo Laredo, Mexico, the two had appeared together in a *corrida* in Bogotá, Colombia.

Ordóñez kept eying Sidney's toupee. Sidney called it his "anti-macassar" (a Jackson Place locution conjuring immigrant gentility if ever there was one). "Try it on," he said. After some hesitation, Ordóñez picked up the toupee and arranged in on his head. "It took twenty years off him," Conrad said. Ordóñez became transfixed by his image in the bureau mirror, drawing himself up in a bullfighter's haughty posture, then pantomiming the placing of *banderillas* into an imaginary bull. As long as he had Sidney's false hair on his head, he was the man he had once been so long before. After several minutes of this, he modestly replaced the toupee on the stand, resumed his slump, and wordlessly left the room. (Conrad employed a fictional version of the episode to good effect when he wrote his novel *Matador* a few years later.)

July 18, 1945: Luis Gómez, the matador known as "El Estudiante," stood facing Sidney just outside the matadors' *burladero* on the sands of Madrid's Plaza Monumental. El Estudiante carried a *muleta* and sword. Sidney hugged his *capote*. This was it. The first two acts, the *suerte de varas* and the *suerte de banderillas*, had been completed for the first bull of the afternoon, and the trumpets' blare had just announced the third act, the *faena*. That first bull, Tallealto from the *ganadería* of Sánchez Fabrés, would normally belong to El Estudiante as the day's senior matador, although this had been the animal that Sidney had caped as his own as custom dictated. Here, in the ceremony of the *alternativa*, El Estudiante as senior man and Sidney's sponsor — his *padrino* — ceremonially cedes that bull to the *novillero* as his own. Sidney, the *novillero* at forty-two, was eight years older than his *padrino*, but El Estudiante had already been a full matador for thirteen years, since he was twenty-one, and had been the star and workhorse of the 1938 season. That some aficionados now say that he too was gay somehow seems a meaningless fact, especially at such a moment. Granted, this information — outside the bullring — might have mattered to some if it were true. It would, however, be meaningless to the ceremony of the *alternativa*, meaningless to Sidney's sense of accomplishment and relief at finally having this truly historic achievement behind him, meaningless to the crowd, who would have been oblivious in any case, and certainly meaningless to Tallealto, whose blood was dripping from his withers onto the sand.

The second matador in seniority, Emiliano de La Casa — "Morenito de Talavera" — stood a few feet away, performing his role as the ceremony's *testigo*, or witness. He watched as the *novillero* and his *padrino* took off their *monteras* and paused. Morenito de Talavera could note that Sidney's toupee remained planted squarely on his head. This was the moment, so simple yet profound, for which

Sidney had long waited: since he and "society bloods" trained with Gaona dodging slaughterhouse horns held by serious little boys; since he first stepped into Plaza de Chapultepec in 1923; and since his triumph in Sevilla in 1929. It was the moment he thought he had lost forever when he was lashed to the infirmary bed with the rectal wound here in the same city in 1930. It was what he thought was beyond his grasp when his arm blew up from the anti-tetanus serum in the Laredo, Texas, hospital in 1931 with only the presence of Ross Dennison to keep him from going crazy. It was what was still missing when he had cavorted in front of Eddie Cantor and a 35-millimeter camera for Sam Goldwyn in 1932, and what he wished he could have shoved in Martha Gellhorn's face five years after that when the shells whistled past the Hotel Florida just blocks away from where he now stood.

Both men held their *monteras* in their right hands. El Estudiante cradled the *muleta* and sword in his left and presented them to Sidney. Sidney gathered them in and handed El Estudiante his *capote*. Next, as was the custom, the two friends shared a traditional *abrazo*, then Sidney turned and shook hands with Morenito de Talavera, and it was over. After twenty-two years in the ring, Sidney had at last become a *matador de toros*. Then, to shouts from the stands of "Viva America!" and "Viva Truman!" Sidney went on to kill — or not kill — the bull, depending on who is telling the story. (The origin of the rumor that Sidney could not kill his bulls that day may have been an August 1952 fight in Tangier, where Sidney was indeed unable to make the kill of his first bull, a dangerous Miura, and came close to repeating the disgrace with his second. He did, apparently, dispatch Tallealto adequately that day in Madrid.) As important as his *alternativa* was to Sidney, the world of official bullfighting in Spain took little notice, which makes it impossible to chronicle some specifics of events in the ring that afternoon. This was the ninth anniversary of Franco's kickoff of the Spanish civil war; so the festival may have had definite political overtones, considering that it was organized by the state headquarters of something called the Youth Front. July 18 was a day of celebration for the Falange Party, and there are aficionados today who speculate that the party arranged the belated *alternativa* for Sidney as payback to an old friend who had done favors for them, or that so late in his career this low-key event was the only appearance in Madrid available to him. (At the peak of his game during an appearance in San Sebastián in the 1929 season, Sidney dedicated a bull to a young army officer, a Colonel Franco. Why, other than courtesy or the cultivation of an up-and-comer, is anyone's guess.) An extant *cartel* for this corrida is certainly modest. Rather than a large poster with a stylized painting of the afternoon's top matador (which may have also existed), it is a simple handbill with a small engraving of a bull in the upper corner, nothing more. The whole thing only measures eight-by-twenty inches. As the usual custom for one taking the *alternativa*, Sidney was the third *espada*, or sword, listed. Above the names of the matadors was that of a *rejoneador*, don Alvaro Domecq, a talented young aristocrat from the famous sherry-making family who was to fight the first of the day's seven bulls in the Portuguese style. After this *corrida*, neither of the two main bullfighting papers of the day, *El Ruedo* and *Dígame*, made any mention of the bullfight at all. Years later, Cossío stated in *Los Toros* only that Sidney's performance that day was not a colorful event.

As the new *matador de toros*, Sidney entered the list — at the bottom of course — of every matador in history going back to Francisco Romero in the town of Ronda two centuries before. He became the oldest matador in the twentieth century to have confirmed his *alternativa* in Madrid. And he secured his unique place in bullfighting history by becoming the first American to do so — just as he had bragged he could after dinner at that Mexico City restaurant back in 1923. However, as one door opened, another one closed. Following this appearance on July 18, Sidney fought once in Portugal, then returned to the United States. Having finally taken his *alternativa* in Madrid, Sidney Franklin would never again appear professionally in a bullring in Spain. That life was over.

18

The New Man

SIDNEY'S STORY IS ONE OF transformation, just as the bull-fight itself is a ritual of transformation as a modern man with a tailored sports coat, sunglasses, and a convertible puts on the archaic suit of lights for the centuries-old rite of bravery and death. Even as Sidney became the new matador of the bullfighting world, he was forced by age and circumstance to accept the role of elder statesman. One insurmountable fact was that there would always be a new crop of matadors. Manolete was killed in 1947, becoming, like Joselito a generation before, an instant legend. But Carlos Arruza, who would go on for years both as matador then *rejoneador,* was seventeen years younger than Sidney. Luis Miguel González, or "Dominguín," who was to dominate the art for a decade, was twenty-three years younger than Sidney, yet still managed to confirm his *alternativa* a month before Sidney's own. Dominguín's rival in the late 1950s was Antonio Ordóñez, the son of Sidney's old friend Cayetano, "Niño de la Palma," who borrowed the toupee. (The *father* was still a year younger than Sid.) Also, the nonbull-fighting years, the pain of frequent operations, the strain of personal and financial trouble had aged Sidney, and others could not help but notice. It was time to find new parts to play.

As the first American bullfighter, Sidney would always have celebrity in an era when, unlike our own, actual accomplishments were required for such recognition. Even as he struggled to get by while reinventing himself, Sidney Franklin was *known*. In Madrid he was invited to parties at the American embassy. In New York nightclubs he played *toreo de salón* with Rita Hayworth acting the part of the bull. He compared *verónicas* with Charlie Chaplin, who said the bullfight was as graceful as dance. *Time* magazine would occasionally print little blurbs about his exploits both in and out of the ring. He was, after all, America's bullfighter. *New Yorker* editor William Shawn suggested to his staff writer and longtime lover Lillian Ross that Sidney's life would not just make a great movie, but a Technicolor musical, and seriously suggested a project with Gene Kelly for the lead. (Perhaps Oscar Levant would play the part of the bull. The mind reels.)

While in New York some time in 1939 staying as usual with one of his sisters, Sidney reconnected with Hemingway's friend, the Spanish artist Luis Quintanilla, and sat for a portrait. A political exile from Franco's Spain, Quintanilla described drinking California wine, eating Florida olives, and listening to music as his studio was flooded with sunshine, the bright colors of the *corrida*, and memories of Andalucía as Sidney posed in his suit of lights. "I don't know why I painted gaily the American bullfighter: the Kid from Brooklyn," Quintanilla said. Sidney was still able to light up a room. The portrait glows with reds, pinks, golds, and the priestlike black of the bull which Sidney appears to manhandle, if not actually straddle. In Sidney's face, Quintanilla captures both the insouciance and the wariness that existed side by side in his personality, a face that had known both exhilaration and deep disappointment. The painting was part of a 1939 exhibition of Quintanilla's work at the Associated American Artists Gallery in

New York. It was subsequently reproduced in the March 1940 issue of *Town & Country* magazine, just the sort of "swank" publication in which Sidney felt he belonged. ("Real Estate and Kennel Sections appear regularly at the back of the magazine," it proclaimed.) Hemingway wrote a short blurb to accompany the full-page portrait. On the surface he is cheery and gracious, praising (some might say over-praising) Sidney's skills with the cape as some of the best he had ever witnessed, but then he pointedly and perhaps unnecessarily reminds readers of the downward plunge of Sid's career by saying that he was no longer to be seen in the plazas of Sevilla or Madrid, but instead only in Mexican border towns or an upcoming rodeo in Idaho. "I haven't seen Sidney fight in a long time now but if he is still as good as he says he is when Quintanilla and he and I get together . . . at the Stork, he is, to put it mildly, terrific." The painter's son Paul Quintanilla says that the original of the portrait no longer exists; it was cut in half and painted over by his father long ago.

After taking the *alternativa* in 1945, Sidney soon found himself back in Mexico, where, as Hemingway noted, he could still get bookings, however modest. He was there in 1947, traveling with a young Brooklyn protégé, Julian Faria, when Lillian Ross caught up with him for her *New Yorker* profile. Fighting in those small-town bullrings was much the same as it had been twenty years before, only now the posters declared that Sidney Franklin was "El Único Matador Norteamericano."

There was another redheaded American bullfighter down in Mexico at the end of the 1940s, film director Budd Boetticher, who was preparing the production of a movie inspired by his own experience called *Bullfighter and the Lady*. Sidney was on hand for much of the filming, and it did not take long for conflict to arise between the two competitive men. Boetticher, the adopted son of a well-to-do Indiana family, had gone to Culver Military Academy and then Ohio State. Recovering from a football injury in the late 1930s, he took the family LaSalle and a college pal and cruised down to Mexico City to recuperate. There, a beautiful and wealthy Mexican madam his mother's age took him under her wing — among other things — and when he expressed interest in bullfighting, she arranged for his training with some of Mexico's finest matadors, including the colorful and hot-tempered Lorenzo Garza. Like Sidney in the 1920s and Barnaby Conrad somewhat later, Boetticher was smitten with Mexico City's taurine world, and like them he trained hard, the only Yankee in a crowd of young Mexican aspirants. His idyll ended when his mother found out and ordered him home. It was a tossup whether Mrs. Boetticher was more concerned about the potential damage to her boy by the bulls or by the beautiful brothel owner. She arranged with comedy producer Hal Roach, the father of a Culver chum, to get young Budd a job in Hollywood; so in 1940 Boetticher found himself lugging *muletas* and *estoques* into Darryl Zanuck's office at Twentieth Century Fox, where he was hired as technical advisor on director Rouben Mamoulian's Tyrone Power vehicle, *Blood and Sand*. Throughout the 1940s Boetticher worked his way up to directing first at Columbia, and then at Universal. *Bullfighter and the Lady* (a title he hated, his original was *Torero*) was a modestly budgeted independent feature produced by John Wayne's company to be shot entirely on location in Mexico — a dream project for Boetticher. Robert Stack was the star, playing a cocky young American, somewhat based on the director, who trains to be a *torero* under the direction of an experienced Mexican matador, played by Gilbert Roland. It is curious just exactly what Sidney was doing there. Robert Stack implied years later at a screening of the film that Sidney was on the set in a loosely defined capacity for technical advice, but when it came to the bulls, Boetticher felt he needn't take a back seat to anyone. "I made the mistake of telling him, 'mi casa es su casa,'" he said later, "and Sidney took me literally. I finally had to throw him out."

Problems arose as Sidney saw the story unfold of the naive American who goes to Mexico City and trains to become a matador. Sidney could not help but feel that Boetticher was, if not telling his story, at least poaching on his legend, and it galled him no end. He soon threatened legal action to stop the production.

This was not idle sword rattling from Sidney. He was a man who jealously nurtured his myth and stature as *the* American matador. In 1934 Sidney hauled Harry Cohn's Columbia Pictures into a Manhattan Court, suing for several hundred thousand because of the studio's film that he claimed defamed him by giving the public the impression he was "an impostor, liar, falsifier and humbug unworthy of serious consideration." The cause for his complaint was a Columbia comedy short with the cheeky title *Throwing the Bull*. The film, which employed newsreel footage of Sidney in the ring without his permission, began with the narration, "Now folks, meet Sidney Franklin, one of the greatest bull-throwers — I mean, bull-fighters — born under the sunny skies of Brooklyn." In a letter to Hemingway in late 1935, Sidney states that he won the lawsuit and was awarded "seven grand" and that he then planned legal action against Fox Movietone and a company called Bray, Inc., for similar transgressions. He wrote, "Although I really don't like this sort of thing at all, I've got to do something to protect myself, Verdad?" Columbia appealed the judgment. Whether Sid ever collected from them he did not say.

Boetticher claims that he responded to Sidney's threats with a threat of his own: either drop the subject or be outed for his conduct with various "nephews" — the young Latin men with whom Sidney was by now known to associate. (One source of this term was an incident that began when an *Esquire* magazine editor, George Wiswell, after an introduction to Sidney from Barnaby Conrad in the mid-1940s, asked the American matador to lunch in New York. Wiswell enjoyed Sidney's company so much that he invited him up for a weekend at his home in Westport, Connecticut. Sidney accepted, but asked if he could bring along a nephew who was visiting him at the time. Wiswell generously agreed. Sidney showed up with the "nephew" — a young bullfighting protégé of about eighteen — on a Friday afternoon. The two houseguests were each assigned their own bedrooms. On Sunday morning Wiswell walked into Sidney's room with a cup of coffee for his guest. He found the middle-aged matador *flagrante delicto* with the young man. Sidney began a lame explanation about his nephew getting cold during the night, but it was one of the rare times in his life when he was truly at a loss for words.)

His sex life was therefore, by his forties, a subject of discussion, whether due to Sidney becoming more comfortable with it, or just being more careless. Keeping secrets is a weary business. Sidney's cheerful bachelorhood had for years been an object of curiosity among casual acquaintances, a topic he fended off at times with humor, such as the claim that he had seen far too much animal breeding to have much use for the institution of marriage. Other times he adopted the tone of a detached professional man in control of his appetites with no time for such folderol. When Barnaby Conrad somewhat naively asked Sidney when they first met why he had never married, Sid launched into a long explanation, saying that he had yet to find the perfect woman. When the then twenty-two-year-old pressed the matador on what such a woman would be like, Sidney described his ideal as possessing a combination of great beauty, refined education, and wealth equal to his own — or at least equal to that which he had once possessed. He annoyed some homesick boys of the Abraham Lincoln Brigade in 1937 during a late-night discussion of women by claiming that sex was no more important to him than a glass of water. He was a guy who could take it or leave it. In his autobiography he describes — or, according to his niece Eve, invents — a beautiful, titian-haired, and quite amorous American girlfriend named Helen, whom Rodolfo Gaona supposedly blames for Sidney's career stall in the mid-1920s. The way Sid tells it, having a sexual relationship with a frisky young woman was to be a "whoremaster" and drained a man to the point of moral and physical exhaustion. Gaona conveniently tells him he must give up the girl if he intends to have a career as a matador. Thus, according to Sidney, a woman in a bullfighter's life makes for an either-or situation. A guy's gotta choose. (Obviously, the rakish Domingín never got *that* memo.) It was as if bullfighting were a calling like the priesthood that allowed a young man of confused, troubled, or secret sexuality to claim a higher purpose than heterosexual passion and thus escape embarrassing questions about his single status, even as he strutted around in brocade and silk (fabrics common to both professions, come to think of it). So by the late 1940s in Mexico, rumors of Sidney's homosexuality circulated among both bullfighters and fans, but this was a different age than our own. As with speculations about the sex lives of movie stars, such things although spoken of privately were considered one's own business. As long as a person was not overt, rumors notwithstanding, the public was more inclined to accept that person in their chosen public role.

Bullfighter and the Lady turned out to be the best film ever made on the subject. There is an immediate, almost documentary, feel to the scenes of the *corridas* shot in black-and-white in the huge Plaza Mexico, and several matador friends of Boetticher appear in the movie. The film shows the life and culture of the bullfighting world and the people devoted to it with seriousness, insight, and great respect. It is not about the fame; it is about the art, the tradition, and the mystery. Robert Stack, stiff to the point of caricature in some roles later in his career, is charming and natural as the self-centered rich-boy hero whose learning curve into manhood is tragically a step too slow. It is one of his best film roles. Gilbert Roland, by middle age too often hired simply to portray a stereotype of preening machismo, is relaxed and quite human as the hero's matador mentor. (Roland was himself the son of a matador and an acquaintance of Manolete's.) Katy Jurado, already a star in Mexico, is both sensual and dignified in her first English-speaking role as Roland's proud but much younger wife.

Stack's hair is dyed blond in the film, which somehow accentuates the intended frivolousness of his character. Boetticher's reason for this, however, was simple and ingenious: in long shots of actual bullfighting, he could plop a blond wig on matador Luis Briones, a shorter and darker man than Stack, and the viewer's eye would be drawn to the light hair, aiding the illusion that it is Stack in the arena. In one scene, however, Stack himself had to get into an informal festival ring with real fighting calves. It is a long sequence where the would-be American *torero* must perform at a *tienta* where amateurs and aspirants are displaying their ability with the cape for the amusement of invited guests, including some drunken vaqueros. At an American Cinematique memorial to Boetticher at Hollywood's Egyptian Theater after the director's death in 2001, Stack described his worry about the physical danger to himself in that scene. He said that Boetticher reassured him, saying that he would not ask Stack to do anything that he himself would not do.

Then Stack remembered that the director had been extensively trained to fight bulls, so he might be asked to do any number of dangerous things. He recounted with humor his realization that he'd been had. With both Budd Boetticher and Sidney Franklin right there encouraging him, he was on the spot. In action shots of the *tienta*, a very recognizable Robert Stack gets battered and knocked around in his character's first go-round with real calves, finally staggering out, bruised and his clothes torn, and happy that he not only survived the public ordeal but also acquitted himself passably well. The scene works because Stack's exhilaration and relief—like his bruises—were real.

Sidney did not convince Budd Boetticher to cease production, but he did come away with something from what he still considered to be *his* story, even if he had to steal it. In his interviews with Lillian Ross in 1947, Sidney describes his own visit to the *ganadería* prior to his first appearance in the ring in 1923. He said señor Guerrero "let me play around with the animals," nothing more. If this were a memorable occasion, he never said so. However, when Sidney got around to writing his own autobiography shortly after the filming of *Bullfighter and the Lady*, which Robert Stack said the matador had indeed witnessed, that short experience at the bull ranch grew into a grand three-day fiesta with Sidney as the star attraction. Sidney's description of the events runs for several pages and is elaborately described with cinematic detail. He wrote of governors, mayors, generals, cabinet ministers, and cowboys coming for miles to see the nervous young gringo perform with not a series of heifer calves, as is usual at a *tienta*, but with full-grown reject bulls. Sidney ends up battered but triumphant before a huge crowd, his street clothes torn to rags. *Bullfighter from Brooklyn* was published in 1952, a year after the release of *Bullfighter and the Lady*.

When asked his opinion of Sidney Franklin one evening in his living room in the fall of 2000, Budd Boetticher thought for a moment, then got a mischievous look in his eye. The old director was by then in his eighties, but he still raised and trained Lusitanos, the horses of the Portuguese bullfighter, the *rejoneador*. "The Spaniards had a saying," he said. "Sidney was gored more times by his 'nephews' than he ever was by any bull." Then he paused, suddenly quite serious. "But you could never take away from Sidney's courage." Boetticher, no stranger to courage himself, nodded gravely. "He was very, very brave."

19

Servalavari

WHEN *BULLFIGHTER FROM BROOKLYN* appeared in New York bookstores in mid-November 1952, Sidney was not in town to bask in the glory of the literary life (a studied disdain perhaps learned from his time with Hemingway). He was eight miles outside of Sevilla in the town of Alcalá de Guadaíra, where he was transforming himself once again, this time into an instructor of would-be matadors. He had set up a school for young Americans drawn by his name and the promise that they too could find success in the profession as he had. Sidney found a large house to rent on a plateau outside of the town, which until then had been known mostly for its olive oil and its matadors, such as the father and son Manuel Martine and Pepin Martine Vasquez, contemporaries of Belmonte and Manolete respectively. (Towns surrounding Sevilla, such as Utrera, Camas, La Algaba, and Tomares were similarly fertile breeding grounds for *toreros* as well.) A few hundred yards across the plateau from Sidney's house was one of Alcalá's two bullrings, a rickety, boarded-up *plaza de toros*, which he had renovated as a practice ring for the students he hoped to attract. A more modern concrete arena built in the early years of the century was nearby. This was bullfight country. It was in the soil. Even the golden sand — the *albero* — of Sevilla's La Maestranza was mined from the hillsides of Alcalá de Guadaíra.

It is worth noting that Sidney was reinventing himself in this way about the time that Hemingway was again turning his attention back to bullfighting as well. By the early 1950s, the writer could be seen once again at some of the plazas that his writing had helped popularize, such as those of Pamplona and Madrid.

Sidney was as serious about this latest enterprise as he had been about any aspect of his bullfighting career. For one thing, he felt a school would establish him as both maestro and mentor, just the role that Rodolfo Gaona had performed for him when he was beginning. And as usual, he needed the money. As all things with Sidney, his approach was bold and showy, and full of self-praise. The result was that the school did attract some students with real potential. One of the last of these was Baron Clements Jr., a drawling former high school quarterback from the east Texas town of Kilgore whose father was a successful welding contractor. He studied under Sidney at Alcalá de Guadaíra in the late 1950s, even putting in a predawn shift at a local slaughterhouse as Sidney had done in Mexico over thirty years before. Clements first professional fights as a *novillero* were, like Sidney's, in Mexico. Again, he emulated Sidney — unintentionally — with a goring in the ring at Nuevo Laredo during Easter week of 1959. Unlike Sidney's 1931 horn to the leg in the same ring, Clements's *cornada* was to the groin. Sidney asked the twenty-year-old boy if he could continue, and just as his mentor hoped, Clements said he would. Only after killing the bull did he go to the infirmary for seven stitches. A month later, Sidney himself was gored at the age of fifty-five.

"Nobody in Mexico has his style and manner in killing," Sidney said of Clements, with his usual understatement. "And only one—Antonio Ordóñez—can match him in Spain." Not only Dominguín but also some of Sidney's own students would disagree.

On August 30, 1959, Sidney presented Clements in Tijuana's bullring El Toreo for the Texan's *alternativa*. As with much of Sidney's career, there remains some lingering controversy about this event. It is claimed that neither of the other two matadors on the program, Jaime Bolaños and Charro Gómez, served as witness for Clements. Gómez himself said later that the afternoon's performance was enhanced when the breeze caught Sidney's toupee as he was caping one of his bulls, causing the rug to flop unglamorously off his bald head to the delight of the heavily American crowd. As with Harper Lee early in the century, Clements's Mexican *alternativa* was never confirmed in Madrid, putting a symbolic asterisk after his accomplishments as the next American matador after Sidney himself.

A student in the earliest days of Sidney's school was a young man from Salem, Massachusetts, with great promise named Porter Tuck. He was an adult before he witnessed his first bullfight during a visit to Mexico City following his army discharge. After an apprenticeship with Sidney at Alcalá de Guadaíra, Tuck performed for two highly regarded seasons as a *novillero* known as "El Rubio de Boston," the blond from Boston. Graceful performances in the ring led Sidney to hope—or perhaps fear—that this was the first American *torero* whose career could surpass his own. Tuck was within reach of taking his *alternativa* in the fall of 1955 when he received a horrible horn wound to the chest in the ring in Valencia. As with Sidney's Madrid *cornada* in 1930, the goring was not quite fatal but it might as well have been. After recovering as much as he could manage, Tuck appeared once more in the Madrid ring, but with less than satisfactory results. He was forced to retire while still in his early twenties, his health and his career ruined. After a decade of physical and emotional struggle, he finally took his own life with a pistol while sitting under a tree in a New York park. He was just thirty-three. Because of his promising beginning and sad end, Porter Tuck is still spoken of with fondness by Americans who follow the bulls.

A third student remembered Tuck fondly as well, but his recollections of his time with Sidney are less pleasant. His name was Patrick Cunningham. A Philadelphia native who, like Budd Boetticher, was a military prep school product (Boetticher went to Indiana's Culver; Cunningham attended Pennsylvania's Valley Forge Academy). He also had a career as a *novillero* after working with Sidney, but after a bad goring fought as an amateur *aficionado práctico*, then moved on to other pursuits, one of them literary. Cunningham wrote a moving and entertaining novel of his days studying to be a bullfighter with Porter Tuck under Sidney's instruction in Sevilla, which was published in 1991. The book was called *A River of Lions*, a title taken from Federico García Lorca's "Lament for Ignacio Sánchez Mejías," (an Andalusian matador, poet, and playwright who received a fatal wound in the Manzanares ring in 1934.) Cunningham's fictional portrayal of Sidney as the former bullfighter "Stanley Philips" is brutal. Philips, the "Torero from Texas," is portrayed as a boorish, money-grubbing braggart for whom the bullfighting community of Spain has no respect. He is also depicted as a greasy pederast whose secret life as a *maricón* is no longer much of a secret.

Cunningham saw his first bullfight while attending the University of Southern California after World War II. Like college boys before and since, Cunningham spent many weekends across the Mexican border. Tijuana's bars, strip joints, and sex shows are timeless lures for San Diego sailors on leave and for college students — who can drink freely although under the age of twenty-one — looking for trouble. For Cunningham the lure was not the notorious Blue Fox Café, but the bullring. Adventurous and athletic, he soon wanted to face this new challenge for himself. After reading *Bullfighter from Brooklyn*, he wrote to Sidney in Spain and received an invitation to come to Alcalá de Guadaíra to study with him — naturally, for a price. Sidney even invited Cunningham to live at his home. The young man could not believe his good fortune.

Cunningham became friends with his fellow student Tuck right away, but Sidney was not the man he had expected from the pages of his autobiography. The matador who spent so much time on his appearance and wardrobe in his younger years is remembered by Cunningham as a shabbily dressed miser wearing a ratty jacket and cloth cap who would drive his students to and fro in an old Chrysler station wagon. In Cunningham's novel, "Stanley's" sole employee at the school was a rank-smelling teenage Spanish boy of limited mental capacity who slept on the floor of Philips's room when he was not, as it seemed obvious to the students, in the matador's bed. For Cunningham and Tuck, familiarity with Sidney — the close proximity of both living and training — bred not just contempt but also scorn. When Sidney tried to appear witty and smart, the boys saw him only as crass and vulgar. Still, the bullfighting pull was strong, and Sidney was by Cunningham's account a fine teacher. He knew his capework; he knew the bulls; and he knew the business. And regardless of how Cunningham said he was perceived, he seemed to know everyone in the Spanish bullfighting world as well. He was still able to impart that insider's insight along with the training that would keep both young men competitive when they went out on their own in the professional ranks as *novilleros*. The two friends worked hard, learned their craft, and stayed with Sidney for close to five months.

Andalucía was not just the heart of the Spanish bullfight country with Belmonte's Sevilla and Manolete's Córdoba as the psychic touchstones. It was also the heart of the bull-breeding country, and thus the place where the *tientas* sprang up like olive trees. Once they felt they had the skills not to embarrass themselves, the two friends hung out in the bullfighters' bars around Sevilla's Calle de Las Sierpes and sought out every *tienta*, every private festival, that they could talk themselves into. As Sidney's star pupils, Cunningham and Tuck did appear once at a *festival-tienta* with their maestro, not at a *ganadería*, but in the plaza of Jerez de la Frontera. A benefit for the poor, this event featured the legendary Arruza among others. (The *cartel* for the festival refers to Sidney as the "*ex*-matador de toros norteamericano," and spells his student's name "Cumnighan.") For the most part, however, Cunningham and Tuck declined to share their plans with their teacher, preferring to make these amateur appearances without Sidney.

The great ranches and feudal haciendas of rural Mexico where Sidney learned his trade as a young man and nursed his wounds as he got older were modeled on their counterparts in Spain. Those of Andalucía were truly the old world: aristocratic, genteel, formal. The lineage of the men and women Cunningham and Tuck would meet was as impressive as those of the horses and the bulls they raised. It was also a world closed to outsiders unless they were deemed worthy. The town of Jerez de la Frontera, located between Sevilla and Cádiz, was home to don Alvaro Domecq, whose family was famous for fine bulls of the Vázquez line and even finer sherry and wine. Don Alvaro was also the highly respected *rejoneador* who had performed with Sidney Franklin on the day of his *alternativa* the decade before. Invitations to his *tientas* were prized. To be asked to his table after the festival was even more of a rare thing, especially for a pair of boisterous Yankees.

In *A River of Lions*, Cunningham describes such an invitation extended by don Alvaro to his narrator Mike Cassidy and Parker Todd, his fictionalized Porter Tuck. In the story, the two Americans were fortunate enough to be allowed to participate in a relaxed and informal event where they would perform with two professional matadors to test ten cows. Unlike some *tientas* the Americans attended, which had been large social affairs with titled guests, Rolls-Royces, and chamber music, the shaded stands of the private Domecq testing ring held only a few women spectators that afternoon, and the narrator described half of those as servants. Afterward, the Americans were invited inside by don Alvaro for an impromptu meal with his wife, sister-in-law, the two matadors, and José Flores — "Camará" — a former matador who had become the most influential bullfight manager in Spain. Camará still wore a black necktie in mourning for his client and friend Manolete who had been dead for six years. It was a rare privilege for the two young men, a glimpse inside a very private world. They took their seats in a great hall under wrought iron chandeliers. In the corner of the room, a single candle burned before a niche in which was displayed a statue of the Virgin, around whose waist was wrapped the sash Manolete had worn the afternoon he was killed in Linares. The sash was still encrusted with his blood, like the relic of a saint, which to don Alvaro and Camará, both of whom were at Manolete's bedside when he died, he indeed was. The narrator and Parker Todd ate a meal of bread, cheese, olives, fruits, and sherry. Toasts were made, and the Spaniards' formal reserve slipped away as they slowly accepted the young Americans as worthy companions. Then, the spell was broken by one guest who was not invited, Stanley Philips. Their maestro had tracked his boys down to crash the party. The narrator describes the Spaniards stiffening as Philips greets the displeased don Alvaro with "this is some wigwam you got here, Al." After being greeted as "Joe," Camará refuses to shake Philips's hand, a slight that Philips ignores as he makes the rounds of the table with his "sour-smelling houseboy," handing out copies of the newest *Reader's Digest*, in which a condensed version of *The Torero from Texas* was printed. It is a scene to make the reader cringe along with the American students and the Domecq family. When Philips goes on to denigrate Manolete in front of Camará, the Americans are left alone in the great hall in a chilling display of aristocratic dismissal. When asked decades later how true to life this fictional scene was, Patrick Cunningham said it happened just as he wrote it.

Those who knew Sidney, even longtime friends such as Barnaby Conrad, admit that this unfortunate portrait is a fairly accurate look at the man Sidney had become at this point in his career. It also demonstrates an almost willful need to be taken on his own terms, pushing the boundaries of taste and good sense when custom and experience should have taught him better. In 1954 when a certain don Plácido, the mule wrangler whom Sidney hired to perform the *arrastre*, the dragging of the bull carcasses from the student ring at Alcalá de Guadaíra, demanded higher pay as well as free tickets to Sidney's festivals, Sidney turned him down. When don Plácido then refused to work for him, Sidney simply proceeded without him. After the first bull of the next festival was killed, Sidney drove the Chrysler station wagon into the bullring, snagged the dead animal's horns with his catch rope, took his dallies around the car bumper, and circled the arena with a screw-you-all grin aimed at his aghast spectators as he dragged the bull away. This was such an arrogant violation of tradition that Sidney later had to make amends. He obviously knew better, but, as with his soured relationship with Hemingway, Sidney felt a hurt that created an inelegant chip on his shoulder. If the Spanish bullfighting world no longer valued him as it had in the past, he'd show 'em. This bizarre display was not reported by a disgruntled student, but by a writer for *Time* magazine, who found it funny.

It was during those months in 1953 that Cunningham saw Ernest Hemingway and his fourth wife, Mary, leaving a Pamplona café. The writer had transformed from the burley, dark-mustached athletic man of the 1930s into the iconic Papa Hemingway of the long-billed fishing cap and white beard, but he remained vibrant, unlike the more frail and boozy image he would project during the famous 1959 season. Cunningham, his left arm in a sling after taking a horn to his armpit, introduced himself to Hemingway, who led a small group of friends while his wife and others walked several steps behind. Hemingway asked the young stranger about his injured arm. Cunningham explained that it was a recent bullfighting injury, as he was studying to become a matador under the instruction of Sidney Franklin. Hemingway's manner changed, and his response was a gruff, "Oh. Sidney." This scene is described in Barnaby Conrad's introduction to *A River of Lions*. A decade and a half after his novel's publication, Cunningham said that, knowing Sidney and Hemingway no longer spoke, he brought up Sidney's name deliberately to see what the reaction would be, and that the author's response was, "I don't want to talk about it!" said with an emphatic scowl.

Patrick Cunningham, a charming self-described "red-nosed Irishman," still had one last thing to learn about Sidney as late as 2007. A dinner companion mentioned that Sidney was born on July 11. Cunningham, in mock horror, reached across the booth and grabbed his companion's forearm in a grip that, at eighty-one, could still swing a *capote* with ease and said, in so many words, say it ain't so. July 11 was Cunningham's birthday as well, and he was not pleased to have even a coincidental connection to his old nemesis fifty-four years after his time in Alcalá de Guadaíra.

There is one episode from this last Spanish period of Sidney's life about which the matador did not brag. In 1957 — perhaps trying to replace that old Chrysler station wagon — he was arrested for bringing an automobile into Spain, apparently without the proper papers or payment of import duties. This was a jailing offence under a Franco regime trying to clamp down on illegal trade and smuggling. According to Sidney's obituary in the *New York Times*, he served nine months of a twenty-three-month sentence, hard time for a man of fifty-four, and an obvious humiliation for the one-time Idol of Spain. (Sidney might have found jail time preferable to his job of the moment — managing a cafeteria at the U.S. Strategic Air Command headquarters in Morón de la Frontera — one of the few times in his life that the matador was reduced to working for wages.) The only consolation for Sidney was that as he faded from the public consciousness, this incident was not very newsworthy in the United States. It was not mentioned in contemporary articles about Sidney, such as *Time*'s 1959 piece on Sidney and Baron Clements, which appeared roughly a year after Sidney would have been released from prison.

The increasing number of aspiring American toreros in the 1950s demonstrates the enduring popularity of the *corrida* in this country. It is also indicative of a postwar American conceit that anything was possible for us in a world we had just tamed then claimed as our own. It was a time not unlike the 1920s, when Sidney as the can-do American first took on the Mexican bullfighting establishment. And it specifically was a testament to the example set by Sidney himself, proving that a Yanqui could beat the odds and achieve the highest rank. Then, there was the undeniable glamour of the thing, popularized somewhat by *Bullfighter from Brooklyn*, but more so by films. One of the better-known American bullfighters of this era was John Fulton Short. Short had been infected by the passion of the bulls, the *gusanillo*, when as a boy he saw Tyrone Power in *Blood and Sand*. Short was a Philadelphian, like Patrick Cunningham, and went on to fight bulls under the name "John Fulton." (Supposedly, Mexican promoters could not pronounce the name "Short.") His path was familiar and hard: training on Mexican ranches, performing well in *novilladas* in Spain beginning in 1958, struggling for decent bookings with the difficult Spanish impresarios, receiving his *alternativa* in Sevilla in 1963 but not confirming it in Madrid until 1967. Fulton always felt that despite these successes, his career was stifled by being an American, and that Yankee bullfighters would always be men without a country. Fulton was also highly regarded as an artist, opening a successful studio in Sevilla toward the end of his bullfighting life in a reverse of Sidney's career trajectory. Sidney could not miss the irony that the one aspirant of the 1950s who joined him as only the second American to confirm the *alternativa* in Madrid was not only a fellow artist, he was — according to many acquaintances — gay as well, and the one promising young American who had *not* trained under him at Alcalá de Guadaíra.

As he spent the decade shuttling back and forth between Mexico and Spain, promoting his students and keeping his name before the public, Sidney remained a presence, if only as a figure from the past. And there were people who, unlike some of those former students such as Cunningham and Tuck, remembered Sidney fondly. Tony Brand, a longtime resident of Sevilla, tells a story, which took place late in the 1950s, of an old man who sat in a bullfighters' café in that city. Perhaps the café was Los Corales on the Vía San

Jose a block off the Calle de Las Sierpes. Perhaps it was La Punta del Diamante on the corner of Constitution and Alemanes (now a Starbucks) across the street from the cathedral. Wherever it was, the man sat alone at his table in the quiet of the late afternoon. From his flamenco manner and his flat-brimmed sombrero *cordobés*, he was obviously a veteran of the taurine world. He smoked his thin cigar peacefully in the cool shadows until a young man came into the establishment and stood at the bar ordering a drink. The old man would not take his eyes off him, staring and then trying not to stare into the oblivious stranger's face, even as the barman brought another sherry to his table. The old man left the new glass untouched. The man at the bar, by his clothing, his manners, and his gestures was certainly a member of the profession as well, but obviously not a Spaniard. Like the old man, the stranger wore a sombrero *cordobés*, although perhaps not at so dangerous an angle. When his curiosity became more than he could bear, the old man discretely waved the barman over and asked him the identity of the seemingly familiar foreigner. Why that, said the barman, is the famous American matador. The old man nodded in confirmation as he pushed himself up from his table. He knew it—he just *knew* it. He crossed the room with tears in his eyes and stopped before the surprised young man, his open hands gesturing in amazement. "Ah, Seed-ney, Seed-ney, los años no pasan por ti!" (Roughly, "Sidney, the years have not touched you!") Indeed, they had not. The handsome young man at the bar was John Fulton.

20

Recuerdos

A SPARSE AFTERNOON CROWD gathered in the ballroom of Mexico City's Hotel Montejo. The place was known as a bullfighters' hangout, but the chatting audience arranging themselves in the rows of straight-backed chairs was a mixed bunch of non-bullfighting Americans and Mexicans, sportily dressed with the growing casualness of the early 1960s. Movement behind the velvet curtain at the edge of the stage caught the attention of the crowd, settling them. Then, over the ballroom's public address system, an odd-sounding trumpet blared a fanfare: "Da-da-da-dah-duh-da-duh, da-dahhh!" The crowd quieted. An overblown announcer's voice—more carny barker than concert hall—crackled through the speakers, "Ladies and gentlemen, presenting the famous American matador . . . Sidney Franklin!" The curtain opened revealing the man behind it. Alone, like the Mighty Oz, was the Kid from Brooklyn. There had been no trumpet, just a sixty-year-old guy blowing into his hand; no announcer, simply the man himself proclaiming his own fame. Unlike the Wizard, Sidney was pleased to step from behind the screen and expose his own deception, and was completely at ease in the corny spotlight he created as he literally tooted his own horn. He strode to the edge of the stage in a crisp shirt, ascot, and Basque beret and began a lecture on *toreo* with a self-absorbed intensity that a few in the audience actually found off-putting. Once again, Sidney had transformed himself, this time riding his celebrity into his sunset years. He for some time had been broadcasting English language commentary on Mexican bullfights, first on radio and then, by the late 1950s, on television. Those who heard them said he was a natural on-air personality — knowledgeable, accurate, and full of anecdotes and insights that only an experienced professional could provide. It made sense. For the English-speaking aficionado from Mexico City to Miami, or the uninitiated viewer watching the black-and-white action rebroadcast from a local TV station in Los Angeles between the Felix Chevrolet commercials, Sidney made the *corrida* both accessible and enjoyable while keeping his name before the public a full forty years since he began it all with Gaona.

So how, after all those years of self-promotion and reinvention, did Sidney Franklin stack up with the rest of the bullfighting world? How did the matadors of Spain and Mexico regard him? The reviews are mixed. He obviously had the friendship and respect of many, traveling in their circle, sharing their risks, indisputably part of a tight fraternity that no outsider — not even an Ernest Hemingway — could successfully penetrate. One was either a *torero* or one wasn't. Sidney Franklin was, and that bestowed a status that at times was all he had to cling to.

In Mexico after Sidney had taken the *alternativa* in 1945, there was a feeling among some younger fans that Sidney Franklin was more of a joke than a matador. (Unlike Spain, at least Sidney could get bookings in Mexico, although not usually of the first tier.) Part of this reaction to him was because his best years were a full generation in the past and current fans were not seeing the *torero* at his best, and part was simply the fact that he was neither Mexican nor Spanish. As John Fulton was finding out, the old notion that a non-Latin could never compete on the same level with those born to the culture persisted — just as it had with Sidney's dinner companions back in 1923. Among a faction of the Mexican bullfighting public, as an American, a Jew, and a rumored homosexual, Sidney would always be somewhat of a pretender. By the early 1950s even Hemingway concluded that any non-Spaniard or non-Mexican had little chance of acceptance. If one were good, he told Patrick Cunningham during their short meeting outside the Pamplona café, the crowds would not show up to see you outshine their countrymen. If one were not so good, they would only show up to watch you die. If the public was fickle, the taurine establishment was worse. As American aspirants who followed Sidney's path would also learn, opportunity was hard won. It was not unknown for the novice to have to finance his own appearance, including buying the bull — usually inferior, or worse, spoiled from previous use — who would be trying to kill him (or her) later in the afternoon. The pay, when offered at all, was sometimes insultingly low, a handful of pesos for risking one's life for the crowd. The Mexican bullfight weekly *El Redondel* was run by two critics, señors Bitar and Icaza, who were considered to be fair and, according to some, even kind. Their coverage of Sidney in those years was grudging with an almost deadpan nod to his bravery, but following the accepted line in Mexico by the 1940s that he lacked true artistry. Sidney's thick hide seemed to protect him from such judgments, whether from the press or the aficionados and matadors past and present whose hangouts he frequented. Of one fight, *El Redondel* praised his killing thrusts, but said that the overall performance was all that could be expected of a matador already past his prime. As with all opinions of Sidney in any era, his courage was always a given.

Ultimately, it was the judgment of the other matadors, not the critics, the crowd, or the impresarios, that mattered. While appearing with Sidney in the Tijuana bullring back in the 1940s, the other two matadors on the program, Luis Castro — "El Soldado" — and Andrés Blando, each more than a decade younger than Sid, were watching the American with the toupee as he prepared to enter the arena. In a moment of mischief not uncommon with death so near, El Soldado, the day's senior matador, told Blando that he would give him one thousand pesos — a fair amount of money in those days — if he would run over and rip the wig off Sidney's bald head. It would be a great joke but an even greater humiliation. Blando thought about this tempting image for a moment, but then decided against it. After all, the middle-aged Norteamericano was another pro. No matter what they thought of his activities outside of the ring, he was one of them.

Others were not so charitable. The fiercely proud Dominguín stated that Sidney had no status whatsoever among the bullfighters of Spain. But then of course all bullfighters worth the time to mention are fiercely proud and equally disdainful. Carlos Arruza joked in his autobiography that any matador, when asked to rate one's contemporaries, always put oneself at the top of the list as if this were the natural order of things and then began rating downward from there. Such a lack of humility was not only second nature, it seemed essential to survival in the profession. The truth was that Dominguín was using a slam at Sidney to get at Hemingway, who had taken up the cause of Dominguín's contemporary and brother-in-law, Antonio Ordóñez, during their rivalry — an exciting series of *mano a mano* during the 1959 season, which Hemingway subsequently turned into the book *The Dangerous Summer* after first covering them for *Life* magazine. Dominguín resented the Hemingway pose as supreme bullfight authority and felt that

he had inflated a series of sober performances between two professionals into a dangerous grudge match, which indeed those *corridas*
became. Hemingway had provoked Dominguín further by deni-
grating not only him, but worse, by making a disparaging remark
about the sainted Manolete as well. Dominguín was especially
touchy on the subject of Manolete, as many aficionados felt that
he had pushed the once-retired matador to take dangerous chances
late in his career that ended in his death in the Linares ring in 1947.
Hemingway had been attacked for the Manolete remark, among
other reasons, because he supposedly had never seen the man in
the bullring, and thus had no firsthand knowledge on which to
base his criticism. (Actually, Hemingway and his wife Mary had
traveled from Cuba to the Yucatan peninsula to catch the last Mexican *corrida* of Manolete's in Mérida, Mexico, in 1947 before one of
the frequent disputes between the Spanish and Mexican taurine
establishments cancelled further trans-Atlantic appearances for a
time.) For Dominguín to denigrate Sidney in retaliation against
Hemingway was to dismiss the accuracy and importance of *Death
in the Afternoon*, to question the judgment of its author and the
mystique surrounding him, and thus to belittle the whole Hemingway point of view as resting on the shaky foundations of Sidney Franklin's opinions. (Tomás Orts-Ramos had gently chastised
Hemingway on this last point in his contemporary review of *Death
in the Afternoon*.) Whether either Sidney or Hemingway wanted to
acknowledge it, the two remained linked because of that book and
their own dangerous summers that preceded the writing of it.

In remembering the life of Sidney Franklin there remains this
connection, this crosspollination in the stories told and written
by the two men that is impossible to escape. One example of
this intertwining is the Hemingway short story "The Mother of
a Queen," about a homosexual matador. Sources as diverse as bi-

ographer James Mellow and *aficionado práctico* Tony Brand support Hemingway's contention that the gay matador, Paco, was based on *torero* José Ortiz. Ortiz was born in Guadalajara, Mexico, in 1908 and was obviously known to Sidney. He is mentioned in *Bullfighter from Brooklyn* as a top young *novillero* whose friendship Sidney cultivates, supposedly to further his own career. He figures in a fanciful story about short-sheeting and other practical jokes played on Sidney when the two shared a room at the Xajay ranch during a grand *tienta*. As "The Mother of a Queen" came out in 1933 in the collection *Winner Take Nothing*, Sidney was certainly a source for gossip and anecdote about Ortiz as he and Hemingway had spent much time together in those few years following his 1930 goring. Still, to discuss the sexuality of another matador with Hemingway, especially one known to be a close friend, seems curious, a venture onto dangerous ground. Was Sidney testing his friend's reaction to the idea of a gay *torero*; was he indulging his friend's homophobia to appear straight and disdainful as well; was he just toying with someone too thick to see the truth about Sidney himself? Or was Hemingway, always a bit obsessed with such things as the nature and quality of one's manhood, drawing out information from a reluctant Sidney? The latter case would have forced Sidney to ask himself, "What does he know?" Sidney was of great help to Hemingway as he catalogued the bullfighters' vernacular in the glossary of *Death in the Afternoon*. One entry, however, seems to display Hemingway's own prejudices: the entry for *maricón*. His synonyms include such American slang as "nance" and "fag," and he states that of the more than forty matadors with whom he was acquainted, he knew of only two who would fit that description. He then proceeds to describe personal attributes of the two, which would have made their identities easily guessed by aficionados of the day. One — presumably Ortiz — is described as so extremely adept and precise with the cape as to be an "exterior decorator" of the ring, but miserly with money. One could guess at the identity of the other *maricón*, but the assumption can be made that it is not Sidney, as he was most likely the source of such information, and inclusion in such a negative glossary entry would seem a cruel jab at a close friend. Still, the description of the second homosexual matador as a man who "has a reputation for great valor and awkwardness and who has been unable to save a peseta" could certainly be applied to Sidney. Hemingway's assessment of Sidney fifty-five pages later as "very brave but very awkward," coupled with Sidney's ongoing financial slide, is a sharp horn hooking uncomfortably close to the heart. His assertion in the *maricón* entry that "there are many very, very funny Spanish fairy stories" might not seem so funny to one who is the butt of such humor. Can the identity of the second *maricón* be known for sure? Sometimes, all that is revealed when reading too closely between the lines is empty space after all.

The title of the story refers to the central incident where the narrator, the matador's exasperated friend Roger, tries to get the miserly *torero* Paco to pay for the permanent interment of his mother, already five years dead. When the matador ignores Roger's entreaties, spending his money on expensive suits of lights and "punks," the mother's body is disinterred by the cemetery and dumped on a local ash heap. (Mellow's speculation that Hemingway was exploring his troubled relationship with his own mother has nothing to do with Sidney or Ortiz, and perhaps nothing to do with "The Mother of a Queen" either.) He does speculate that Roger, gossipy on sexual matters, quarrelsome but always in the know, might have been inspired by Sidney. (Chatty gossip from Sidney about an unnamed woman's penchant for oral sex is recorded in *Death in the Afternoon*.) Mellow then muses that he might have been the model for Paco as well, noting Sidney's well-known love of expensive *trajes de luces* and the fact that the fictional Paco was so careless with the packing of his outfits that they were "spoiled by salt water" on the voyage back to Mexico from a season in Spain, an echo of Sidney's claim in *Bullfighter from Brooklyn* that his suitcases were covered in mold and his swords oxidized "beyond recognition" after his fantastic hurricane and shipwreck episode on a return voyage to Veracruz. Did Hemingway borrow from Sidney's tall tales in 1933, or nineteen years later did Sidney lift this telling detail from "The Mother of a Queen" for his own outlandish yarn? As all fiction is a blend of the observed and the imagined, it almost doesn't matter. What came first was the friendship. Beyond that, all lines between the two tend to blur. One could accuse Sidney Franklin of many things but poor packing of his beloved costumes would not be one of them. As with his discussion of Sidney, Ernest, and the whores on the Manzanares River, Mellow's analysis of "The Mother of a Queen" would certainly have taken on a different caste were he aware of Sidney's sexual orientation. And what of Ortiz, the model for Paco? According to Barnaby Conrad, he retired to become a respected raiser of fighting stock and occasional instructor of bullfighters on a Mexican *ganadería* following a career renowned for exquisite capework that supposedly, but perhaps not certainly, was the source of his nickname, "El Torero de Seda," the silken bullfighter.

A similar question arises in Sidney's tale as told to Conrad of Hemingway crossing the Sevilla street to punch out the "Nancy-boy." This also has an echo if not an origin in Hemingway's fiction. When Jake Barnes first sees Brett Ashley in *The Sun Also Rises*, she is surrounded by an entourage of young gay men. As they pour out of two taxis outside a *bal-musette*, Jake notices that they wear not jackets and ties as he and his men friends do, but instead are set apart by their choice of pullover jerseys or shirtsleeves. Jake notices the whiteness of their hands and that their wavy hair is freshly washed. The mere sight of them, their facial expressions and gestures, infuriates him.

> Somehow they always made me angry. I know they are supposed to be amusing, and you should be tolerant, but I wanted to swing on one, any one, anything to shatter that superior, simpering composure.

This passage helped solidify the image of Ernest Hemingway as the prototypical literary gay-basher for a generation of critics. It is worth repeating the words Sidney told Barnaby Conrad seventeen years later:

> We see a Nancy-boy walking along on the other sidewalk — a real hair-dyed, limp-wristed type, but just minding his business. "Watch this," says Ernie. He crosses the street and knocks the poor maricón down, hurts him, with no warning.

Literary chicken or egg? Even Sidney's wonderful phrase, "all the sexes," as in "all the sexes throw themselves at you" conjures a throwaway line Hemingway used in print at least once. In the introduction to the 1930 autobiography of a notorious Parisian girl-about-town, *Kiki's Memoirs*, Hemingway refers to "lady writers of all sexes." As with Sidney's use in the 1940s, the "all" clearly is meant to include *all* ranges of sexual experience within the gender, a specific if jokey reference to the homosexual. Perhaps this was simply a common usage of the day, original with neither man.

The long relationship of these two physically active men, Sidney Franklin and Ernest Hemingway, was at first held together by the muscle and bone of a strong friendship. Over the years as the muscle atrophied, first Sidney then Hemingway tended to claw irritably at the remaining sinew and cartilage that kept them connected. As Lillian Ross has said, other than those first few years, the friendship was always an unequal one between a great man and a lesser one.

After years of pulling his punches where Sidney was concerned, Hemingway finally hit back — rewriting the story himself to create some daylight between Sidney's past and his own legend. In interviews conducted both in Cuba and New York toward the end of his life when his health was poor and his spirits often down, he told writer and *Atlantic* editor Robert Manning of his annoyance with Sidney. This was prompted by a series of interviews and reminiscences with past acquaintances recorded for an NBC radio program on Hemingway and his world. To Manning, Hemingway contradicted Sidney's version of their shared past, claiming that he had never traveled with Sidney's entourage in Spain in the fall 1929. He called the assertion that he had once been on the road with Sid's *cuadrilla* "ballroom bananas," as if the hard-traveling picadors, *banderilleros*, and *mozos* were nothing more than a bunch of gaudy theatrical vagabonds. He was clearly uncomfortable with Sidney trading on their friendship, even if Sidney's remembrances happened to be true. Lillian Ross stated that by this time Hemingway resented Sidney's proprietary attitude toward him, acting as if he somehow "owned" Hemingway.

What also seemed to make him uncomfortable was the fact that he had been such pals — on the road in 1929, in the cafés and bullfights and Manzanares beaches of the early 1930s, in New York nightclubs in the middle of the decade, and at the Hotel Florida during the Spanish civil war — with a fellow who was later acknowledged to be homosexual. Hemingway may have been a beast to some, but he was a social beast, and he is on the record saying repeatedly what good company Sidney Franklin could be. He saw value and enjoyment in that comradeship. It may have been an unequal friendship, but a friendship it was. By the late 1940s or early 1950s Hemingway would have to have known what the rest of the bullfighting world, even the most casual fan, knew about Sidney. Had Hemingway known all along? Was his homophobic pose just that—only a pose? He may have put out the image of himself as the hunter, the warrior, the boxer, but he was only secondarily those things. He was not primarily a warrior; he was an artist. He did not have the soul of a boxer; he had the soul of a poet. We do not still read him because he had a good left hook. An insensitive palooka did not write that first paragraph of *A Farewell to Arms*, with all its painful offhand beauty, an artist did. Or write story after story brimming with emotion because he could convey emotion so clearly without ever needing to speak of it. Many thoughtful Hemingway biographers, such as Jeffrey Meyers, have thoroughly covered this ground of his image overtaking his art, and of the gruff pose used to hide the sensitive nature. So when it came to Sidney, perhaps old Ernie knew from the beginning and simply didn't care. Even before his maiden visit to Pamplona, Hemingway had traveled to Madrid in 1923 to see his first bullfight with two companions, one of whom was the openly bisexual Robert McAlmon. But then Hemingway was not yet famous and could have had no clue just how famous he would become. So, was Sidney an acceptable companion to a young artist while in the closet, and an embarrassment to an aging icon only once he stumbled out? Was Hemingway confident enough of himself and his judgments in the 1930s to have Sidney as a friend, but less so as his own doubts and demons overtook him by the 1950s? We can never really know.

Both in his writing and his life, Hemingway was a painstaking reviser. In the interviews with Manning, he downplayed the friendship and stressed instead his generosity to Sid, how he paid for one of his operations and gave him cash to keep his costumes out of hock when times were hard. To the old writer looking back, perhaps covering his tracks, the image he wanted to create for posterity was clear: Hemingway was the senior partner in the relationship, and the loyal friend, Sidney was not.

So we know why Hemingway matters, but why does Sidney? Why are we speaking of him more than three decades after his death, and almost eighty years after the peak of his career? He would certainly declare that he was worthy of such attention. But it is not because he was one of the twentieth century's great bullfighters. He was by most estimates very good for a very short time. Then he was much less effective for quite a long time. It is impossible to say what his career would have been like had he not turned his back on that bull in the Madrid spring of 1930, any more than one can say what sort of movie career James Dean would have experienced had he not driven his Porsche to Salinas; or what direction Elvis's music would have taken had he not been drafted into the army at the height of his fame. (Patrick Cunningham stated that Sidney alluded to the rectal goring as altering his "perspective" on sexual matters as well — a gruesome thing to contemplate.) We do not speak of Sidney simply because he was the first American bullfighter to take his *alternativa*, either. Harper Lee preceded him and was extremely well thought of by Rodolfo Gaona himself, despite only taking the *alternativa* in Mexico; and John Fulton was by some accounts a better matador, although such comparisons are as pointless as saying that Mohammed Ali was a better heavyweight than Jack Dempsey, or that Dempsey was better than Jack Johnson. Did Sidney really invent the modern,

low and slow *verónica* as he claimed in self-aggrandizing articles
he wrote for the magazine *Toros* in the late 1950s and early 1960s,
or did Cagancho and Francisco Vega de Los Reyes — "Gitanillo de
Triana" — precede him by half a decade in this style in the 1920s, as
Tony Brand pointed out in his written rebuttals? (Brand says that
Sidney's response to his contradiction was a humorous, "forgive
'em Father for they know not what they do.") These are arguments
best left to the aficionados and are perhaps too arcane for the rest
of us. (It is a fact that Sidney's career and ranking are still argued
by those same aficionados: just look at the 2002 history *Yankees
in the Afternoon*, by former *aficionado práctico* Lyn Sherwood. After
a chapter on bullfighting's influence on Hollywood, then one on
Harper Lee, Sidney gets chapter three all to himself with an account that purports to correct the "Hemingway" version. By the
late 1980s, Tony Brand and John Fulton began their own informal
investigation into the specifics of Sidney's career to set the record
straight in their own minds, scouring Spanish sources to deter-
mine just where and when and with whom Sidney appeared, and
what was said about those appearances. This book has benefited
greatly from their sweat and scholarship.)

What we are left with is Sidney Franklin the man in all his infuriating complexity. His capacity to make people smile was only
exceeded by his ability to piss people off. Sidney was a fascinating
person who lived many lives in a way that was indeed unbelievable, just as Hemingway wrote. It was the breadth of his experience that makes him matter, not only what he did, but with whom
he did it — and not just Hemingway, but John Dos Passos, Martha Gellhorn, Governor Tom Campbell, Constancia de La Mora,
Archibald MacLeish, Joris Ivens, Janet Flanner, Rita Hayworth,
Stephen Spender, Josephine Herbst, Dr. Norman Bethune, Errol
Flynn, Herbert Matthews, Barnaby Conrad, Charlie Chaplin, Lil-

lian Ross, Luis Quintanilla, Budd Boetticher, and the rest, legends big and small of the past century. Bullfighters have always traveled with a celebrity crowd, but Sidney's circle was, because of the Hemingway friendship, wider, more literary, and more political, and thus of more interest. His injuries pushed him to companions and situations he might not have experienced had his career not crashed so early. So had he been more successful as a matador, we might find him less interesting as a person. The goring taught him that there were more ways than one to shed the brave blood. It is his courage, spoken about by everyone from Hemingway to Boetticher to Cossío, that matters. And courage, coupled with his thick-hided perseverance, makes Sidney interesting and turns him into a true twentieth-century character. He grew up with that new century, and his life witnessed its promise and its violent excess. He fought bulls for thirty years after he should have quit, simply because bullfighting was not just what he did but how he had come to define himself, the mask that he had chosen to wear. He could no more safely turn his back on that identity than he could turn his back on another bull. Sidney's homosexuality was certainly an aspect of his complexity and probably a spur to his relentless bravado and sense of destiny, but again not its only cause. His secret life was just another worm that prowled through his soul, competing with that worm of *afición*, the *gusanillo* also eating away at him, keeping him going not just as a bullfighter but as a man. Attribute this to an unquenchable human spirit or to a nauseating lack of self-awareness, but Sidney Franklin never gave up on his grand vision of himself or indulged in self-pity when the reality did not always fit that vision. In the end it was a matter of noblesse oblige after all.

21

Sol y Sombra

SIDNEY FRANKLIN DIED MONDAY, April 26, 1976, a few months before his seventy-third birthday, in the Manhattan nursing home where he had been living for seven years. He had been suffering through health problems since the Madrid goring at the age of twenty-six, living on borrowed time for forty-six years. That he lasted this long is a testament to his stubborn refusal to settle for anything less than a full life as a bullfighter and nothing but a bullfighter. To be gored in Mexico as late as 1959 at the age of almost fifty-six was proof that the passion did not fade. Tossed by the bull, Sid may have gone one way and his toupee another, but he was still out there on the sand with students, such as Baron Clements, who were a full generation younger. Of course many matadors over the decades, such as the great gypsy Cagancho, have refused to cut the pigtail, performing well into middle age, either for fun, for money, or simply because they cannot let go of either the spotlight or the excitement — the life — of the bulls. The worm keeps eating away and will not be denied. Carlos Arruza supposedly promised his wife that at a given point in his life he would never set foot in a *plaza de toros* again. Bullfight legend — and the truth — was that he kept his promise by training to become a *rejoneador*, letting his horse do the stepping into the ring with Carlos on its back. He became an accomplished *rejoneador* because, although he wanted to be true to his wife's wishes, he could not give up the life he had lived since he was a child. It must be said that Arruza then often cheated a bit on the promise by stepping down from his horse at the crowd's pleading to fight the bull on foot. (He did eventually die a violent death, but on a rural highway, not in a bullring.) That passion, so foreign to those of us from other cultures, was shared by Sidney, and as an outsider in so many ways, it was accentuated by his need to always prove that in this world if no other he truly belonged.

Bullfighting still had a strong pull for Americans when Sidney's life ended. In the 1960s a new generation of celebrities could be seen if not in Spain at least at the *barrera* seats of the Tijuana bullrings. Although these new fans may have tended more to young television stars lacking the cachet of an Orson Welles, an Ava Gardner, or a Rita Hayworth, their *afición* was just as great as they watched their own contemporaries, such as Californians Robert Ryan, Jeff Ramsey, and teenage phenomenon Walter de la Brosse.

Now, a full generation after that, bullfighting still has a new crop of passionate adherents following *toreros* who would be stars in any age, such as matador Enrique Ponce or *rejoneador* Pablo Hermoso de Mendoza. The ready acceptance of the culture — that rakish pose of *un tipo flamenco*, the knowledge of the bulls, that *afición* shared by an entire nation — is, however, not so assured. Spain has undergone its own ritual of transformation by finally modernizing, diversifying, and becoming more integrated into the new Europe. In turn, the European Parliament in 2007 passed a resolution calling on Spain to end bullfighting altogether as the practice was becoming more and more controversial. There is more at work here than just the growing demand for animal rights demonstrated by protestors who gather outside the bullrings. The city government of Barcelona, although still possessing active *plazas de toros*, in 2004 took an official position formally condemning bullfighting, a thing that would have seemed both bizarre and tragic in 1930. (But perhaps not surprising to aficionados from Andalucía, who, as Barnaby Conrad observed, always felt there was *something* about Barcelona: too industrious, too Catalán, not Spanish or flamenco enough for their taste.) Then, in 2007, the state-run Televisón Española dropped live coverage of bullfights—which it had been providing to Spaniards since its inception in 1948—from all its channels, relegating taped highlights of the national pastime to late night. The stated reason was to protect children from violence on television in the late afternoon and early evening hours—just the time of day when the first bull runs through the *toril* gate. Pay television services and regionally owned stations still carried live *corridas*, but the move was part of a larger trend that was upsetting to aficionados. In a mini-echo of the civil war, the decision to end live broadcasts came from a socialist government and was fought by the conservative opposition, who felt that traditional Spanish values and national identity were under siege. Although bullfight promoters claimed that the year before the ban attendance had reached sixty-five million fans, their audience is growing older and older, and few attend the bullfights with regularity as they did in the many golden ages of the twentieth century. As with baseball in this country, the price of tickets has increased substantially just as the public's available free time to spend in long afternoon pursuits has decreased. Instead of matadors, whose disdainful pose seemed hopelessly retro, young Spaniards became more seduced by soccer icons and pop stars.

The landscape itself changed. Some breeding ranches are now crowded by subdivisions. The concrete bullring of Alcalá de Guadaíra has been torn down, the land covered with modest apartments and condos. Sidney's ramshackle wooden arena on the plateau where Porter Tuck and Patrick Cunningham once practiced with the maestro has been converted into a restaurant. But the Spanish art, like Sidney, would not be kept down for long. Just as the death of Joselito in 1920 seemed to signal the end of the entire pastime ("Joselito is dead, long live football," proclaimed a huge sign in Sevilla), it bounced back almost immediately as Belmonte refused to stay retired. Then Niño de la Palma, Cagancho, Manolete, Arruza, Dominguín, and Ordóñez began packing in the crowds over the next several decades. So it was in 2007. After a five-year retirement, beloved matador José Tomás staged a comeback at age thirty-one, and the country once again went bullfight crazy. Leftist newspapers that had dropped coverage of *corridas* printed page after page on the return of Tomás, a product of the town of Galapagar, whose calm reserve and close work with the horns reminded old timers of Manolete himself. Tomás's debut performance in the spring of 2007 filled the arena in indifferent old Barcelona. For his last appearance of the season — also in Barcelona — Televisón Española ignored its own ban and gave aficionados a live satellite hookup of the event.

As both a bullfighter and a broadcaster, Sidney found that the world had changed greatly by the time of his death. He was by then an artifact of another age — the roaring twenties in New York, post-revolutionary Mexico, and between-the-wars Europe as he lived his three lives. The headlines of the edition of the *New York Times* that carried his obituary proclaimed Reagan's victory over Ford in the 1976 Texas presidential primary, and something that might have been of more interest to Sidney, Angel Cordero riding Bold Forbes to a win in the Kentucky Derby the day before, beating Honest Pleasure by over a length. The obituary of course quotes "his good friend Ernest Hemingway" from the pages of *Death in the Afternoon*, joining the two once again in the public mind as friends forever.

The Brooklyn of Sidney's past continues to change with new waves of immigration: African Americans from the South before and during World War II, Puerto Ricans after the war, non-Jewish Russians after the cold war, and even Vietnamese and Laotians among many others. Brooklyn's loss of the Dodgers and Ebbets Field has been told many times. The *Brooklyn Eagle*, which printed stories of their local bullfighting boy, stopped publication in 1955, was resurrected in 1960, then closed for good in 1963. The Frumpkin's house on Jackson Place however still stands. It is well kept, renovated, and modernized, but with its familiar front windows and narrow staircase as they once were, it is still a home that Sidney would recognize from his boyhood, although the smells drifting out from the kitchen would tend more toward gourmet coffee than boiled cabbage.

Sidney suffered a stroke that immobilized his right side and robbed him of the two things he had counted on his whole life: his nimble feet and the quick tongue that Hemingway had once counted on to talk them both out of trouble. His surviving siblings and their children had set him up in the Village Nursing Home, at 607 Hudson Street, where he waited out his days. According to his niece Eve Frumkin, there was no longtime companion in evidence, no man on whom he could lean to help him face the end without shame or fear of reproach. His was a different era, and knowing Sidney, he was probably fine with relying on only a loving, supportive family, a few old friends, and the occasional fans — those aficionados who sought him out and came to visit although the maestro could no longer speak. So Sidney went out of this life as he had gone through it: independent but not alone, following his own instincts, taking his own counsel. It had been a decade and a half since Hemingway's suicide in Idaho.

Toward the end Barnaby Conrad came to visit accompanied by Sidney's brother Milton, the accountant. By this time Sidney and Conrad had been friends for thirty-two years. To this day Conrad has an inscribed photo of a somewhat stocky, tentative-looking Sidney, taken about the time of his *alternativa*, hanging on the wall of his lovely beachfront home south of Santa Barbara. When a visitor asked Conrad about bullfighters he had known, he directed the visitor to a matador's *capote* displayed in the entryway of the house, referring to it as a "piece of the true cross." Stenciled across the yellow ducking in faded block letters was the name Sidney Franklin. Covering the back and shoulders of the cape were autographs of the great names of twentieth-century bullfighting: Juan Belmonte, Manolete, Conchita Cintrón, Carlos Arruza, and many more. For an aficionado this was truly a sacred garment. The visitor expressed amazement that Sidney had parted with this remarkable artifact, even to give it to such a valued friend. At this Conrad only smiled indulgently and said, "Sidney never *gave* anybody anything."

When Conrad and Milton Frumpkin entered Sidney's sixth-floor room, he was propped in his wheelchair and cleaned up for visitors, the great freckled left hand that had once gripped that cape now holding on to the wheel rim, as always, ready for the next move, even as his age-spotted head tilted a bit. His immobile right arm lay across his chest, the hand stuffed into the front of his shirt to keep it from dangling uselessly. It could have been a sad scene — old folks in room after room, sitting in their own pee, staring at the linoleum, waiting to die, whole lifetimes of action and experience and anguish locked in their silent heads. Instead, Sidney retained some of the jaunty optimism that had seen him through so many hard times. When he saw Milt and Barney, he brightened up. On his wall was a calendar with color photographs of bullfighting scenes in Sevilla. Sidney grinned a lopsided grin, his mouth sagging to one side from the stroke, pointed to Conrad and then to himself and finally to the calendar, rolling his finger over to indicate the passing of months, the turning of the page. From his wheelchair he then pantomimed a perfect *verónica*, as he had performed the *verónica* so beautifully so many times in the past, as if to say "you and me, next summer at the bullfights in Sevilla." He would not live to see that summer, but even then, for Sidney Franklin, the matador's life was everything.

Acknowledgments and Afterthoughts

AS ANY AFICIONADO CAN TELL, I am no aficionado and do not pretend otherwise. At least I was not one when I began this. But after years of digging out the facts and lies and simple truths of Sidney Franklin's life, I at least understand that passion, that *afición*, and have a hint of its source. But this is not a book about bullfighting. It is a book about a bullfighter who was, in so many ways, the man apart—el único matador.

In the beginning my only knowledge of the life had come from watching my new friend Budd Boetticher in an arena on Riverside Drive in Burbank, California, train his Lusitano stallion, Piropo, for the *rejoneo*. As a young aspiring horseman myself (a city boy who had worked on ranches and pack stations through high school and college), Budd's skill and enthusiasm in this pursuit made sense to me, and stuck with me over the years. Just as quickly as I got to know this legendary old director, Budd moved south, and I did not see him again for over two decades—shortly before his death. But I took from him this oblique window into bullfighting, which, if nothing else, gave me a few minutes of useless cocktail party knowledge. That was just enough to convince a film producer to ask me to help research a picture pitch on Sidney Franklin's life — a man about whom I knew nothing but his name. The film project quickly died, but my interest did not. There was much I had learned about Sidney that I had not found in any book — most especially his. If I could not write a script for my producer friend, then maybe I could write an article, maybe even a book of my own. The *gusanillo* had begun to do its work.

As I wrote this, there were moments when I truly felt I understood the world of *los toros*. Then there were times I felt like a Laplander trying explain the infield fly rule. As much of the world of the bulls centers around the life of the ranch — fine cattle and blooded horses and the people who raise them — I instantly felt at home. Stockmen, from Mongolia to Merced, from Andalucía to Buenos Aires to Bridgeport, speak the same language and live — at one level — similar lives. The first four years of a bull's existence then were a part of my own experience. It was those last twenty minutes in the ring that took some psychic explaining.

I could not have written this book without Barnaby Conrad and Tony Brand. Period. Barnaby is a most gracious host — generous with his time, his knowledge, his perspective, his *afición*, and his remarkable stories of just about anyone who mattered in the twentieth century. He is a man of impeccable taste and unfailing kindness. What Hemingway said of Barnaby's friend Sidney in *Death in the Afternoon* I think applies much more to Barnaby: "He is a charming companion, one of the best story tellers I have ever heard, [and] has enormous and omnivorous curiosity about everything." But one needn't take my word for it. I don't think Bernabé ever made a friend he did not keep.

One such friend is Tony Brand, who met Barnaby when he was still in high school, and whom I met through Barnaby. Tony was invaluable in filling in those spaces later in Sidney's life: the lecturing, the self-serving articles, the wild stories. Tony not only fought bulls as an *aficionado práctico* and played flamenco guitar professionally but he is also a fine scholar who has worked with Professor Miriam Mandel on such meticulously researched works as Hemingway's Death in the Afternoon: *The Complete Annotations*, and Hemingway's The Dangerous Summer: *The Complete Annotations*, and more. After a few phone calls over the years — Tony lives much of the year in Sevilla — I finally met him in person the summer of 2007 when the book was almost written. Or so I thought. After every long lunch at Jerry's Deli on Ventura Boulevard, or after every long and funny phone call, I would have to open up the manuscript and add another line, another scene, another chapter. Or, as we walked out to the parking lot, Tony would pop open his trunk and unroll not just any *cartel*, but the very one announcing Sidney's *alternativa*. He became like a long lost uncle — tío Tony — who although was raised in LA, keeps a Spaniard's body language, and hours. It was not until the end of the process that he casually let slip that two decades before, he and matador John Fulton had methodically researched Sidney's career in Spanish libraries and archives. Everything Tony had, he shared.

Through Tony I met online the renowned Hemingway scholar Miriam Mandel of the English Department of Tel Aviv University, who constantly pointed me in the right direction, kept me from fundamental goofs, and encouraged me with her knowledge and enthusiasm. Part of the Conrad-Brand-Mandel nexus is the wonderful Valerie Hemingway, the author's last secretary and future daughter-in-law, who was always available by phone or e-mail, always encouraging, and whose memoir, *Running with the Bulls*, gave a true look at the artist's last years. Another friend of Barnaby's, Sidney's former student Patrick Cunningham, gave immediacy to

Sidney's darker years while remaining a great dinner companion (although I still need to ask him about the time he supposedly decked Brando on the set of *Mutiny on the Bounty*.)

This project also introduced me to a man who had been president of *Los Aficionados de Los Angeles*, Mariusz Olbrychowsky, who generously took me to my first bullfight (featuring the fine Spanish *rejoneador* Pablo Hermoso de Mendoza), who gave me information from the technical to the mundane (such as what the market neighborhoods of Mexico City smell like at 3 a.m.), and who remains a friend and collaborator on films and documentaries. As with the others, Mariusz is a man of great knowledge and taste because he possesses great curiosity. (I told him that as a boy he must have read Hemingway in the original Polish.)

Then there was former *novillero* Dr. Walter de la Brosse, whom I had known for years as a horseshow judge before learning that he had been a teenage sensation in the bullring. Walter told me where in my own Los Angeles, just a few miles from my home, I could find aspiring matadors practicing their capework on a Saturday morning, just as Sidney had done those mornings at Nativitas almost ninety years earlier.

Finally, I was fortunate to speak and correspond several times with the legendary Lillian Ross who cut her journalistic teeth on the flamboyant Sid, and who generously shared many insights, both funny and true.

The people of this strange interconnected bullfighting world are, like *Bos taurus ibericus*, their own species — open, confident, generous to strangers, and cheerfully brave. And they all know each other. Their *afición* is not just for the bulls, or for the life of the bulls, but for life itself. In the fall of 2007, Walter asked if I wanted to accompany him and a loose group of two dozen or so friends to a weekend of *corridas* in Tijuana. He said that, along with some actor pals of his, I would probably see people I knew such as Barnaby and Mary Conrad. I asked if there were still seats available for my wife and myself. Speaking as the matador he once was, Walter said, "there's always room at the top."

In addition to the people mentioned above, I would like to thank Paul Quintanilla for permission to use his father Luis's wonderful portrait of Sidney in this work, and for his enthusiasm for this resurrection of the lost painting; my old mountain climbing friend Pete Mann, who, as a Dartmouth boy on holiday, saw Sidney perform in Mexico many times and told me what the fans of that era thought; the writer Tom Fuchs, for his stories of his father Daniel's boyhood in Brooklyn and for his unstinting encouragement through the long years of putting this together; film producer Jenny Lew Tugend, who first introduced me to Sidney's life; my boyhood friend Oliver Ocskay for clarifying the stories of his mother, Elsa Jaeger Ocskay, and her life in Spain in the 1930s; Melodee Spevack for her cultural and linguistic critique of the dialects and subdialects of her native Brooklyn; and the late Robert Stack for graciously taking a few minutes to talk to a stranger about his time with Sidney.

I also would like to acknowledge the hard work and cooperation of Susan Wrynn, James Hill, Laurie Austin, and Morgan Miller of the John Fitzgerald Kennedy Library; Holly Jones and Mike Letourneau of AP Wide World Photos; Jamie Montalvo of Corbis; and the staff of the main branch of the Los Angeles Public Library, and their George B. Smith Biblioteca Taurina.

I am indebted to the Hemingway biographers: Carlos Baker, Jeffrey Meyers, Michael Reynolds, Bernice Kert, James Mellow, Peter Griffin, Denis Brian, and Alice Sokoloff; the Gellhorn biographers Caroline Moorehead and Carl Rollyson; and Dos Passos chronicler Stephen Koch. The Hemingway part of Sidney's story lay scattered through their pages like bits of broken mirror waiting only for me to assemble the fragmented image, flaws and all. I am grateful for their scholarship and insights, on which I gladly relied.

At the University of Nebraska Press I would like to thank my editors, Rob Taylor and Katie Neubauer, for their hard work and patience (it's only one more photo!), and to thank my great copy editor, Sarah Steinke. In Los Angeles, thanks to my Spanish translator Mary McFadden-Rossetto. And finally, my affection and gratitude to my agent and lawyer at Kaye & Mills, the incomparable Jessica Kaye for never giving up, for critiquing and cajoling, and for making all this happen.

Lastly to my family: my patient wife, Heidi, and my wonderful and wild children, Bonnie and Robert, who kept the faith.

Budd Boetticher, Bob Stack, Eve Frumkin, and Elsa Ocskay are gone, but my gratitude, like the *gusanillo*, remains.

NOTES

Bullfighting terms and usages, such as those for *verónica, monos-abio, quite, rebolera, padrino,* and *querencia,* are taken from Barnaby Conrad, *Encyclopedia of Bullfighting* (Houghton Mifflin, 1961).

Introduction: *The Alternative*

xvii **It was July 18**—José María de Cossío, *Los Toros,* tomo IV, p. 454. The date of Sidney's *alternativa,* who his fellow matadors were, the breeder and name and color of the bull are all provided in this definitive (but not error-free) Madrid encyclopedia of bullfighting.

xx **Some old aficionados say**—Tony Brand, in discussion with author, March 5, 2001. Tony mentioned this several times during our many conversations over the years. On September 11, 2007, he provided me with the *cartel* (poster) for this 1945 bullfight, which confirmed that it was a performance for the "Youth Front" on the anniversary of Franco's start of the civil war.

xx **Others insist — incorrectly**—Barnaby Conrad, in discussion with author, January 26, 2001. During a telephone conversation on December 31, 2007, he stated that he might have been thinking of Sidney's 1952 *corrida* in Tangier when his bulls did indeed leave the ring alive.

xxi **almost all mainstream biographies**—Meyers, *Hemingway: A Biography,* p. 231. In 1985 Meyers is the first, to my knowledge, to mention in a Hemingway biography that Sidney was a homosexual, and he cites his source as Barnaby Conrad from the taurine community where details of Sidney's personal life were well known.

xxi **the mincing gentry**—Ernest Hemingway, *Death in the Afternoon,* p. 205.

xxiv **One was a genius**—Lillian Ross, in discussion with author, April 10, 2003.

xxv **There are still those of a certain age**—Pete Mann, in discussion with author, August 1, 2007.

1. The Bull

3 **one of nine surviving children**—Ross, *Lillian Ross: Reporting*, pp. 167, 168.

3 **By the time the Frumpkin's fifth child**—Eve Frumkin, in discussion with author, April 5, 2001.

4 **She sits there like a little mouse**—Brian, *The True Gen*, p. 204.

5 **Of course it's all bullshit**—Conrad, in discussion with author, February 15, 2001.

6 **Sidney asserts that it was he**—Franklin, *Bullfighter from Brooklyn*, p. 188.

6 **Sidney likewise casts himself**—Franklin, *Bullfighter from Brooklyn*, pp. 81–86.

6 **Sidney was a small child**—Ross, *Lillian Ross*, pp. 168–69. Citation includes the claims that his sister Bella, a high school teacher, tried out educational theories on him; that his brother Sam, a physician, let him cut up cadavers as a child; his brothers' professions; the Freudian implications of bullfighting within his family; and Sidney's description of boyhood theatrics.

7 **Sidney's niece Eve Frumkin**—Frumkin, in discussion with author, April 5, 2001.

7 **Sidney claimed that his own father**—Ross, *Lillian Ross*, p. 168.

7 **She described one**—Frumkin, in discussion with author, April 5, 2001.

9 **Still there was nothing swishy**—Conrad, in discussion with author, January 26, 2001.

10 **For example, locals said**—Melodee Spevack (Brooklyn native and voiceover professional specializing in dialects), in discussion with author, February 17, 2008.

10 **Williamsburg was home to**—Tom Fuchs, in discussion with author, November 15, 2007.

13 **So he cleaned out his bank account**—Ross, *Lillian Ross*, p. 172; Franklin, *Bullfighter from Brooklyn*, p. 5.

2. Que Viva Mexico

14 **I am the sun, moon and stars**—Ross, *Lillian Ross*, p. 160.

14 **There is a story**—Innes, *The Conquistadors*, p. 73.

15 **Sidney had met a young man**—Franklin, *Bullfighter from Brooklyn*, p. 5.

16 **Now the locomotive chugged**—Dunn, *The Crimson Jester: Zapata of Mexico*, period Mexican National Railway map inside cover.

18 **He took a cab**—Franklin, *Bullfighter from Brooklyn*, p. 6.

18 **the smell of the previous day's vegetables**—Mariusz Olbrychowsky, in discussion with author, May 8, 2006.

18 **He secured a storefront studio**—Franklin, *Bullfighter from Brooklyn*, pp. 6–7. Citation includes Sidney's description of setting up shop, teasing shoeshine boys, eating at El Gallo de Oro, motoring to the countryside, and printing his first bullfight poster.

19 **European society bloods**—Ross, *Lillian Ross*, p. 173.

20 **it's a matter of noblesse oblige**—Ross, *Lillian Ross*, p. 146.

21 **strikingly lithe and graceful**—Franklin, *Bullfighter from Brooklyn*, p. 2.

21 **There are aficionados who dispute this**—Tony Brand's personal research indicates no such *corrida* for the year of 1922.

3. The Wisdom of the Aztec

24 **he stuck his foot in it**—Ross, *Lillian Ross*, p. 173; Franklin, *Bullfighter from Brooklyn*, pp. 9–10. Sidney tells two versions of this dinner conversation. To Ross he was dining with society bloods at the Fénix; in his autobiography he was with his newspaper and theatrical crowd at an unnamed location.

24 **Americans have more guts**—Franklin, *Bullfighter from Brooklyn*, p. 9.

25 **the Great Indian was superstitious**—Ross, *Lillian Ross*, p. 173;

Franklin, *Bullfighter from Brooklyn*, p. 11. The detail of the stationary with the cats' heads is repeated in both.

25 **They teased him with lurid stories**—Franklin, *Bullfighter from Brooklyn*, p. 12.

29 **The well-known Xajay ranch**—Cossío confirms the name of the Xajay owner as Guerrero in *Los Toros*, tomo III, s.v. "Francklin [*sic*], Sidney," p. 288.

31 **I looked like a Christmas tree**—Ross, *Lillian Ross*, p. 175.

32 **a late-morning preliminary exhibition on September 30, 1923**—Franklin, *Bullfighter from Brooklyn*, p. 29. Sidney told Lillian Ross the date was September 19.

4. El Niño de la Synagoga

40 **Sidney shut the poster shop down**—Franklin, *Bullfighter from Brooklyn*, p. 56.

40 **General Adolfo de La Huerta**—Franklin, *Bullfighter from Brooklyn*, p. 45.

41 **he was invited by well-known matador Luis Freg**—Franklin, *Bullfighter from Brooklyn*, p. 54. Citation includes his description of fights in Chihuahua and Tampico.

41 **he worked at a large slaughterhouse**—Franklin, *Bullfighter from Brooklyn*, p. 48.

42 **something called a Mexican Breakfast**—Wentworth and Flexner, *The Pocket Dictionary of American Slang*, p. 217.

43 **It was finally a regional impresario**—Franklin, *Bullfighter from Brooklyn*, p. 57.

43 **matadors with colorful names**—Brand, "Corridas of Sidney Franklin," p. 2.

43 **he was befriended by a fabulously wealthy expatriate American stranger**—Franklin, *Bullfighter from Brooklyn*, pp. 69–75. This friendship began three of the most fanciful chapters of Sidney's autobiography: fights, arrests, handsome male companions, jungle expeditions, sex with Indian maidens, shipwreck, and even some bullfighting.

44 **For the first time, Sidney asked for**—Ross, *Lillian Ross*, p. 177.

44 **A photo of Sid**—Ross, *Lillian Ross*, p. 177.

45 **Officer Frumpkin demanded that his son quit**—Ross, *Lillian Ross*, p. 177.

45 **Despite Sidney's claims**—Brand, "Corridas of Sidney Franklin," p. 2.

45 **considered the first American matador**—Conrad, *Encyclopedia of Bullfighting*, p. 131.

5. Thanks, Ma

48 **Sidney caught the ss *Monterrey***—Franklin, *Bullfighter from Brooklyn*, p. 119.

48 **His reception in Brooklyn**—Frumkin, in discussion with author, April 5, 2001.

49 **It was just hello and goodbye with him**—Ross, *Lillian Ross*, p. 178.

49 **the incessant whine of the accented English**—Franklin, *Bullfighter from Brooklyn*, p. 120.

49 **Her auburn hair had turned gray**—Franklin, *Bullfighter from Brooklyn*, p. 120.

49 **Lubba staked Sidney to a five-thousand-dollar loan**—Franklin, *Bullfighter from Brooklyn*, p. 122.

50 **In February he boarded the liner *Rochambeau***—Franklin, *Bullfighter from Brooklyn*, p. 123.

50 **They are their own species**—Cossío, *Los Toros*, tomo I, pp. 133–40.

51 **The councils of Toledo**—*Enclyclopaedia Britannica Online*, s.v. "councils of Toledo," http://www.britannica.com/EBchecked/topic/598567/councils-of-toledo (accessed February 14, 2007).

51 **The Hellenistic mystery cult of the god Mithras**—*Encyclopaedia Britannica Online*, s.v. "Mithra," http://www.Britannica.com/EBchecked/topic/253490/mithra (accessed February 14, 2007).

51 **the earliest recorded epic**—Mason, *Gilgamesh*, p. 45.

52 **The invaders brought two essentials**—Beatie, *Saddles*, p. 31.

53 **Legend says emperor Shih Huang Ti of the Ch'in (Qin) Dynasty**—Dupuy and Dupuy, *The Encyclopedia of Military History*, p. 79.

53 **the *estribo*, or stirrup board**—Conrad, *Encyclopedia of Bullfighting*, p. 91.

54 **this became a sport of the new Moslem ruling class**—Conrad, *La Fiesta Brava*, p. 15.

54 **Spanish legend has the great warrior El Cid**—Conrad, *La Fiesta Brava*, p. 15.

54 **in Spain, bullfighting became entwined with saints' days**—Marks, *To The Bullfight*, pp. 136–40.

55 **Aficionados speculate that the poorer towns with plazas of dirt**—Olbrychowsky, in discussion with author, May 8, 2006.

56 **a family of carpenters from Ronda**—Conrad, *La Fiesta Brava*, p. 16.

6. Yanqui Flamenco

60 **the Espinosa brothers, Juan and Fermín**—Franklin, *Bullfighter from Brooklyn*, p. 123.

60 **he soon was spending his mornings with fellow Mexican *toreros***—Ross, *Lillian Ross*, p. 178.

61 **the country's top promoter don Eduardo Pagés**—Franklin, *Bullfighter from Brooklyn*, pp. 127–28.

62 **at that time no American had ever set foot in a Spanish ring**—Cossío, *Los Toros*, tomo III, p. 289.

62 **His name was F. Ross Dennison**—Ross, *Lillian Ross*, p. 179; Franklin, *Bullfighter from Brooklyn*, p. 133. For a change, both Ross and Sidney's accounts are quite similar regarding Dennison's pivotal role in securing Sidney's all important first fight in Spain, and their subsequent celebrations.

62 **Ross came to the rescue**—Ross, *Lillian Ross*, p. 179.

63 **as Mexican matador Carlos Arruza would claim**—Aruzza, *My Life as a Matador*, p. 148.

63 **the bullfighter's chapel under the stands**—Franklin, *Bullfighter from Brooklyn*, p. 142. Sidney explained to Conrad why he, a Jewish bullfighter, could often be seen wearing a cross around his neck. "The bulls are Catholic." Conrad, in discussion with author, September 27, 2008.

64 **My decision is history**—Ross, *Lillian Ross*, p. 179.

64 **mimicking the distinctive stride**—Franklin, *Bullfighter from Brooklyn*, p. 142.

64 **fitted as though painted on me**—Franklin, *Bullfighter from Brooklyn*, 142.

64 **bulls from the ranch of don José Rufino Moreno Santamaría**—Cossío, *Los Toros*, tomo IV, p. 454. Citation includes the particulars of Sidney's first Spanish *corrida*, including participating matadors.

66 ***La Union* of Sevilla said that Sidney was a born bullfighter**—Ross, *Lillian Ross*, p. 144.

66 **Sidney claims that strangers even stripped naked and joined him**—Conrad, letter to author, September 26, 2008.

66 **All the sexes throw themselves at you**—Ross, *Lillian Ross*, p. 158.

67 **I wondered as I ate the magnificent banquet**—Franklin, *Bullfighter from Brooklyn*, p. 153.

67 **His debut performance in the Spanish capitol**—Cossío, *Los Toros*, tomo IV, p. 454.

67 **Hemingway wrote that Sidney**—Hemingway, *Death in the Afternoon*, p. 474.

68 **Barnaby Conrad wrote that the Sevilla headlines**—Conrad, letter to author, September 26, 2008.

68 **Sidney performed well in his Madrid debut**—Cossío, *Los Toros*, tomo III, p. 289.

68 **is a term of encomium**—Conrad, *Encyclopedia of Bullfighting*, p. 98.

7. Death in the Afternoon — with Drinks and Dinner to Follow

70 **his regular entourage included, among others, a Spanish duke**—Franklin, *Bullfighter from Brooklyn*, p. 169.

70 **Sidney noticed a big American in rumpled tweeds and bedroom slippers**—Ross, *Lillian Ross*, p. 182; Franklin, *Bullfighter from Brooklyn*, pp. 170–77. The meeting of Sidney and Hemingway differs depending on who is doing the telling.

72 **Sidney claimed to read only the *Saturday Evening Post***—Hemingway, *Death in the Afternoon*, p. 475.

72 **One telling detail of Sidney's account**—Mellow, *Hemingway: A Life without Consequences*, p. 389.

72 **The long afternoons in the scalding heat**—Reynolds, *Hemingway: The 1930s*, p. 24.

73 **according to several Hemingway biographers, bisexual**—Brian, *The True Gen*, p. 190.

74 **they would simply share his double bed**—Franklin, *Bullfighter from Brooklyn*, p. 178.

74 **Sidney always took a long time to dress in the morning**—Ross, *Lillian Ross*, p. 149.

74 **I always had to wait for him**—Ross, *Lillian Ross*, p. 149.

75 **This direction from him was the cause**—Franklin, *Bullfighter from Brooklyn*, p. 179.

75 **He'd just go in and wham!**—Ross, *Lillian Ross*, p. 183.

75 **Sidney has no grace because he has a terrific behind**—Ross, *Lillian Ross*, p. 147.

75 **Hemingway and Pauline saw Sidney fight in Madrid**—Kert, *The Hemingway Women*, p. 222.

75 **by September 12 the Hemingways were driving**—Reynolds, *Hemingway: An Annotated Chronology*, p. 58.

76 **Franklin is brave with a cold, serene and intelligent valor**—Hemingway, *Death in the Afternoon*, p. 473.

76 **He correctly points out**—Hemingway, *Death in the Afternoon*, p. 199.

76 **I just figured, Hell**—Ross, *Lillian Ross*, p. 164.

77 **he is a charming companion**—Hemingway, *Death in the Afternoon*, p. 475.

77 **Sidney's cousin, critic Clifton Fadiman**—Kert, *The Hemingway Women*, p. 223.

77 **Fadiman would soon perceptively codify**—Reynolds, *Hemingway: The 1930s*, p. 118.

77 **the unhappy warrior that men would like to be**—Fadiman, "Ernest Hemingway," *Nation*, January 18, 1933, pp. 63-64.

78 **Arruza, had the respect not to**—Conrad, foreword to Arruza, *My Life as a Matador*, p. 24.

78 **Cossío's *Los Toros* puts Sidney's 1929 total at 14**—Cossío, *Los Toros*, tomo IV, p. 454.

78 **The Spanish press at the time**—Cossío, *Los Toros*, tomo III, p. 289.

8. To the Ear

79 **Sidney is a marvelous fighter**—Reynolds, *Hemingway: The 1930s*, p. 76.

79 **The bulls Sidney would be facing**—Cossío, *Los Toros*, tomo IV, p. 454; Conrad, *Encyclopedia of Bullfighting*, p. 106. In his autobiography, Sidney states that the bulls come from "the Murube Ranch" (p. 189). They were more precisely young Murube bulls (*novillos*) from the ranch of doña Carmen de Federico.

80 **Sidney had fought the prior Sunday**—Brand, "Corridas of Sidney Franklin," p. 27.

80 **to the ear**—Franklin, *Bullfighter from Brooklyn*, p. 191.

81 **he managed to assuage his sorrow with another trip to Tortugas**—Baker, *Ernest Hemingway: A Life Story*, p. 269.

82 **I was gored by a dead bull**—Ross, *Lillian Ross*, p. 184.

82 **Ignoring his doctor's advice, he left the hospital**—Brand, "Corridas of Sidney Franklin," p. 27.

82 **he tried to vault the *barrera* from the stirrup board**—Franklin, *Bullfighter from Brooklyn*, p. 194.

82 **To give himself relief**—Franklin, *Bullfighter from Brooklyn*, p. 194.

83 **the fans, sticklers for tradition, pointed and booed**—"Names make news," *Time*, August 25, 1930, http://www.time.com/time/magazine/article/0,9171,740168-2,00.html (accessed November 5, 2007.

83 **he again felt like an outsider with his family**—Ross, *Lillian Ross*, pp. 185–86.

84 **a fact that Lalanda confirms in his own writing**—Lalanda, *La Tauromaquia de Marcial Lalanda*, p. 339.

85 **Hemingway wrote of the calf injury**—Hemingway, *Death in the Afternoon*, p. 475. Citation includes the detail about the anti-tetanus injection.

86 **Because of his bad wound he lost the real in bullfighting**—Ross, *Lillian Ross*, p. 183.

9. Hard Times

87 **bullfighters shed the brave blood first**—Arruza, *My Life as a Matador*, p. 176.

88 **the fight promoters and arena officials**—Hemingway, *Death in the Afternoon*, p. 475.

88 **There was nothing left to do**—Hemingway, *Death in the Afternoon*, p. 475.

88 **Hemingway pronounced the young man's performance lousy**—Hemingway, *Death in the Afternoon*, p. 169.

88 **Hemingway would later say that Ortega even modeled his style**—Ross, *Lillian Ross*, p. 162.

89 **Both Sidney and Hemingway write of this idyllic time**—Franklin, *Bullfighter from Brooklyn*, p. 205; Hemingway, *Death in the Afternoon*, p. 271.

89 **Hemingway, Sidney, Luis Crovetto, and four other bullfighters**—Tony Brand and Professor Miriam Mandell have identified three of the four other bullfighters as Palmeño II, Francisco "Curro" Prieto, and Francisco Royo "Lagarito." The squatting man with the bota remains unidentified.

90 **Professor Mellow seems completely unaware of Sidney's sexual orientation**—Mellow, *Hemingway*, pp. 407–8.

91 **The scene on the Manzanares is from the last chapter**—Hemingway, *Death in the Afternoon*, pp. 270–78.

92 **another role model of Hemingway's boyhood, Theodore Roosevelt**—Brian, *The True Gen*, p. 67.

93 **It's all been changed for me**—Hemingway, *Death in the Afternoon*, p. 278.

93 **he attempted a winter tour of South America**—Franklin, *Bullfighter from Brooklyn*, p. 206. This attempt is confirmed by Brand, "Corridas of Sidney Franklin," p. 2.

93 **he co-wrote with veteran journalist and poet Arthur Chapman**—*Saturday Evening Post*, April 11, 1931.

95 **he used his Spanish language skills**—Baker, *Ernest Hemingway: A Life Story*, p. 805.

95 **Hemingway found his work assisting Sidney wearying**—Baker, *Ernest Hemingway: A Life Story*, p. 805.

95 **He looks sort of shoddy in Spain sometimes**—Reynolds, *Hemingway: The 1930s*, p. 118.

96 **The writer Max Eastman**—Baker, *Ernest Hemingway: A Life Story*, p. 403.

96 **reviews in the Spanish press by Nancy Bredendick**—March 22, 2005. This thorough and important examination of the hitherto unexamined Spanish reaction to Hemingway's work shows the regard in which the book was held, but also, in Orts-Ramos's case, shows the problems inherent in relying too much on a fellow named Franklin.

98 **Bernice Kert in *The Hemingway Women***—Kert, *The Hemingway Women*, p. 272.

98 **Eve, however, scoffed at this detail**—Frumkin, in discussion with author, April 5, 2001.

98 **Sidney, along with one of his sisters**—Reynolds, *Hemingway: The 1930s*, p. 179.

99 **He told Hemingway in a June 27 letter**—Ernest Hemingway Collection, John F. Kennedy Library, Boston (hereafter cited as Hemingway Collection).

100 **He complained to Hemingway a full year and a half later**—Franklin, letter to Hemingway, September 11, 1935, Hemingway Collection. This letter includes "the old ash can still leaks," referring to his old wound; "it smelled bad," referring to an attempt at a memoir; "our agreement that someday you'd do it," another reference to the memoir; and "I'm up against a stone wall."

102 **He admits that the idle life back in New York**—Franklin, letter to Hemingway, September 11, 1935, Hemingway Collection.

102 **he met Douglas Fairbanks during a trip to Los Angeles**—Franklin, *Bullfighter from Brooklyn*, pp. 111–13.

10. The Big Parade

107 **'Lo, kid, said Hemingway, want to go to the war in Spain**—Eby, *Between the Bullet and the Lie*, p. 89.

108 **his first book to earn spotty reviews**—Reynolds, *Hemingway: An Annotated Chronology*, p. 68.

108 **His second non-fiction work, *Green Hills of Africa***—Baker, *Ernest Hemingway: A Life Story*, p. 359.

109 **He was a great listener before he moved to Key West**—Meyers, *Hemingway*, p. 237.

109 **Mason was driving Patrick**—Reynolds, *Hemingway: An Annotated Chronology*, p. 72.

110 **he had just spotted his old pal fifty bucks**—Reynolds, *Hemingway: The 1930s*, p. 242.

110 **Wish there were some market for what I know**—Reynolds, *Hemingway: The 1930s*, p. 72.

113 **Even journalist Paul Mower**—Reynolds, *Hemingway: The 1930s*, p. 240.

113 **I've got this nice house and boat in Key West**—Meyers, *Hemingway*, p. 302.

113 **Pauline doesn't like the idea**—Franklin, *Bullfighter from Brooklyn*, p. 215.

114 **Sidney Franklin is going with me**—Baker, *Ernest Hemingway: Selected Letters*, February 9, 1937, pp. 457–58.

114 **Ernest Hemingway had a new girlfriend**—Kert, *The Hemingway Women*, pp. 285–94; Reynolds, *Hemingway: The 1930s*, pp. 243–61; Mellow, *Hemingway*, pp. 283–85; Baker, *Ernest Hemingway: A Life Story*, pp. 379–81; Rollyson, *Beautiful Exile*, pp. 61–66; Moorehead, *Gellhorn*, pp. 102–7; Meyers, *Hemingway*, pp. 298–301. The meeting of Ernest Hemingway and Martha Gellhorn, plus Gellhorn's background and the beginning of their affair, is drawn from these sources. The details and emphases vary somewhat, but the events are basically the same and form the basis for this account.

116 **a beautiful blond in a black dress**—Kert, *The Hemingway Women*, p. 282.

116 **Pauline was grumpy**—Kert, *The Hemingway Women*, p. 290.

116 **You could see she was making a play for him**—Rollyson, *Beautiful Exile*, p. 63.

117 **Pauline seemed sharp-edged**—Reynolds, *Hemingway: The 1930s*, p. 243.

117 **I suppose Ernest is busy again helping Miss Gellhorn**—Rollyson, *Beautiful Exile*, p. 64.

118 **Hemingway had also agreed to collaborate on a film**—Mellow, *Hemingway*, pp. 488–89.

118 **I watched Miss Gellhorn, Archibald MacLeish said**—Rollyson, *Beautiful Exile*, p. 63.

119 **Angel, Martha wrote, I have so much to tell you**—Kert, *The Hemingway Women*, p. 294.

120 **Hadley told of a typical morning**—Griffin, *Less than a Treason*, pp. 141–44.

120 **Here it was . . . that the three breakfast trays**—Meyers, *Hemingway*, p. 177.

11. A Fine Romance

121 **His sisters Bella, Helen, and the twins**—Baker, *Ernest Hemingway: A Life Story*, p. 383.

121 **Biographer Carlos Baker describes**—Baker, *Ernest Hemingway: A Life Story*, p. 383.

122 **In a letter to Hemingway three weeks before they sailed**—Franklin, letter to Hemingway, February 3, 1937, Hemingway Collection.

123 **Shipman's intention was not to write about Spain**—Mellow, *Hemingway*, p. 490.

123 **I was destined to lead**—Ross, *Lillian Ross*, p. 146.

124 **Twenty-five years after the fact**—Baker, *Ernest Hemingway: A Life Story*, p. 383.

125 **the Italians had recently sent over ten thousand troops**—Baker, *Ernest Hemingway: A Life Story*, p. 385.

125 **Hemingway had met his previous blond temptation**—Reynolds, *Hemingway: An Annotated Chronology*, p. 65.

126 **She has made arrangements to join Ernest Hemingway**—Kert, *The Hemingway Women*, p. 295.

126 **his first meeting with an imperious and somewhat ditzy woman**—Franklin, *Bullfighter from Brooklyn*, pp. 219–21.

126 **Gellhorn herself pointed out the absurdity of such a tale**—Kert, *The Hemingway Women*, pp. 295–96.

126 **Carl Rollyson, mentions that female writers in Spain**—Rollyson, *Beautiful Exile*, p. 67.

127 **a duffle bag full of canned food**—Moorehead, *Gellhorn*, p. 112.

127 **She bristled at the assertion**—Rollyson, *Beautiful Exile*, pp. 214–15. Gellhorn's quoted complaints to Baker are all from this entry.

128 **Baker? Oh groan. *Groan!***—Ross, in discussion with author, April 10, 2003.

128 **Balls!**—Rollyson, *Beautiful Exile*, p. 215.

128 **Matthews, however, apparently had a yen for Martha himself**—Moorehead, *Gellhorn*, p. 188.

129 **Sidney recounts a night border crossing on foot**—Franklin, *Bullfighter from Brooklyn*, p. 223.

129 **like the palm of my hand**—Ross, *Lillian Ross*, p. 148.

129 **He relied on a method more Brooklyn than Bolshevik**—Franklin, *Bullfighter from Brooklyn*, p. 225.

130 **There was utter disregard for property and order**—Franklin, *Bullfighter from Brooklyn*, pp. 227–28.

130 **an aristocratic leftist, Constancia de La Mora**—Baker, *Ernest Hemingway: A Life Story*, p. 385.

131 **Sidney and his driver pulled up**—Kert, *The Hemingway Women*, p. 296.

131 **I absolutely flipped for her**—Kert, *The Hemingway Women*, p. 296.

132 **he and Gellhorn necked and fondled for much of the trip**—Norman Allan, "Ted," unpublished online biography, chapter 1, 2008. Ted Allan also co-authored a biography of Dr. Norman Bethune called *The Scalpel, the Sword* in 1952.

12. The Beard

133 **the frazzled couple Ilsa Kulcsar and Arturo Barea**—Baker, *Ernest Hemingway: A Life Story*, p. 387.

133 **sleek woman with a halo of fair hair**—Baker, *Ernest Hemingway: A Life Story*, p. 387.

134 **Martha's *Collier's* credentials were essentially bogus**—Baker, *Ernest Hemingway: A Life Story*, p. 387.

134 **My beautiful girlfriend is coming**—Rollyson, *Beautiful Exile*, p. 66.

134 **I knew you'd get here daughter, because I fixed it so you could**—Rollyson, *Beautiful Exile*, p. 66. This incident is repeated by Baker, *Ernest Hemingway*, p. 387; Kert, *The Hemingway Women*, p. 296; Moorehead, *Gellhorn*, p. 113; etc., and has become a staple of the Hemingway-Gellhorn legend. Rollyson provided the detail of the possessive hand on the head.

135 **Koch, relying partly on Moorehead's account**—*Gellhorn*, pp. 106–7.

135 **Koch completely vindicates Sidney's version of events**—Koch, *The Breaking Point*, pp. 97–98.

136 **he heard the scream and explosion of an artillery shell**—Franklin, *Bullfighter from Brooklyn*, p. 231.

136 **Paintings in the Prado had been packed up for safekeeping**—Eby, *Between the Bullet and the Lie*, p. 86.

138 **He would stand at the foot of the staircase**—Baker, *Ernest Hemingway: A Life Story*, p. 393.

138 **a fussy, stamp collecting desk clerk**—Eby, *Between the Bullet and the Lie*, pp. 86–87.

138 **Hemingway jokingly referred to these women as whores de combat**—Kert, *The Hemingway Women*, p. 297.

139 **To add to Martha Gellhorn's list of outrages**—Rollyson, *Beautiful Exile*, p. 68.

139 **with a green chiffon scarf wound around her head**—Herbst, *The Starched Blue Sky of Spain*, p. 138.

140 **No matter how often you do it, Gellhorn said**—Meyers, *Hemingway*, p. 306.

140 **Hemingway christened the empty shell the Old Homestead**—Baker, *Ernest Hemingway: A Life Story*, p. 392.

141 **How do you like it now, gentlemen**—Rollyson, *Beautiful Exile*, p. 70.

142 **brave and good and fine in a somewhat murky world**—Rollyson, *Beautiful Exile*, p. 70.

142 **Hemingway drank and sang and became the Hemingway character again**—Mellow, *Hemingway*, p. 504.

142 **when he was not the most important thing there was**—Kert, *The Hemingway Women*, p. 299.

142 **who came out of Hemingway's room**—Reynolds, *Hemingway: The 1930s*, p. 263.

143 **the corks popping were not for you**—Herbst, *The Starched Blue Sky of Spain*, p. 151.

143 **I didn't like the sex at all**—Moorehead, *Gellhorn*, pp. 408–9. This and other comments about her sex life are from Gellhorn's letters.

144 **See if you can dig up some hypodermic needles, Sidney**—Brian, *The True Gen*, p. 118.

144 **Hemingway himself remembers Sidney as the invaluable one**—Mellow, *Hemingway*, pp. 494–95.

144 **He would tell stories about his bullfighting triumphs**—Herbst, *The Starched Blue Sky of Spain*, pp. 158–59.

145 **a fascist victory would set the country back**—Herbst, *The Starched Blue Sky of Spain*, p. 172.

13. The Master Horn

147 **With Ginny [Cowles], went and priced silver foxes**—Moorehead, *Gellhorn* p. 120.

148 **George Seldes remembers Hemingway in Paris**—Brian, *The True Gen*, p. 118.

149 **A traveling California college grad fresh from Berkeley**—Elsa Ocskay, in discussion with author, 1968.

149 **a Law of Historical Memory**—Tracy Wilkinson, "Poised to confront the past," *Los Angeles Times*, October 31, 2007.

149 **the Vatican beatified 498 priests and nuns**—Tracy Wilkerson, "Beatifications lay bare an old divide," *Los Angeles Times*, October, 29, 2007.

150 **Spender found disillusionment common among younger volunteers**—Eby, *Between the Bullet and the Lie*, p. 74.

151 **soviet influence in the loyalist cause cost him**—Koch, *The*

Breaking Point, pp. 130–31; Herbst, *The Starched Blue Sky of Spain*, pp. 154–55. It is Koch's contention that the well-respected Herbst, who witnessed the affair, was an agent of soviet propaganda.

152 **On the day Dos Passos returned to Madrid**—Koch, *The Breaking Point*, p. 125.

153 **Josephine Herbst had found this out from government sources**—Herbst, *The Starched Blue Sky of Spain*, pp. 154–57.

14. The Sword

156 **By late April, when they had been in the city about a month**—Baker, *Ernest Hemingway: A Life Story*, p. 396.

156 **who had serious work to do**—Kert, *The Hemingway Women*, p. 297.

156 **Cecil Eby describes her striding through the American volunteers**—Eby, *Between the Bullet and the Lie*, p. 74.

156 **immersing herself personally in the war**—Herbst, *The Starched Blue Sky of Spain*, pp. 140–47.

157 **under the title Only the Shells Whine**—Kert, *The Hemingway Women*, p. 298.

157 **when she, Ernest, and Sidney would arrive at small villages**—Kert, *The Hemingway Women*, p. 297.

158 **Barnaby Conrad tells a story of a particularly noble bull**—Conrad, *Encyclopedia of Bullfighting*, p. 55.

159 **Ernest and Martha left Sidney in Madrid**—Baker, *Ernest Hemingway: A Life Story*, p. 396

160 **they traveled on horseback where there were no roads**—Mellow, *Hemingway*, p. 495.

161 **I was not in Guernica, but I was in Mora del Ebro**—Mellow, *Hemingway*, 495.

162 **According to Sidney, Flynn came to Spain**—Franklin, *Bullfighter from Brooklyn*, pp. 233–35.

162 **Joris Ivens wrote to Sidney and cameraman John Ferno**—Baker, *Ernest Hemingway: A Life Story*, pp. 396–97.

15. Separate Trails

163 **About seven months after I got to Madrid**—Franklin, *Bull-fighter from Brooklyn*, pp. 234–35.

164 **For Hemingway, first it was Paris**—Baker, *Ernest Hemingway: A Life Story*, pp. 397–99.

164 **Hemingway from the unfinished manuscript of *To Have and Have Not***—Reynolds, *Hemingway: The 1930s*, p. 267. Baker claims it was the short story "Fathers and Sons."

164 **By March 18 his liner docked in New York**—Reynolds, *Hemingway: An Annotated Chronology*, pp. 87–88.

164 **the second American Writer's Conference**—Reynolds, *Hemingway: The 1930s*, pp. 270–71.

165 **Fascism, he said, is a lie told by bullies**—Reynolds, *Hemingway: The 1930s*, p. 270.

165 **pretty nice and a lot better than sitting around in a hot hall**—Reynolds, *Hemingway: The 1930s*, pp. 270–71. Citation includes the Dawn Powell quotes as reported by Reynolds.

166 **Hemingway took time to visit with Scott Fitzgerald**—Baker, *Ernest Hemingway: A Life Story*, p. 399.

167 **This replacement would cause friction between Hemingway and Welles**—Hemingway, *Running with the Bulls*, pp. 75–76.

167 **the evidence is contradictory**—Baker, *Ernest Hemingway: A Life Story*, p. 402; Reynolds, *Hemingway: The 1930s*, p. 272; Franklin, telegram to Hemingway, July 15, 1937, Hemingway Collection.

168 **even this house, designed by architect Wallace Neff**—Ryon, "A Neff, but Enough Is Enough," *Los Angeles Times*, October 2, 2005. The Neff house was in recent years mentioned in the press due to the occupancy of architecturally savvy Brad Pitt and Jennifer Aniston.

168 **The picture was beyond praise**—Baker, *Ernest Hemingway: A Life Story*, p. 402.

168 **Sylvia Sidney supposedly donated one of the thousand-dollar bills**—Koch, *The Breaking Point*, pp. 229–30. Koch also reports that other screenings of the film were held at the homes of

Darryl Zanuck, Joan Crawford, and iconic director John Ford. This last might seem odd, but Ford had loyalist painter Luis Quintanilla as his guest on the set of his 1940 screen adaptation of Eugene O'Neill's *The Long Voyage Home*. The painter's son Paul Quintanilla has some rare photos of his father with Ford, John Wayne, Thomas Mitchell, John Qualen, and others on the website he has created that is dedicated to his father's life and work. (A meaningless bit of circuitous trivia the cinematographer on *The Long Voyage Home* was Gregg Toland, who filmed Sid in 1932 in *The Kid from Spain*.)

169 **Ernest Hemingway spent a total of three weeks in Key West**—Reynolds, *Hemingway: The 1930s*, p. 282.

170 **Driving the big Lincoln was their traveling companion and guide**—Reynolds, *Hemingway: The 1930s*, pp. 274–75.

170 **Franklin was a fascinating fellow with a lot of bullshit**—Brian, *The True Gen*, p. 87.

170 **He wired Hemingway from Brooklyn, advising that a new Ford**—Franklin, telegram to Hemingway, July 15, 1937, Hemingway Collection.

16. Hemingway's Gay Blade

172 **Ernest was concerned about the size of his penis**—Conrad, *Fun While It Lasted*, p. 102.

172 **He had been raised in the leafy, stucco-ed gentility of Hillsborough**—Conrad, in discussion with author, January 26, 2001.

174 **He had returned for the first time**—Conrad, *Fun While It Lasted*, pp. 101–14. Conrad is the most reliable source for details of Sidney's return to Spain during the war. They saw much of one another in the two years Sidney spent restarting his career prior to taking his *alternativa* in 1945. Unless otherwise noted, the specifics of those days are from *Fun While It Lasted*.

175 **When asked years later**—Conrad, in discussion with author, January 2001–September 2008. Conrad said that—unlike a few other matadors he could name—there was *no* indication from his comportment that Sidney was gay.

176 **There was the time in mid-December 1940**—"Author in the Forenoon," *New Yorker*, December 28, 1940.

177 **He's changed. Something's changed**—Conrad, *Fun While It Lasted*, p. 102.

178 **The particulars of this last wartime rendezvous**—Brand, in discussion with author, July 16, 2007, Los Angeles.

178 **On that trip he had met another Jewish soldier of fortune**—Baker, *Ernest Hemingway: A Life Story*, p. 457.

179 **His offer to John Wheeler**—Baker, *Ernest Hemingway: A Life Story*, pp. 471–72.

179 **He conceived of a Havana-based counterespionage unit**—Baker, *Ernest Hemingway: A Life Story*, pp. 472–73.

180 **Bill Davis was a large, thick-featured, balding man**—Hemingway, *Running with the Bulls*, p. 37.

180 **was convinced Davis was trying to kill him**—Hemingway, *Running with the Bulls*, p. 142.

180 **There was some talk among fellow expatriates**—Brand, in discussion with author, July 16, 2007.

180 **Supported first by Bob Joyce and Ellis Briggs**—Baker, *Ernest Hemingway: A Life Story*, pp. 472–73.

181 **Director J. Edgar Hoover himself requested**—Robins, "The Secret War Against American Writers," *Esquire*, March 1992, p. 109.

181 **Hemingway had dreamed up an even more exciting job**—Baker, *Ernest Hemingway: A Life Story*, pp. 473–75.

182 **I weighed Ernest in the balance and found him wanting**—Ross, *Lillian Ross*, p. 150.

183 **That is why never re-negged**—Baker, *Ernest Hemingway: Selected Letters*, July 2, 1948, p. 646.

183 **they were both adequately and normally equipped**—Brian, *The True Gen*, p. 65.

183 **John Dos Passos, when he was still speaking to Hemingway**—Meyers, *Hemingway*, p. 255.

184 **Gingrich accepted and published new short stories of Fitzgerald's**—Dardis, *Some Time in the Sun*, p. 69.

184 **Gingrich eventually married Hemingway's former mistress**—Meyers, *Hemingway*, pp. 255–56.

17. The Alternativa

185 **Watching that first *corrida* with Conrad**—Conrad, *Fun While It Lasted*, p. 109.

187 **the Sidney Franklin of the ballet**—Mellow, *Hemingway*, p. 404.

187 **Sidney was sipping sherry with Barnaby Conrad**—Conrad, *Fun While It Lasted*, p. 112.

188 **All the sexes were wild about him**—Ross, *Lillian Ross*, p. 150.

188 **the two had appeared together in a corrida in Bogotá**—Brand, "Corridas of Sidney Franklin," p. 27.

189 **Luis Gómez, the matador known as El Estudiante, stood facing Sidney**—Cossío, *Los Toros*, tomo IV, p. 454.

189 **some aficionados now say that he too was gay**—Conrad, in discussion with author, January 26, 2001.

191 **the party arranged the belated *alternativa***—Brand, "Corridas of Sidney Franklin," p. 26. It was after the famous eight-bull corrida in San Sebastián on July 21, 1929, that Sidney dedicated his *novillo* to a certain Colonel Franco.

191 **neither of the two main bullfighting papers of the day**—Tony Brand and John Fulton, unpublished research, early 1990s.

191 **He became the oldest matador in the twentieth century**—Conrad, *Encyclopedia of Bullfighting*, pp. 142–59.

192 **Sidney Franklin would never again appear professionally**—Cossío, *Los Toros*, tomo IV, p. 454.

18. The New Man

194 **Charlie Chaplin, who said the bullfight was as graceful as dance**—Ross, in discussion with author, April 10, 2003. When Conrad asked the great Juan Belmonte who performed the best *verónica* he'd ever seen, he said, "Chaplin, with calves on my ranch—incredible!"

194 **I don't know why I painted gaily the American bullfighter**—
Paul Quintanilla, e-mail to author, February 10, 2007. Quintanilla
quotes from his father's contribution to the catalogue of his 1939
show at the Associated American Artists Gallery, New York.

195 **I haven't seen Sidney fight in a long time now**—Hemingway,
caption to "Sidney Franklin by Luis Quintanilla," *Town & Country*,
March 1940.

196 **cruised down to Mexico City to recuperate**—Boetticher,
When in Disgrace, p. 9. Citation includes the Mexico City and early
Hollywood events, plus the conflict with Sidney.

197 **I made the mistake of telling him, mi casa es su casa**—
Boetticher, in discussion with author, October 15, 2000; *When in
Disgrace*, p. 78.

197 **Sidney hauled Harry Cohn's Columbia Pictures into a Manhattan Court**—"Names make news," *Time*, December 31, 1934
www.time.com/time/magazine/article/0,9171,754490,00.html
(accessed February 17, 2007).

197 **I've got to do something to protect myself, Verdad**—Franklin,
letter to Hemingway, September 11, 1935, Hemingway Collection.

198 **One source of this term was an incident**—Conrad, in discussion with author, December 31, 2007. Conrad had heard the
details from Wiswell, the editor at *Esquire*, who accepted Conrad's
first bullfighting story.

198 **he had seen far too much animal breeding**—Ross, *Lillian Ross*,
p. 155.

198 **When Barnaby Conrad somewhat naively asked Sidney**—
Conrad, in discussion with author, December 31, 2007.

199 **He annoyed some homesick boys of the Abraham Lincoln
Brigade**—Herbst, *The Starched Blue Sky of Spain*, pp. 172–73.

199 **Gaona conveniently tells him he must give up the girl**—
Franklin, *Bullfighter from Brooklyn*, p. 109.

199 **rumors of Sidney's homosexuality circulated**—Mann, in discussion with author, August 1, 2007.

201 **Stack's exhilaration and relief—like his bruises—were
real**—Robert Stack, in discussion with author, Aug. 25, 2000.
The conversation followed a UCLA screening of the film.

201 **let me play around with the animals**—Ross, *Lillian Ross*, p. 174.

201 **Sidney's description of the events runs for several pages**—Franklin, *Bullfighter from Brooklyn*, pp. 21–28.

202 **Sidney was gored more times by his nephews**—Boetticher, in discussion with author, October 15, 2000.

19. Servalavari

203 **Sidney found a large house to rent**—Brand, in discussion with author, February 18, 2008; Cunningham, *A River of Lions*, p. 5. Citation includes the description of his house, the town, its heritage and surroundings.

204 **Baron Clements Jr., a drawling former high school quarterback**—"Matador from Texas," *Time*, May 4, 1959, http://www .time.com/time/magazine/article/0,9171,892529,00html (accessed August 8, 2007). Citation includes details of Clements's career with Sidney, including Sidney's quote about his ability.

205 **when the breeze caught Sidney's toupee**—Brand, in discussion with author, February 18, 2008. Brand was told this story by Charro Gómez.

205 **a horrible horn wound to the chest**—Conrad, in discussion with author, September 27, 2008. Manolete's doctor told Conrad that Tuck's horn wound to the chest—from back to front—was the worst he had ever seen.

206 **he finally took his own life with a pistol**—Sherwood, *Yankees in the Afternoon*, p. 89; Conrad, in discussion with author, September 27, 2008. There is more than one version of this: Tuck's sister told Tony Brand there was no suicide at all; Barnaby Conrad, who employed Tuck in San Francisco shortly before his death, said that he heard that Tuck was found standing against a wall in lower Manhattan, dead of a gunshot wound. As Tuck supposedly bought illegal drugs to deal with his constant pain, Conrad wondered who would shoot himself on such a busy street.

206 **His name was Patrick Cunningham**—Cunningham, in discussion with author, August 27, 2007. Conversation included incidents of life studying with Sidney.

208 **Cunningham and Tuck did appear once at a festival-tienta**—Brand, in discussion with author, February 18, 2008. Brand shared with me the *cartel* for this event as described in the text.

210 **In 1954 when a certain don Plácido**—"Blood & a Station Wagon," *Time*, March 29, 1954, http://www.time.com/time/magazine/article/0,9171,819689.html (accessed January 24, 2008).

211 **he brought up Sidney's name deliberately**—Cunningham, in discussion with author, August 27, 2007.

212 **he was arrested for bringing an automobile into Spain**—Obituary of Sidney Franklin, *New York Times*, May 2, 1976.

213 **he was — according to many acquaintances — gay as well**—Brand, in discussion with author, February 18, 2008; Conrad, in discussion with author, September 27, 2008.

214 **The handsome young man at the bar was John Fulton**—Brand, in discussion with author, July 16, 2007. This charming story was told to Brand by his good friend John Fulton.

20. Recuerdos

215 **Ladies and gentlemen, presenting the famous American matador**—Brand, in discussion with author, June 28, 2007. Brand attended the lecture described here and provided the details of it and of Sidney's broadcasting career in the 1960s.

216 **there was a feeling among some younger fans**—Mann, in discussion with author, August 1, 2007.

217 ***El Redondel* was run by two critics**—Cintrón, *Memoirs of a Bullfighter*, pp. 127–28.

217 **all that could be expected of a matador**—Ross, *Lillian Ross*, pp. 162–63.

218 **While appearing with Sidney in the Tijuana bullring**—Brand, in discussion with author, July 16, 2007. This story was told to Brand by Andrés Blando.

218 **Domínguín stated that Sidney had no status whatsoever**—Meyers, *Hemingway*, pp. 525–26.

218 **Carlos Arruza joked in his autobiography**—Arruza, *My Life as a Matador*, p. 22 (footnote).

219 **Hemingway and his wife Mary had traveled from Cuba**— Brand, in discussion with author, July 16, 2007.

210 **biographer James Mellow and aficionado práctico Tony Brand support**—Mellow, *Hemingway*, pp. 411–12; Brand, in discussion with author, February 18, 2008. Conrad also said that Ortiz's mannerisms were as obvious as Liberace's. In a September 26, 2008, letter, Conrad stated that when he met him in 1955, Ortiz "positively swished."

220 **He figures in a fanciful story about short-sheeting**—Franklin, *Bullfighter from Brooklyn*, pp. 51–53.

220 **the entry for maricón**—Hemingway, *Death in the Afternoon*, pp. 417–18.

221 **an unnamed woman's penchant for oral sex**—Hemingway, *Death in the Afternoon*, p. 277.

222 **his swords oxidized beyond recognition**—Franklin, *Bullfighter from Brooklyn*, p. 98.

223 **Somehow they always made me angry**—Hemingway, *The Sun Also Rises*, p. 20.

223 **Hemingway refers to lady writers of all sexes**—Mellow, *Hemingway*, p. 399.

224 **the friendship was always an unequal one**—Ross, in discussion with author, April 10, 2003.

224 **he told writer and Atlantic editor Robert Manning**—Manning, "Hemingway in Cuba," *Atlantic Monthly*, August 1965, http://www.theatlantic.com/issues/65aug/6508manning.htm (accessed February 16, 2009).

224 **Hemingway resented Sidney's proprietary attitude**—Ross, in discussion with author, April 10, 2003.

225 **Hemingway would have to have known**—Mann, in discussion with author, August 1, 2007.

226 **Patrick Cunningham stated that Sidney alluded to the rectal goring**—Cunningham, in discussion with author, August 27, 2007.

227 **forgive 'em Father for they know not what they do**—Brand, in discussion with author, September 11, 2007.

21. Sol y Sombra

229 **Carlos Arruza supposedly promised his wife**—Conrad, letter to author, September 26, 2008. Conrad states that Carlos could not help but repeatedly cheat on this promise, "acceding to the pleadings of the crowd to get off the horse and fight on foot."

230 **In the 1960s a new generation of celebrities**—Walter de la Brosse, in discussion with author, April 12, 2007.

231 **state-run Televisón Española dropped live coverage of bullfights**—Woolls, "Spanish TV pulls the plug on live bullfight coverage," *Los Angeles Times*, August, 27 2007.

232 **The concrete bullring of Alcalá de Guadaíra**—Brand, in discussion with author, September 11, 2007.

232 **beloved matador José Tomás staged a comeback**—Tracy Wilkinson, "Rebirth in the arena," *Los Angeles Times*, June 18, 2007.

233 **The obituary of course quotes his good friend Ernest Hemingway**—*New York Times*, May 2, 1976.

233 **According to his niece Eve Frumkin**—Frumkin, in discussion with author, April 5, 2001.

234 **Sidney never gave anybody anything**—Conrad, in discussion with author, January 26, 2001. In the September 26, 2008, letter, Conrad expressed how valuable the cape was to him. "If this house were to catch fire I would grab it and run to safety. Then I would go back for Mary, my wife of 45 years."

234 **When Conrad and Milton Frumpkin entered Sidney's sixth-floor room**—Conrad, in discussion with author, January 26, 2001. Conrad has told this wonderful scene to me several times since, adding bits of detail and emphasis. From the first time I heard it, I knew I had my ending. Gracias, Bernabé.

BIBLIOGRAPHY

Arruza, Carlos. *My Life as a Matador: The Autobiography of Carlos Arruza*, with *Barnaby Conrad*. Boston: Houghton Mifflin, 1956.

Baker, Carlos. *Ernest Hemingway: A Life Story*. New York: Avon, 1968.

Baker, Carlos, ed. *Ernest Hemingway: Selected Letters 1917–1961*. New York: Charles Scribner's Sons, 1981.

Beatie, Russel H. *Saddles*. Norman: University of Oklahoma Press, 1981.

Boetticher, Budd. *When in Disgrace*. Santa Barbara: Neville, 1989.

Brand, Tony. "Corridas of Sidney Franklin." Unpublished monograph, Sevilla, 1996.

Brian, Denis. *The True Gen: An Intimate Portrait of Ernest Hemingway by Those Who Knew Him*. New York: Grove, 1988.

Cintrón, Conchita. *Memoirs of a Bullfighter*. New York: Holt, Rinehart, & Winston, 1968.

Conrad, Barnaby. *Encyclopedia of Bullfighting*. Boston: Houghton Mifflin, 1961.

———. *Fun While It Lasted*. New York: Random House, 1969.

———. *La Fiesta Brava*. Boston: Houghton Mifflin, 1950.

Cossío, José María de. *Los Toros: Tratado Técnico E Histórico* — tomo I, Quinta Edición. Madrid: Espasa-Calpe, 1964.

———. *Los Toros: Tratado Técnico E Histórico* — tomo III, Quinta Edición. Madrid: Espasa-Calpe, 1965.

———. *Los Toros: Tratado Técnico E Histórico* — tomo IV, Madrid: Espasa-Calpe, 1961.

Cunningham, Patrick. *A River of Lions*. Santa Barbara: Neville, 1991.

Dardis, Tom. *Some Time in the Sun*. New York: Charles Scribner's Sons, 1976.

Dunn, H. H. *The Crimson Jester: Zapata of Mexico*. A. Neil Sawyer, New
  York: National Travel Club, 1934.

Dupuy, R. Ernest, and Trevor N. Dupuy. *The Encyclopedia of Military History from 3500 BC to the Present*. New York: Harper & Row, 1970.

Eby, Cecil. *Between the Bullet and the Lie: American Volunteers in the Spanish
  Civil War*. New York: Holt, Rinehard, & Winston, 1969.

Griffin, Peter. *Less than a Treason: Hemingway in Paris*. New York: Oxford
  University Press, 1990.

Franklin, Sidney. *Bullfighter from Brooklyn: The Amazing Autobiography of
  Sidney Franklin*. New York: Prentice Hall, 1952.

Hemingway, Ernest. *Death in the Afternoon*. New York: Charles Scribner's
  Sons, 1932.

———. *The Fifth Column and Four Stories of the Spanish Civil War*. New York:
  Charles Scribner's Sons, 1969.

———. *The Sun Also Rises*. New York: Charles Scribner's Sons, 1926.

———. *Winner Take Nothing*. New York: Charles Scribner's Sons, 1933.

Hemingway, Valerie. *Running with the Bulls: My Years with the Hemingways*.
  New York: Ballantine, 2004.

Herbst, Josephine. *The Starched Blue Sky of Spain*. New York: HarperCol-
  lins, 1991.

Innes, Hammond. *The Conquistadors*. New York: Alfred A. Knopf, 1969.

Kehoe, Vincent J-R. *Aficionado! The Pictorial Encyclopedia of the Fiesta de
  Toros of Spain*. New York: Hastings House, 1959.

Kert, Bernice. *The Hemingway Women*. New York: W. W. Norton, 1983.

Koch, Stephen. *The Breaking Point: Hemingway, Dos Passos, and the Murder
  of José Robles*. New York: Counterpoint, 2005.

Lalanda, Marcial y Andres Amorós. *La Tauromaquia de Marcial Lalanda*.
  Madrid: Espasa-Calpe, 1988.

Marks, John. *To the Bullfight*. New York: Alfred A. Knopf, 1953.

Mason, Herbert. *Gilgamesh: A Verse Narrative*. Boston: Houghton Mifflin,
  1970.

Mellow, James R. *Hemingway: A Life without Consequences*. Reading MA:
  Addison-Wesley, 1992.

Meyers, Jeffrey. *Hemingway: A Biography*. New York: Harper & Row, 1985.

Moorehead, Caroline. *Gellhorn: A Twentieth-Century Life*. New York: Henry Holt, 2003.

Pinchon, Edgcumb. *Viva Villa!: A Recovery of the Real Pancho Villa, Peon, Bandit, Soldier, Patriot*. New York: Grosset & Dunlap, 1934.

Reed, John. *Insurgent Mexico*. New York: International Publishers, 1969.

Reynolds, Michael. *Hemingway: The 1930s*. New York: Norton, 1997.

———. *Hemingway: An Annotated Chronology*. Detroit: Omnigraphics, 1991.

———. *Hemingway: The Paris Years*. New York: W. W. Norton, 1989.

Rollyson, Carl. *Beautiful Exile: The Life of Martha Gellhorn*. London: Aurum, 2001.

Ross, Lillian. *Lillian Ross: Reporting*. New York: Prentice Hall, 1952.

Sherwood, Lyn. *Yankees in the Afternoon: An Illustrated History of American Bullfighters*. Jefferson NC: McFarland, 2008.

Sokoloff, Alice Hunt. *Hadley: The First Mrs. Hemingway*. New York: Dodd Mead, 1973.

Wentworth, Harold, and Stuart Berg Flexner. *The Pocket Dictionary of American Slang*. New York: Pocket, 1968.

INDEX